"Inner Coach: Outer Power" is an extraordinarily compelling view of higher possibilities. Keith Varnum uses his own experience as a springboard to a guided tour of the upper reaches of human potential. I was glued to the stories and principles as they unfolded.

ALAN COHEN

Best-selling author of
The Dragon Doesn't Live Here Anymore

There is an awakening taking place on Earth and people are beginning to realize that what we once perceived as supernatural is really natural. Keith's book clearly reveals that truth in a fun and informative way. His method of storytelling lifts the heart and inspires the reader to connect with his or her own Divine Power. I highly recommend this enlightening and entertaining book.

PATRICIA DIANE COTA-ROBLES

New Age Study of Humanity's Purpose, Inc.

D0199995

ALSO BY KEITH VARNUM
WITH MARK CONRAD

Living the Dream—It's Time

Keith Varnum's web sites:

www.thedream.com
www.sedonavisionquest.com

Inner Coach
Outer Power

K e i t h   V a r n u m

New Dimensions Publishing
Phoenix, Arizona

Edited by Candice de Bar, Judee Pouncey and Sulana Stone
Cover design by Edward Sean Hampton-Gross
Illustrations by Casey Cook

For information:

New Dimensions Publishing
11248 N. 11ᵗʰ St.
Phoenix, AZ 85020
800.736.7367

Email: keith@thedream.com
Web sites: www.thedream.com
www.sedonavisionquest.com

Printed in the United States of America

Publisher's Cataloging-in-Publication
(Provided by Quality Books, Inc.)

Varnum, Keith.
    Inner coach : outer power / Keith Varnum. – 1ˢᵗ ed.

    p. cm.
    LCCN 2001097678
    ISBN 1-891569-49-X

    1.   Self-actualization (Psychology) 2.   Spirituality.
I.   Title.

BF637.S4V37 2002   158
                            QB101-1309

To my mentors and best buddies:

St. Germain, Michio, Lester and Medicine Cloud—
who allowed me to drink from their wisdom,
grow from their honesty and
blossom from their love.

Foreword

Within the first two pages of Keith Varnum's book, I found the answer to one of the most perplexing puzzles of my life. I'd struggled for years to understand why my son, now 23 years old, never seemed to get ahead. We had talks together. He created a dynamite action plan, but he never followed through with it. Time and again, this baffling syndrome occurred. As his mother, I became totally exasperated, attempting to assist him, yet knowing I had to let him grow by making his own decisions.

When I picked up this book, a clear distinction hit me right between the eyes—the vast difference between the soul and the personality:

> If these two aspects of ourselves don't know each other, don't communicate and don't work together, then we must be prepared for frustration, endless toil and exhaustion.

> Once these two components are aligned—WOW! We *gain* energy instead of having it sucked from us. We see our dreams and desires unfold *effortlessly!*

Having these revelations inspired me to be more compassionate with my son and gave me the strength and insight to give him the freedom to find his own way to unfold his unique destiny.

As I participated in Keith's workshops for more than three years, I became empowered to create the alignment and fruition of my own dreams. I became very focused and found the courage to go for what I really desired in my life. Miracles happened—in my physical body, as well as in my mental, emotional and spiritual worlds.

Trained in traditional Western medicine, I had only that orthodox background from which to view disease, aging and other natural functions. Keith helped me to see a panoramic picture with a wide-angle lens instead of the narrow view of my training. As a result of expanding my expectations of what is physically and medically possible, I experienced profound positive physical changes in myself that I never thought possible. I shifted a 15-year-old medical condition that was an expected, but unwanted, result of previous pelvic surgery. I know that mental and emotional alterations are definitely possible as a result of relieving stress and unresolved feelings, but my physical condition reverting back to that of 15 years earlier absolutely astonished me! My body now feels—and functions—as it did when I was a vivacious young woman!

Also, I have been able to take these concepts—of connecting to my true knowing and of transforming old, fixed realities—back into my professional practice. As a specialist in Internal Medicine, I'm now able to assist others to effect wonderful and lasting changes in their lives. I am forever grateful!

The experiences Keith shares, marking the milestones of his own transformation, are described so vividly, they leave the reader anxious to know more:

What does he do next in *this* episode?

How does he handle this person or predicament?

How does he get out of this dilemma?

You mean, I create stuff like this too?

Hmmm.

And I know from my personal creation of miracles that the principles behind these most amazing stories are valid and true.

In *Inner Coach: Outer Power*, dynamic writing details a compelling account of one man's journey. Keith inspires courage—*your* courage! A book you'll want to keep reading until the wee hours of the morning.

If you dare to live your dream, begin *now* to pay close attention to *your* inner coach. Then watch your life take off in exciting, new directions!

MAGGIE MEARS, M.D.

Founder of *Write From Your Heart-A Creative Writing Workshop*

Contents

PART IV – Following the Inner Coach

PART V – Living in the Outer Power

Preface

"How'd they do that?" I asked myself time and time again.

As a journalist and documentary filmmaker, I witnessed ordinary people performing extraordinary feats on countless occasions. I documented individuals in moments of crisis and emergency going beyond the limits they and society believed possible. Caught up in earthquakes, floods, hurricanes and accidents, I watched mild-mannered people become super-heroes.

When extreme circumstances demand action, paranormal abilities arise from normal folks. Women lift two-ton trucks and hold them aloft until their child or husband is freed from beneath the vehicle. Young boys perform successful medical procedures as if they were trained professionals. Men lead victims to safety through burning buildings, pitch-black forests and raging floods. Teenagers bend steel and rip open closed elevator doors to liberate loved ones. Scared people jump ten feet over a chasm to safety. Given a death sentence by doctors, people heal themselves spontaneously.

"Where do human beings get the power and knowledge to perform such implausible feats?" I wondered. I observed that when life offers a person a choice between their beliefs in what is possible and the necessity to save another from harm, people often scrap their perceived limitations and choose to do whatever needs to be done. Very often, people choose life, caring and rescue over the restrictions of their belief systems.

"If we can break out of our belief box when life has us up against the wall, why can't we release our limiting beliefs at will when we are not in a crisis?" I inquired within myself.

I looked around in my world for examples of people who know how to free themselves from tribal collective limitations—mainstream cultural beliefs—in order to access fresh possibilities of human potential. I discovered my models through reading biographies of dynamic individuals and interviewing adventurous people. I found that people who are forerunners, pioneers and explorers in social, political and artistic expression invariably refer to one or more moments in their lives in which they opened to a peak experience. And not only do these resourceful people *make reference* to these extraordinary moments, they *draw* strength, wisdom and compassion from these glimpses of their true power. They have learned how to tap into these past moments of heightened awareness and achievement in order to surmount present life challenges. Whether it be excellence in athletic or artistic expression, or success in business or romance, these potent moments of "transcendence of the ordinary" act as wells of inspiration and inventiveness that enable people to handle current predicaments.

With a degree of benevolent innocence, I decided that if these people could break free of their restrictive belief systems and tap into the power of previous peak experiences, then I could as well. Their successes inspired me to try this approach myself—to reach beyond my perceived boundaries. The stories in this book report my exploration of inviting magic into my life and welcoming miracles into my world. It is my heartfelt wish that my stories inspire you to go beyond your own self-created limits.

Keith Varnum
Phoenix, Arizona

INTRODUCTION

There Is Only One Story

The Universe is made of stories, not atoms.

MURIEL RUKEYSER

There is only One Story:

Having . . . losing . . . finding,

Knowing . . . forgetting . . . remembering,

Hide and seek—

The drama of the outer personality and the inner coach,

The interplay of the external and the internal,

The dance of form and essence.

From the beginning of time, the One Story is told and retold in every culture in the form of books, movies, songs, myths, dances, rituals, games and art.

We keep telling the One Story through all these varied outer forms, so one day, when we are ready to remember, we will hear the One Story again:

One People, One Spirit, One Destiny.

If you listen to these stories with your heart, you will hear the One Story, and you will remember Your Story—

the story your inner coach has to tell.

Enjoy.

My Story

This book is my expression of the One Story.

These pages tell the simple version and the complicated version.

The simple version is my life from the point of view of the inner coach, the real self. This rendition is the same as everyone else's story. Every inner coach has the same story. Every spirit is on the same inner journey.

The complex version tells my life from the perspective of my outer personality. This rendition is different from everyone else's story. Every personal identity has its special saga with its own unique plot. Every personality is on a different outer journey.

The inner coach uses multisensory perception to enjoy its world. The personality usually limits itself to the five external senses.

The real self interacts with the physical and nonphysical worlds. The personality confines itself to the world of outer physical sight, sound, smell, taste and touch.

The spirit's story is full of similarity, connection and coincidence. The personality's tale is full of difference, division and happenstance.

The scenario of the real self focuses on unity, compassion and joy. The script of the personality focuses on separation, anxiety and regret.

The goals of the real self are harmony, cooperation and understanding. The personality's agenda is conflict, competition and confusion.

The inner coach is into fun, ease and freedom. The personality thrives on drama, trauma and karma.

Spirit's story is guts and glory.
The personality's yarn is guts and gore.

It takes guts to fully experience and embrace your personality's epic struggle.

It takes even more courage to fully explore and embrace the triumph of your soul.

Through telling the story of my inner coach, I hope to remind you of the story of your own inner coach.

As the spirit of my tale shines through the surface details, it may remind you of Spirit working behind the details of your personality's fable.

As the outer appearances of my narration reveal the inner agenda of my real self, you may begin to see the common thread of soul intention running through the surface appearances of your life.

Believe It or Not

Many individuals don't believe my story.

It is too "farfetched." Too far out.

I agree. I had to live far out to fetch such a story.

Usually, those same people reconnect with me years later to tell me they now understand what I was talking about.

What transpired in those intervening years to change these people's perspective?

These folks had a far out occurrence of their own. Life presented them with an experience beyond their belief box—outside their personality's old framework, envelope, paradigm or range of previous experiences.

Once our world is expanded outside of our old boundaries, we realize all manner of stories are possible, even probable.

Really good stories entice the personality so far out of its ordinary prison of perception that a person encounters his or her real self.

My intention in telling you my story is to catalyze the reunion of your personality with your real self.

The Bridge

The real self is too smart to leave the hearing of its story to chance.

The inner coach loads the dice. The gig is rigged.

When we travel away from the unified field of multisensory awareness into the complexity of the personality, the inner coach leaves a trail of markers for us to find our way back to the simple knowing of Who We Are.

These soul clues are hidden along our personality path so we will stumble across them just when we need the encouragement of a wider perspective to get through our next life challenge.

This is the original message of the fairy tale, "Hansel and Gretel." Hansel, our adventurous personality, takes us on an exploration of the mysterious forest, the vast world of surface difference and diversity. Gretel, our intuitive real self, marks with pebbles the route we take going away from home, Spirit. When we get lost in the confusion of the surface appearances, Hansel and Gretel unite to find the way home. When our personality and inner coach communicate, we find our way back to Oneness and knowing Who We Are.

The stories in this book are real-life exploits of mine.

As I tell these candid tales to people, the stories have the effect of triggering people's memories of actual, extraordinary events in their own lives.

People recall events in their lives that, at the time they occurred, were too farfetched to fit into any known category of personal experience.

These far out, socially unacceptable encounters were buried, misinterpreted, discounted, denied, forgotten, or, by some other device, shoved into a mental closet.

As I openly relate my extraordinary encounters, people listening become comfortable enough to remember the forgotten out-of-the-ordinary events that have happened to them.

As the personality senses the space of acceptance of extraordinary life adventures, it feels safe enough to recall its own unusual, extrasensory exploits.

We have all had hundreds of direct personal experiences of multisensory, nonphysical awareness and extra-normal powers this lifetime.

Using our innate connection to our inner coach, these amazing exploits can be recollected from the closets and graves in which we buried them.

As a storyteller—in the guise of a therapist, healer, journalist, talk show host and filmmaker—my stories have assisted thousands of people to recall their own inner coach: outer power stories.

May the muse of True Memory shine on you as you read my story.

PART I

Starting Fresh All Over Again

My Friend the Ascended Master

*We must be willing to let go of the life we have planned,
so as to have the life that is waiting for us.*

JOSEPH CAMPBELL

This book is the story of my personality's relationship with my inner coach. My story begins where most people's stories end—when the child enters society.

Of course, a person's inner coach story never ends. However, a person's awareness of what is happening on the nonphysical, multisensory level often comes to an abrupt halt if that inner awareness is not nurtured. This premature shutdown to experiencing the full consciousness of our true nature is the fate of most people. The closedown usually occurs in early childhood, just about the time we are entering the world of adults in preschool or kindergarten. We're told to "put away the things of childhood" by the people nearest us. Our parents, relatives, friends and teachers have already hidden from themselves their abilities to see nonphysical reality—angels, fairies, invisible friends, spirit guides, deceased Grandma or Grandpa at the family dinner table or the shimmering glow around loving people. Because most parents no longer remember the magic and power of their own extrasensory perception, the natural multisensory abilities of children in our Western culture are usually suppressed for the sake of social acceptability.

This cutoff from expanded consciousness would have been my fate as well, if it weren't for the valiant and persistent efforts of one Ascended Master named St. Germain. Throughout my childhood, this loving nonphysical being visited me at night right after my parents tucked me in and before I went off to dreamland. His presence filled me with a warm sensation. I discerned him as a faint pulsating light in the corner of my bedroom. In later years, as I got comfortable with his enveloping energy in my room, I was able to perceive the form of his body and the features of his face. Eventually, I conversed with him as one talks to an old friend.

St. Germain is a nonphysical being referred to as an "Ascended Master." Ascended Masters are human beings who have mastered and ascended the influence of their human emotions and the limitations of cultural, psychological conditioning. When this mastery reaches a certain level, these regular, physical people ascend from the limitations of the physical universe and become nonphysical beings with multisensory and multidimensional awareness. Other Ascended Masters include Jesus, Buddha, Lao Tzu, Mother Mary and Sai Baba. These wise and experienced friends make themselves available to people through meditation for spiritual guidance and counsel. (By the way, the "St." is simply part of St. Germain's name; it does not mean he is a saint in any religious sense.)

My spiritual mentorship with St. Germain has been a constant in my life since childhood, although it took me a long while to evolve my relationship with him into a conscious exchange between equals.

At first, I experienced my mentor as a kind of guardian angel, comforting me with soothing vibrations by night and saving me from human danger and disaster by day. In my youth, I was especially aware that a divine force intervened many times to prevent injury and accidents during my teenage driving years.

In my twenties, as I became more accustomed to extrasensory phenomena and my own spiritual nature, my connection with St. Germain became more conscious. I developed my self-esteem and courage to a degree where I interacted with this awakened being as a good buddy and confidant. This is when my training for my life's work began in a deliberate and detailed way.

On every nocturnal visit, St. Germain would show me aspects of my inner coach game plan, the scenario my real self had laid out for my future. As my friend described coming events, I observed these prophesies as an "awake vision." I witnessed scenes of my future self—speaking to large groups of people, practicing various healing arts, and teaching yoga and other meditation techniques. St. Germain told me how these events would come to pass and how I could prepare myself for my chosen destiny. However, usually by the next day, I'd unconsciously water down the reality of our meetings, disguising our lessons as vague memories. Or I'd shake off the nighttime visitations as provocative, enlightening dreams—but dreams, nonetheless.

For years, I felt blessed—and hounded—by my friendship with this helpful counselor. I was enthused—and scared—by my soul's enlightened plan. Because I didn't yet have a way to deal with the fear, I often resisted the counsel of my ascended buddy.

Searching for some understanding or explanation of my nightly visits, I tried to discuss my connection to St. Germain with friends and family. All I got back was an incredulous look that screamed, "You're kidding, right?" Quickly I resigned myself to keeping this wondrous part of my life a private matter.

During my youth, I experienced many extraordinary events, which I share in this book. These miraculous occurrences were exhilarating, yet terrifying. I carried a lot of doubt about my capacity to psychologically handle multisensory realities and my worthiness to receive miracles. With hindsight, I see that it simply wasn't time for me to own my personal power and wisdom. Nor was it time for me to begin the public expression of my gifts. Then something so undeniable happened that I was no longer able to pretend my exalted friend and prophesied destiny were a fantasy.

Orlando, Florida, was the perfect setting for my awakening. What better place for magic to thrust itself permanently into my life than the home of Walt Disney's "Magic Kingdom." The experience began when a new acquaintance, Jerry, asked me to dinner during a human potential workshop we were both attending. Proud and confident, Jerry was a self-made man, a successful entrepreneur. A former NHL hockey player, he stood tall and stalwart, still brawny from his days with the Detroit Red Wings. His firm jaw and rough-cut features struck an imposing profile as we discussed very mundane, comfortable and safe subjects such as business and sports. As we sauntered outside after the meal at the hotel restaurant, Jerry proposed we trek down the street to a 7-11 convenience store to purchase some spring water. The market was barely visible about a mile down the busy thoroughfare. I glanced at my watch for the time. Since it wasn't late, I said, "Sure, why not?"

As we took our first step in the direction of our destination, Jerry casually inquired, "What do you know about St. Germain?"

His question struck me as totally out of the blue. Even though we'd met at a personal growth seminar, Jerry and I hadn't touched on anything even faintly metaphysical in our supper conversation. Now he was asking me about the most important, yet secret relationship of my life.

When our feet hit the ground taking our first step, we were standing in front of the 7-11 convenience store—over a mile away from the restaurant! We had gone that distance in one step! Instinctively, we both looked at our watches. No time had gone by! When we went inside, I double-checked the time with the store's wall clock. It also verified that mile-long journey from the restaurant to the store had occurred in a matter of seconds! We bought the water. In stunned silence, we returned to the hotel the normal way—we walked. Our return trek took about twenty minutes.

Back in my hotel room, Jerry spoke first, "Did you notice anything unusual on our walk to the 7-11?"

Of course, I had, but my mind was still spinning with the inexplicable wonder of it all. I mumbled under my breath, "It seemed to me, it didn't take any time to go from the restaurant to the store."

Jerry was also in a state of shock and disbelief. "I know. I checked the time when we got to the store. Zilch. Nada. No time had gone by. It doesn't make any sense."

"You know, Jerry, I have on rare occasions experienced time contracting and expanding in my life."

"I have too, but not like this. Man, we went a mile in a split second! And, Keith, I don't remember the trek to the store either. There were at least six streets to cross, each with a traffic light. I certainly noticed crossing the streets and waiting for the lights to change on the long way back!"

"Me, too. I can't recall walking to the store at all. It was like just POP! and we were there, standing in front of the store. The time jump happened right when you asked me about St. Germain."

That was it. St. Germain's name was the key, the secret password, that literally opened the gates of Heaven on that balmy night in Florida. A soft, golden light began to fill the hotel room from one corner. From the other side of the room, a piercing violet light reached out to encircle us.

Both radiating energies felt safe to invite into my space. Jerry also slipped into a calm, relaxed posture on one of the beds.

"Do you see that yellow glow in the corner?" he asked me.

"Yes, do you see that purple light over there?" I asked right back.

"Yes, it feels extremely familiar, like I know it, like I've felt it before," Jerry replied.

"Yeah, I do recognize the feeling, but I can't tell you from where," I agreed.

Soon the source of the two pulsating glows became all too apparent. The beams were emanating from two old friends coming to visit. Their calling cards were the lights radiating from the corners of the room. They were trying to announce themselves gracefully.

We should have known who it was. Given the portal we'd just gone through—the instant, one-mile jump in time and space at the drop of a name—who else could have pulled off such a stunt?

As my new friend and I simultaneously took a deep breath, we found ourselves fully aware of sitting in the presence of our oldest and dearest spiritual mentors, St. Germain for me and Jesus for Jerry. Jerry had encountered Ascended Master Jesus several times over the previous years—in a childhood lightning strike during which Jerry was unconscious for hours, and, later in life, in meditation and prayer.

Once we identified the sources of the emanations, Jerry and I felt very comfortable sitting with St. Germain and Jesus in the hotel room. The intimacy was intense, but ecstatic. St. Germain and Jesus conversed with us very informally, as casual friends, with great affection and humor. The masters spoke to us about our individual missions on Earth this lifetime and about our relationship to each other, to the Council of Ascended Masters and to God. In intricate, colorful detail, they painted the pictures of our futures: my friend and I would each teach our inner wisdom to large numbers of people around the world. Jerry would lecture and convey his truth in a more traditional, formal way. I'd develop a more egalitarian, flexible manner of presentation.

For an entire week our nonphysical mentors met with us in the hotel room each evening. Much of what they said I'd heard before from St. Germain, but never when I was in such an awake state. Jerry and I were very present and alert for each evening's session. Previously, we'd both veiled over our meetings with our cosmic buddies, discounting or disguising the encounters by the next day. However, the fact that we met with our esteemed friends for several evenings—and that we were so conscious during these meetings—made these visitations impossible to deny or forget. Jerry and I have retained full recall of the information and the aura of grace that was bestowed on us that week.

Another factor in our lasting retention and acceptance of these extraordinary events was that it is now, finally, time on Earth to remember—to wake up, to know.

During the concluding evening's conversation with our two enlightened friends, I discovered the meaning of a curious message that had been floating in my consciousness since my youth. Never before did I have a clue what the recurring soul memo meant. Finally, I knew in my heart the true import of the enigmatic phrase:

We are the failsafe seeds to ensure
the creation does not go on forever.

Repeating verbatim this inner message, our mentors reminded us of the design of our shared destiny with all of humanity. They elaborated:

"Within each of you humans is the failsafe seed of knowing how to undo this particular creation—this creation of being unconscious, of forgetting who you are and why you are here on Earth. Within each of you is the seed of knowing your unique plan and special purpose—your personal contribution to the unfolding of the collective plan. The seed of knowing is within you and when given the right environment at the predetermined time, the seed will sprout and grow."

For Jerry and me the right environment and time were there and then in that hotel room. Our instantaneous one-mile leap in space had catapulted each of us into a new stage of personal, spiritual blossoming. This new arena was to be a public one. Events played out from that moment empowering Jerry and me to move into conscious public sharing of our distinctive skills and wisdom. The rest of this book is the story of the unfolding of my particular soul expression—from inner preparation to outer presentation.

And St. Germain has always been there behind the scenes, looking after me, coordinating my spiritual experiences, *keeping* me out of trouble in most cases, and *getting* me out of trouble when I follow the dictates of my outer personality instead of my inner coach.

You, too, can open to a divine dialogue and fun friendship with nonphysical teachers. They surround each of us all the time. To get the ball rolling all it takes from you is an invitation from the heart. When you find yourself in a quiet, relaxed, receptive state, simply ask for a communication, connection or exchange from your spirit guides. Give permission for their assistance. Welcome their love and encouragement. Your inner coach will show you how. Your natural instincts know how to do it.

The interaction may begin as a sensation of warmth in your body or a faint glow in the corner of the room. You may sense a presence within you—or outside of you somewhere in your physical space. A new color, symbol or sound may show up in your meditation. A book or song may catch your attention. Our nonphysical friends use whatever avenues they can to reach out and get through to us.

The following stories offer some hints on how to begin your only true journey on Earth—the path back to your real self. You're always in contact with your spirit friends, even when you're not aware of them. You, too, have had extraordinary experiences since the day you were born. Allow your True Memory to return. Open yourself to the magic of your own multisensory awareness and let the good times roll!

Part II

Opening to Possibilities

Advice from Beyond the Grave

What the heart knows today,
the head will know tomorrow.

JAMES STEPHENS

On a brilliant, sunshiny day, there is no place on Earth more alluring and unassuming than Lilydale, New York. The hamlet is the quintessential, picturesque country village. Quaint. Classic. Archaic. Frozen in time. However, it's not Lilydale's physical beauty for which the settlement is renowned; it is the town's metaphysical character that draws thousands of visitors each year. Lilydale is not only enchanting, but enchanted as well—literally.

This irony was not lost on Peter and me after we realized we were tricked into traveling to Lilydale under the pretext of capturing its surface charm on canvas. It was charms of another sort that drew our souls to this idyllic community—the magical charms of Lilydale's spiritualist mediums. It wouldn't be the last time I was conned into opening to an expansive *inner* awakening under the guise of an enticing *outer* attraction. Peter, my comrade-in-arts, and I were set up by Spirit.

A precocious thirteen, I was taking summer art classes at Chautauqua Institution, a cultural resort in upstate New York. Little did I know my real education over the summer months would have nothing to do with oils and watercolors. My art teachers always encouraged me to look beneath the surface of the object of a painting in order to capture the spirit of the subject. It was the spirits of Lilydale I was sent to capture that day—not on my earthly canvas, but on my eternal template.

The people and events of this sleepy burg move at the same leisurely pace as the spring sap oozes from the ancient maples in the thick virgin woods enveloping the town. The remote, quiet hamlet chooses to forget the passing of time. Sprinkled among its meandering lanes and pristine ponds sit well-preserved Victorian homes, fanciful boarding houses and rambling hotels— magnificent edifices of a bygone era protected by enormous ancestral oaks anchored in eternity. As creative artists, our secular assignment was to render the town's unique atmosphere and character on paper.

Our visit coincided with the summer gathering of several hundred spiritualist mediums who set up shop in Lilydale annually. These modern-day soothsayers gave us budding artists something more than the physical landscape to reflect upon. Fascinatingly diverse people came from around the world to contact their dead relatives and friends through these visiting mediums. My classmates and I laughed at the idea of talking to the dead. We considered the spiritualists nothing more than hustlers, their clients sheep begging to be fleeced, and the séances on a par with carnival entertainment.

After a day of drawing, some of us decided to attend a séance just for the fun and novelty of it. On a dare, my friend Peter worked up the nerve to raise his hand and ask the presiding medium for a communication from the spirit world. Peter was a rarity: a fellow who was an aesthete as well as a jock—a sensitive, creative artist in the body of a macho, all-star athlete.

In this moment, his dual nature came together to inspire him to take a bold leap of faith and headlong plunge into another world.

Suddenly, the soft, melodic voice of the petite female medium changed dramatically. A gravelly, resonant and definitely male uttering came from somewhere deep within her: "You really have to quit breaking the law, Peter! Smashing those parking meters was foolish. You're going to get caught next time. I'm telling you this because I love you. I don't want you to make a big mistake you'll regret for the rest of your life."

Peter turned ashen white and started shaking. "That's my Uncle Mike's voice," he blurted. "That's just the way he talked. It's my uncle! And he's dead!"

After the séance, Peter told me how he had destroyed several parking meters just prior to leaving his Wisconsin hometown—

eight hundred or so miles from Lilydale. Not even Peter's closest friends knew he was the vandal. Because his father was the city's chief of police, it was of the utmost importance that his culpability be kept a secret.

Since my birth, my parents taught me there is always a rational explanation for everything. Yet this feat appeared to defy logic. Replaying the séance over and over again in my mind, I was baffled. *Not one of us has ever been to Lilydale before. Not one of the townspeople knows us. The medium has never had any communication with any of us. So how could she be aware of a crime that occurred hundreds of miles away?*

I questioned Peter again the next morning. He was still shaken, and reiterated that he'd told absolutely no one about the parking meters. My mind continued in overdrive. *How was the spiritualist aware Peter had a dead uncle? And how did she reproduce what sounded to Peter like his uncle's voice?*

The more I tried to rationalize what happened, the more the facts refused to fit into my current concept of reality. The incident ripped a tear in the fundamental fabric of my logically woven, explainable world. By the end of the summer, I was no further ahead in understanding the events of the séance than I had been the afternoon it occurred in Lilydale.

For months afterward, I continued to ponder heavily on the enigma of Lilydale. Eventually, I surmised there must be another dimension to life of which I had no knowledge. Logic dictated that if I could learn about this dimension, I'd find the answer to the séance mystery. After much contemplation, I concluded I needed to look for answers *beyond* the physical appearance of events. I began seeking out *meta*physical people and books wherever I could locate them. Somehow, I knew these folks and resources would reveal the key that would unlock the Lilydale puzzle. So began my journey into the many mysteries of the many layers of realities on Earth. It's an adventure that continues to this day.

Stopping Time

One should count each day as a separate life.

SENECA, ROMAN PHILOSOPHER

Six hundred feet straight down! Nothing to break the fall. I've got to switch channels. I don't like my chances on this station. Infused with youthful caprice, I mused to myself about my predicament. Enjoying the intense body rush of imminent danger, I was torn between prolonging the joy-terror and searching for an escape from my imminent demise.

I'd been in similar dire situations before and I'd always evaded the worst. *How did I get out of danger before? Quick, you idiot, think! You don't have all day!*

The impending disaster pumped my adrenaline—and my memory. *I let go,* I reminded myself. *That's what I did in past situations. I just let go of having to control the whole thing. I released my need to be right about how life operates. I allowed the picture to change. That's when circumstances shifted and something unexpected, seemingly impossible, occurred. Let the channel switch, Keith!* I coached myself into letting go into safety once again. Averting the most probable outcome, I robbed death of its prey yet another time.

Yes, rather unceremoniously, I was reminded of the natural malleability of the physical universe by a six-hundred-foot free fall straight down a sheer cliff. The threat of a perilous plunge into empty space re-impressed on my young mind the lessons I learned in similar predicaments: go with the slide on the ice rink, relax into the tackle in football and turn toward the skid in the car. Now I call it "the decision to surrender." Back then, I called it "just letting go."

I was fourteen. The morning mist was lifting after an all-night soaking rain. My girlfriend Cheryl and I decided to go for a hike down a precipitous gorge in upstate New York. We had most of the crisp spring day to play before reporting to work as dinnertime servers at a local restaurant. The trail was winding and steep. Three hours later, we arrived at the bottom of the granite and shale canyon.

Cheryl was an intriguing, rare combination of tomboy and temptress. I was a mix of tenderheart and tomcat. In a wondrous, inexplicable way, we complemented each other, generating a lot of easy, relaxed fun together. After spending an afternoon playing and swimming in the rippling stream, it dawned on us we didn't have enough time to hike back up the zigzagging trail to the top and get to work on time. After discussing our limited options, we concluded we could still make it back to civilization and our job deadline if we climbed straight up the vertical cliff.

Ascending the steep cliff turned out to be quite easy. Protruding from the sheer granite wall were small rock ledges as easy to climb up as rungs on a ladder. Within thirty minutes we were twenty feet from the top. We would have been home free, except that the previous night's rain had soaked the soil near the crest, loosening the shale ledges. As we neared the top, each time we placed a foot or hand on the next rock outcropping, the shale broke away from the cliff. Very quickly, we found ourselves frantically moving our hands and feet from one shelf to another, searching for something solid to support us in order to clamber up the last few feet to safety.

We were very close to the top and firm ground. But we couldn't make any more progress. With total panic on her face, Cheryl looked over at me—a silent plea for guidance screaming over the space between us. I didn't know what to do next. I had no answers. Like her, I'd also run out of ledges within reach to grasp. I felt myself beginning to slide down the cliff.

Suddenly, my whole life flashed in front of my eyes! It was like watching a movie being projected a few feet in front of me. During the first second of my descent into the abyss, I re-experienced every major positive event of my life in full, living color, including all the emotional and physical sensations of each incident. I re-lived every significant birthday party, picnic, vacation, romantic date, school honor, sports achievement and family celebration of my short life. This vivid, instantaneous and comprehensive review was very rich and satisfying. Considering my precarious situation, an incongruous aura of calm and fulfillment swept over me.

The flashback ended as abruptly as it began. Suddenly, I was acutely aware of being suspended in time and space between the life review I'd just experienced and the next moment of present time—me in the midst of my slide down the cliff. During that seemingly eternal moment, the realization hit me like a ten-ton boulder: *I don't want to die!* A wave of acute appreciation flooded over me. *I love life. I want to continue exploring what life has to offer.* I remember whispering to myself, *I want to live,* as if one part of me were informing another part of me.

Then, swoosh! I plummeted into the vast emptiness beneath me. Some alert, unknown aspect of my being spontaneously yelled to Cheryl, "Lie flat! Relax! Let go!" Hearing the words that came unbidden from within me, I, too, obeyed, and consciously chose to surrender to the inevitable.

I don't remember anything after that decision, including what logically should have been a very abrupt and painful landing. All I know is, Cheryl and I were suddenly sitting in the stream at the bottom of the gorge where the current formed a small pool. Although the water in the pool had turned crimson with our blood, neither of us was experiencing any aches or discomfort. Upon close examination, we found the bleeding came from small, razor-thin cuts all over the fronts of our bodies. But we had no broken bones, bruises or other injuries. Our bodies weren't sore or tender—just laced with teeny nicks and slices that quickly stopped bleeding. It was as if the only purpose of the scratches was to remind us that, yes, indeed, we had just gone free falling down a six-hundred-foot cliff.

After a short period of wonderment, we practically danced up the long, circuitous trail to the top of the gorge. We were so thankful—and simply happy to be alive, in one piece and being given a second chance. The climb was effortless. Inexplicably, we were totally refreshed and recharged with energy when we reached the top.

Crisis. Emergency. Danger.

These threats to my well-being were my early teachers. From these seeming enemies, I learned that when faced with an expected outcome I don't like, I have an option. I can open to an alternative scenario, another framework, a different set of rules. I jokingly call my ploy "switching channels." It's an apt metaphor. I simply let go of my old way of viewing the world and allow a fresh perspective to emerge—or not! After all, when we truly let go, anything can happen! More often than not, however, I find myself shifted to a new reality—a different station with a new storyline that has a much better ending! This is the stuff of miracles and alchemy.

I first noticed the saving gift of grace when I was a kid. I've always enjoyed the thrill and challenge of perilous situations. On the ice rink, I discovered that if I completely collapsed into a fall, I came out unscathed. Caught in a precarious position when tackled on the football field, I went with the force of the hit to tumble out of harm's way. When in a sharp skid while driving, I embraced the skid by turning directly into it to straighten the car. When my feet slipped on a rocky trail, I went with the twist or slide and landed—like a cat—upright and stable. Like the proverbial drunk falling safely down the staircase, I used to sled down a steep set of wooden stairs on a makeshift cardboard toboggan, deliberately crashing at the bottom and never getting hurt.

I practiced the knack of letting go in everyday situations, so that I was able to successfully apply the skill in much more urgent and crucial predicaments. As a teenager, the art of "abandonment to the moment" saved my neck in several near-miss car encounters. Attempting to pass a vehicle on the winding mountain roads of my home state of Pennsylvania, I found myself on several occasions eyeball-to-eyeball with the driver of an oncoming auto. With both cars going fifty miles per hour, my next stop in five feet and two seconds was the Pearly Gates. Each time, I instinctively let go—of the steering wheel, my projected scenario and my programmed ideas of physics. Voila! I ended up rattled but untouched on the side of the road.

In my young twenties, as a professional journalist covering floods, hurricanes, earthquakes, accidents and assorted disasters, I observed this miraculous dynamic of super-natural powers on countless occasions. When confronted with a choice between the dire prognosis of their current belief system and an unknown outcome if they let go of those beliefs, people will often choose to let go. They release their preconceptions of how the physical universe works. They let go of their need to have events fit their expectations of cause and effect. The reward for such surrender of one's rigid beliefs and expectations is a much preferable outcome—in fact, a miracle—or, at least, what we call a miracle: an occurrence outside our box, our paradigm, beyond what we think or believe is possible.

I've witnessed people lifting two-ton trucks, ripping open steel elevator doors, and performing medical procedures they had no way of knowing how to conduct. How? By choosing to go with an unknown future instead of a known past. When a person's own life, or the well-being of another, is at stake, people often decide to drop the limitations taught by our culture. When it's dramatically obvious that a known past will lead to a known—but fatal—future, people will often choose to give up their familiar, current beliefs and allow something fresh and new to occur.

As a young journalist, a light bulb lit up inside my head: *If we can tap these super-normal abilities in a crisis, why can't we access these extraordinary powers at will, whenever we want?* Thus began my lifelong quest for the Holy Grail—the sacred vessel that holds the nectar of the gods, the knowledge of how to recapture our true nature.

Traveling Out of Body

The things we know best are
the things we haven't been taught.

VAUVENARGUES

I can see the cops coming! They're a good thousand feet away.
I can clearly make out their uniforms and swinging nightsticks.
How can I be seeing this?

I didn't dare mention it to my underage drinking mates
lounging with me on the grassy knoll in the park. *Am I making this*
up? Projecting it somehow into my vision? Forcefully, I shook my
head back and forth in an effort to free my mind of its strange
perception.

But the view of the two policemen remained in my sight, as
they sauntered closer and closer to our drinking den. In fact, to my
further astonishment, I saw a much wider perspective as I swiveled
my gaze within the picture before me. *I can see myself!*

Frantically blinking my eyes open and shut trying to erase this
impossibility, I still found myself staring at my own physical body
on the ground next to my beer buddies. The place from which I
was viewing was about forty feet in the air! As I shifted my
attention to look at the looker, I saw an airborne body in the form
of a luminous shimmer, much like a ghost is portrayed in a movie.
Then, with the ease of a mere thought, I discovered I could shift
my point of view from my physical body on the ground back to
my ethereal light body in the air. Using my eyes in my subtle
body, I surveyed the scene again from my perch in the air.

Am I making all this up? Do I want to impress my pals so
much, I'm concocting an extrasensory perception to allow me to
warn them of an oncoming bust? My frenetic self-questioning
came to an abrupt halt as I heard one of the officers whisper to his

colleague, "Do you hear that noise? There are some kids in the park."

Whether I was conjuring my supernormal sight and hearing to court favor with my friends or not, I needed to act—and quickly. "Hey, guys, don't ask me how I know, but there are some cops right up the street and they're on to us. Let's split." My three inebriated friends and I quietly sneaked down the hill and out of the park under the helpful cloak of darkness. By a nanosecond, we successfully evaded detection as we heard the policemen slashing at the bushes with their billyclubs right behind us. A close call!

"Hey, how'd ya know the fuzz was there?" my buddy pressed me, as we arrived safely back at our car.

"Uh, I just knew somehow. A guess, I guess," I muttered, covering for myself as best I could under the circumstances.

"Well, a pretty good one, man. We'd be up the creek if they caught us. Thanks. You're all right. We should have you around every time we go drinking."

Ah, music to my ears. And so my young career as a drinking guard began!

My friends, at sixteen, were older than I, but still under the legal drinking age of eighteen in New York State. I was fifteen and considered myself really lucky to be included in this older gang at a time of life when acceptance and belonging was paramount. And to have access to liquor through their connections was heaven for me.

I would do almost anything to please these guys and stay tight with them. I mused to myself, *My newfound super-vision is coming in real handy. If we got busted for underage drinking, we'd all get grounded by our parents, not to mention getting in trouble with the law. I've got to keep this good thing going!*

On that fateful night, my inner coach prompted me to keep developing this burgeoning, new ability that I stumbled across in the line of necessity and opportunity. As I played with my prowess as a night watchman for the gang, I realized I was doing more than clairvoyance, "clear seeing." Each time I playfully sent myself out to scan the scene for police, I was having a bona fide out-of-body experience. I didn't have a name for it then, but I sure knew I was doing it! I was right on the mark every time I called a cop alert. My skill was valued by the friends I valued. Literally, I was flying high!

Behind the Scenes
in Mr. Rogers' Neighborhood

Keep me away from the wisdom that does not cry,
the philosophy which does not laugh and
the greatness which does not bow before children.

KAHLIL GIBRAN

Do . . . you . . . know . . . why . . . Mr. . . . . Rogers . . . of . . .
Mr. . . . . Rogers' . . . Neighbor . . . hood . . . TV . . . show . . . talks
. . . so . . . very . . . slowly . . . and . . . very . . . clearly . . . and . . .
uses . . . little . . . tiny . . . words?

During my college years, I had the privilege of working on the
"Mr. Rogers' Neighborhood" show for WQED Public TV in
Pittsburgh. As an intern, I assisted with the props and sets. One
day while on a break from shooting, I asked Fred Rogers why he
talked in such a leisurely, piecemeal way. What he shared with
me, as well as what I observed being with him, gave me a fresh
appreciation of commitment, compassion and integrity.

"Children understand us when we talk plainly and honestly to
them," explained Mr. Rogers. "I talk very simply to children
because I want to communicate with them as young as possible.
Even before children understand the intellectual definition of
words, they absorb meaning from the vibration of each spoken
word, the energy of the intention of the communication, and the
feelings of the people speaking."

This champion of children has been speaking to the hearts and
spirits of youngsters since the beginning of commercial broadcast

communication. Before television was born, Mr. Rogers was on the first radio station in the world, KDKA in Pittsburgh, with "The Children's Hour." His program later developed into "Mr. Rogers' Neighborhood" on public television. Now his slow-talking children's show is on hundreds of television stations in the United States and in scores of other countries.

Fred Rogers relates to children naturally and intimately. He speaks from his heart directly into their souls. And they intensely love him in return. The depth to which Mr. Rogers touches children reveals itself when kids from around the country come to visit the television studio. Often I watched frightened children timidly step into the huge studio, closely hugging their parents, holding onto a leg or an arm. For a child, a TV studio is an intimidating room full of wires, cables, monitors, bright lights and scores of big people running around yelling orders at each other. Peering through this scary mass of adults, cameras and props, kids would catch a glimpse of Mr. Rogers on the far side of the set. Overwhelmed with raw enthusiasm, they'd tear free from their parents, climb over the cables, weave past all the equipment and jump joyously into Fred's outstretched arms.

Somehow, Mr. Rogers always knew when a child was coming and would drop whatever he was doing to be ready to embrace them. Many times I saw kids leap several feet before reaching him, confident their loving hero would catch them once they reached his waist or chest. And Fred would always snag them— gently, reverently. Those children held onto him so tightly. Crying with delight, the kids would tell him repeatedly how much they loved him. Touching, holding and hugging this gentle, caring person—who had affected them so poignantly over the airwaves— was the thrill of their lives.

Often, after a short while, some parents became visibly jealous of the strong, open affection between their kids and the show's genial host. Usually, Mr. Rogers perceived the emotions emanating from Mom and Dad, and graciously returned the child to the envious parents. However, when Fred missed his cue, parents would physically rip their child away from his embrace, making up some excuse about having to leave.

"Mr. Rogers' Neighborhood" has a very distinct purpose in addition to entertainment. In every episode of the show, Fred weaves a consistent connection of cooperation, caring, fairness, generosity, honesty, mutuality, trust, openness, spontaneity, courage and harmony between himself and the show's characters. These qualities are the spiritual principles by which Fred Rogers lives and expresses himself consistently in word, feeling and action on his program and in his private life. He realizes parents may be lacking in some values or may not be available enough to instill these qualities in their children. Fred uses his interactions with the show's puppet and human characters to introduce and demonstrate these values to kids as early in their lives as possible. Then, when children are older and their world expands beyond their home to adults and other kids, they have a solid spiritual and social foundation to draw upon.

Adroitly, Mr. Rogers never lectures his audience, but rather relies on his regular cast of puppet people and animals to present and implant caring concepts through playful adventures. When Robert Kennedy was assassinated in Los Angeles in 1968, Mr. Rogers noticed most television stations were showing people grieving and wearing solemn dark clothes. In addition, radio outlets were broadcasting very doleful music befitting a nation in mourning. As an adult, he understood this somberness is the primary way our culture deals with death. However, he was concerned about the effect this perspective on death was having on children. Fred feared that the extreme national outpouring of grief and despair was sending a very one-sided, negative message to kids concerning death—one of overwhelming sadness, fear, abandonment and confusion. In order to present an alternative to the nation's morose and bleak cultural perception of mortality, Mr. Rogers engaged the magic of his puppets.

What a great time the puppets were having playing with balloons! The puppets bounced and played catch with the balloons until the balloons became their friends. The puppets became such intimate friends with the balloons, they gave them personal names. Then, in the frolic and spontaneity of play, one by one the balloons were punctured. Some balloons deflated quickly. Others lost their air more slowly. Because the puppets were losing some of their balloon friends, they were sad. All they had left of their friends were limp, lifeless pieces of rubber. Afraid and confused, the puppets went to Wise Owl and asked him what was happening to their balloon buddies.

"Where did our friends go? We were having such fun! Now all of a sudden they're gone," the puppets cried.

Wise Owl explained that their friends were not really gone. They had just changed form. His analogy was straightforward and easy to grasp.

"First," Wise Owl told the puppets, "before your balloon friends arrived, they were part of the Big Air. And when you all blew up the balloons, you helped bring this Big Air into the balloons. As the Big Air came into each balloon, it became one of your balloon friends." Wise Owl tenderly explained to the puppets that in the course of living life, the balloon bodies of their friends were punctured and their essence went back to the Big Air. "Your balloon friends no longer need the balloon bodies because they've changed form. But they're still around—in Spirit, in the Big Air," consoled the feathered sage. "Can you feel them?"

"Yes! Yes! We can feel them!" the puppets exclaimed in unison.

The puppets' fears were alleviated. They understood that a person might grieve when a friend dies, changes form and goes away. But death does not mean the end; it simply means a friend has changed form and gone somewhere else. Once again, Mr. Rogers' young audience was given an alternative way to perceive an important aspect of life on Earth. And, as is his special talent, Mr. Rogers imparts a more compassionate and life-affirming way to embrace life than what is shown in much of ordinary commercial television programming.

Years later, I was delighted to come across an historical fact that revealed more of the casual, canny insight of this playful puppeteer. The word that Jesus of Nazareth used in Biblical times when he referred to death does not literally translate into the English word *death*. The Aramaic word Jesus chose to use means "not here, present elsewhere."

The masterful way Fred Rogers used his puppets and the scope of his understanding of human nature were never more evident than when the puppets would counsel the technical crew of his television show.

The crew—mostly cameramen, grips and technicians—rarely talked directly to Mr. Rogers off the set. They did, however, mercilessly make fun of him behind his back for the emotional and expressive way he communicated on the show and in public. Fred was an easy target for the crew because he was such an open and, to them, vulnerable man who wore his heart on his sleeve.

Amazingly though, while Mr. Rogers was rehearsing the movements of his puppets before each show, these same macho, blue-collar detractors would surreptitiously sneak into the television studio and ask his puppets for personal advice! Speaking through the voices and personalities of Wise Owl, the King, Squirrel and other puppets, Mr. Rogers would dispense guidance to the crew members about extremely personal issues, such as being impotent or having serious marital or health problems.

Fred assigned me the task of keeping everyone else off the set until he, or rather the puppets, finished counseling a worker. From a discreet distance, I observed these "tough" men cry and tell the puppets their most secret fears and weaknesses. The men knew on some level, of course, that inside the puppet was the hand of Fred Rogers. The same men who would not talk to Mr. Rogers to his face would bare their souls to his puppet-covered hands! The genuine concern and compassion Fred expressed through his puppets to these workers was very moving to witness.

Later, in public, the same crew members he had counseled continued to ignore Mr. Rogers, as if the puppet encounters had never occurred. And Fred played along with their detached behavior, not giving any sign of personal connection with the workers other than as ordinary members of his crew. However, I did notice that, over time, the men who got the most counseling from the puppets participated less and less in the mocking of their boss behind his back.

Fred Rogers taught me how to communicate in the most profound and affecting way—heart to heart, soul to soul. He not only showed me how to convey messages through *direct transmission*, he modeled how to do so with clarity, love and integrity. By daily example with the children and crew, he demonstrates how to use authenticity of intention to connect with other human beings on the most fundamental spiritual level. He aligns his eyes, face and voice to instill a potent and consistent tone to his sharing. He utilizes his body and gestures to carry the strength of his conviction. To express the lightness and accepting nature of his presence, he uses spontaneous laughter, play, fun and humor. He employs music, poetry, art and dance to share on still more levels and reach a broader spectrum of children—of all ages! His carefully chosen words, stories and actions were the outer expression of inner eternal truths that have served me well over the years. I was, indeed, honored to hang with Mr. Rogers in his 'hood.

The Secret Teachings of Helen Hayes

"Rabbit's clever," said Pooh thoughtfully.
"Yes," said Piglet, "Rabbit's clever."
"And he has brain."
"Yes," said Piglet, "Rabbit has brain."
There was a long silence.
"I suppose," said Pooh,
"that's why he never understands anything."

WINNIE THE POOH

Do our senses deceive us? Not really. We perceive to the extent that our five senses allow us to perceive. We simply miss a lot of the full spectrum of what is really going on around us. We can't grasp the whole picture employing only our "normal" five senses. A "silent" dog whistle is a prime example. The sound vibrations produced by such a dog whistle are not audible to the normal human eardrum. But they do exist. Just ask a dog! We can't see a television signal, but it flows right by us to produce a picture we can see on a TV screen.

However, our multisensory awareness does absorb information our five senses are not able to pick up. We can train ourselves to be sensitive enough to pick up transmissions outside our "normal" range of perception. Multisensory awareness is a skill that can be developed by anyone.

One of my most practical lessons about extrasensory perception I absorbed—literally—from Helen Hayes, one of the most gifted actresses in the history of the American stage.

I had the inestimable privilege of taking a theater performance class from Ms. Hayes when I was an earnest freshman at the

University of Michigan in Ann Arbor. It is paradoxical, and at the same time fitting, that in an *acting* class, I would master a very effective tool to create what I desire in the *real* world. Acting is the art of creating a specific perception of reality. And what is reality, ultimately, but each person's individual perception and interpretation of the world?

The first morning of class, twenty expectant, would-be thespians sat waiting in an empty theater. Ms. Hayes swept smoothly onto the campus theater stage, as swiftly and silently as a hawk swoops after its prey. Indeed, she had a target: our young, programmed minds. And our rigid mental conditioning was vanquished before we even knew the name of the game.

Without introduction or protocol, she announced, "I'd like you to sit in the front rows as my audience. I'm going to come on stage seven times and would like you to make notes on what you feel, what you notice, and, particularly, what type of character you experience me portraying."

My pen strained at the bit to be let loose. I was about to learn from a master of the craft. With the intensity of a hungry animal, I watched as Ms. Hayes proceeded to come on and off the bare stage seven times. Each time, she walked casually from behind the right curtain to center stage, stood immobile and statuesque for a few minutes, and then glided offstage left. She wore the same plain gray dress in each of the seven walk-ons. Her face was void of makeup. She wore no jewelry. She used no props. Her entire physical manner and bearing appeared to be a repetition of each previous presentation. Each time, she seemed to exactly duplicate the way she carried herself, making the identical arm and body movements. As far as I could see, neither her dress nor her actions ever varied. It was as if the first walk-on had been videotaped and then replayed six times in a row. Each performance *appeared* to be a carbon copy of the previous one.

What I *saw* were seven identical characters. What I *experienced* was something else again: seven quite different portrayals. Surprisingly, I knew immediately, without any doubt, the exact nature of each of the characters she was depicting. I could feel each varying persona she assumed. The personality, mood, disposition and tone were distinct in each instance. In the first scene, she was a downtrodden cleaning woman; in the second, a very proud, self-possessed upper-class snob; in the third, a mean-spirited spinster. Another time, she was a very wise and caring grandmother.

Beaming with a vibrant energy now totally her own, the renowned actress met us in the audience pit. She asked each of us to share what we just witnessed. We discovered we all experienced *simply knowing* the traits of each different personage she was performing on stage. She asked if any of us knew how she was able to convey each distinct character's temperament and personal story so definitively. Not one of us had an answer, a theory or even a clue. As far as we saw, she moved and acted exactly the same way in each of the seven enactments. She didn't appear to do anything differently, in any way, each of the seven times she came on stage. In the overbearing silence, we squirmed uncomfortably in our seats, chewed on our pens and stared at the rafters.

Saying nothing, Ms. Hayes proceeded to show us more fully and specifically what she had just presented on stage. She assumed each of the seven characters one by one, physically demonstrating how she held her head at a slightly different angle during each of the character depictions. In each instance, she moved her arms and shoulders in a unique manner. Her gait was subtly distinct in each entrance and exit. She exhibited how minute body variations and nuances created the effect she wanted to have on the audience. Each cock of her head, twitch of her eyes, turn of her hands and shift of her weight changed our perception of her persona.

Each of us, being the ardent students we were, took copious notes. We felt we had solved the riddle. We now knew how this brilliant actress had created and conveyed the essence of each dissimilar character.

Then the crafty Ms. Hayes oh-so-sweetly and innocently requested, "Now, put your notebooks away. Become a gallery of spectators again. Just relax. I invite you to simply experience me coming on stage again, just as an audience would."

We put our notepads down, but not away. Not one of us was willing to completely relax and let go of being a student at this point. We were determined to deduce her secrets and document her techniques.

Again she walked on and off the stage seven times. This time, of course, we scrutinized her every movement and pose, searching for the subtle body variations she'd demonstrated to us. We were looking for the nuances and hints of the acting craft she'd just shared. Bewildered, I couldn't discern she was using any of those contrivances at all. Even after she revealed the skillful devices an actor can use, it appeared that she was not employing any of those tricks of the trade. Again, to my awe and astonishment, even though I couldn't detect any changes in her movements or expressions from one presentation to another, I still knew what personality the actress was portraying each time!

Upon collaboration afterwards, my fellow students and I agreed the adept Ms. Hayes had kept a couple of the old characters and had introduced five new ones in her second presentation. And we all agreed on the exact order in which she depicted each portrayal. But none of us could decipher the methods the actress used to convey each distinct personality. I scratched my head in wonder, asking myself, *How did we recognize each character with such ease, accuracy and agreement?*

As we students were reeling from our utter failure to discover her devices, Ms. Hayes nonchalantly stepped forward. "Class dismissed," she announced softly. We protested, wanting to ask a million questions, but to no avail. She disappeared as skillfully and mysteriously as she had shifted personas before our eyes.

Ms. Hayes was not only an extremely talented actress, she was also a very wise teacher. She knew we needed time to examine our experiences, our perceptions—and ourselves. We were given a week to ponder what actually had happened on that bare stage.

My friends and I discussed it at great length, but we couldn't figure it out. It wasn't until later in the week, when I finally got myself quiet enough to probe more thoroughly into my own life experience, that I found the answer. Ms. Hayes didn't simply *portray* the various characters. She *became* each character. She merged so totally with the essence of each personage in such a complete way, she radiated the spirit and energy of that character to the audience. We students didn't *see* each character, we *felt* them. We recognized each distinct personality through feeling rather than observation.

Ms. Hayes was a master at using direct transmission to reach her audience. She sent her messages via the channel of extrasensory perception.

When the class met the next week, Ms. Hayes talked about her approach to characterization. She explained that when you allow yourself to *become* the core spirit of a certain type of person you want to portray, you will automatically communicate that essence directly to the audience. When you own, embrace and integrate the essential qualities of a character into your being, you'll naturally convey those attributes. As the character speaks from his or her soul and heart directly into the soul and heart of the audience, a direct transmission occurs. Whenever communication is approached in this direct way, techniques, props, costumes, contrivances and other devices are unnecessary.

Picking up where Mr. Rogers left off, Helen Hayes further demonstrated to me that the most profound communication in life occurs from essence to essence, spirit to spirit—not form to form. When a person *becomes* the essence that they wish to share with the world, the sharing of it happens naturally and automatically. It was a very valuable and liberating lesson from an inspired communicator. It is a dynamic truth and a tool I now employ in all my interactions with others.

Meeting My Inner Coach

Well, I reckon I got to light out for
the territory ahead of the rest,
because Aunt Sally she's going to adopt me and civilize me
and I can't stand it.
I been there before.

HUCKLEBERRY FINN

Throughout our lives, our inner coach guides us into situations where we can gain a clearer vision of ourselves, our world and our future. Sometimes the path can be turbulent, as the personality tries to close its eyes to the grander view. However, when the personality opens again to inner guidance, the light of clarity illuminates the previously darkened world.

To a searching college student, Europe held the promise of some answers to the perennial questions of a nineteen-year-old: *What's the meaning of life? Why am I here? Where do I fit in? What special contributions do I have to offer?*

I desperately needed some corner of the universe to make sense to me. I longed for more meaningful answers to life's important questions than I was finding in American academia or culture. Foreign films were my passion, along with continental cuisine and the early Impressionists. I made my pilgrimage to Europe to immerse myself in the societies that gave birth to the whole of Western civilization. Near the end of my travels, I visited a completely intact, two-thousand-year-old Roman Coliseum in the South of France. The arena was a stunningly symmetrical structure, eternally balanced and bold.

This forum of ancient culture that once showcased gladiator contests, flamboyant circuses and other vehicles for public entertainment for imperial Rome now hosted bullfights for modern Europe. Finding a seat in the crowd, I decided to stay and watch the performance. As I absorbed the brilliant pageantry of color and celebration unfolding within the historic structure, an abounding sense of harmony and beauty swept over me.

The first bull charged into the ring, tossing his noble head from side to side as he ran around the enclosure. The crowd stood as one, cheering wildly. A lithe, brightly costumed matador strode toward the bull in measured, confident steps. He shook his gleaming cape and stamped his feet. An expectant murmur ran through the audience. Waving his cape again, the matador challenged the huge beast before him. The bull charged. I marveled at the elegance of the matador as he calmly pivoted away from the attacking animal a scant few inches from his body. Over and over again, the bull charged and the matador twirled away, barely escaping the sharp horns. It was a dance. The huge bull ferociously attacked and the matador gracefully pirouetted away. I found myself cheering with the other spectators.

By then, I understood the cadence of the crowd. So, when an expectant hush swept over the coliseum, I felt something ominous about to happen. The enraged animal lunged at his tormentor. A reflection of something shiny caught my eye. Then I saw the source of the glare—a honed, steel blade poised in the air to strike. I recoiled in horror as the first blade went into the beast's back. My senses reeled as one sword after another was plunged into the weakening bull. Bitter bile rose in my throat as more gaily beribboned spears were thrust into the bewildered, mortally injured animal. Stunned, I watched as slowly, very slowly, the life force was senselessly drained from a once vibrant creature.

I witnessed three bulls die that afternoon. As the third victim fell to his knees, his blood joining that of the previous two beasts, my numbness gave way to a growing abhorrence of the "civilized massacre" in the ancient arena. Crying out loud, "I can't be part of this! This is not me!" I stumbled blindly out of the coliseum into the street.

My heart pounding against my rib cage, I rushed to the solitude of my car. I'd journeyed to the Old World to find my place in the sun and bask in the glow of the wisdom, principles and traditions of Western civilization. In the coliseum, the realization became quite evident that I had been monstrously misled. A civilization that purported to nurture the immutable qualities of life, liberty, fraternity, equality and compassion was, in fact, dedicating this magnificent classic structure to the systematic destruction of life spirit.

The bullfight was an unavoidable metaphor for the disturbing aspects of Western culture that I didn't want to confront. Still fairly new to the planet, I yearned to remain optimistic and trusting. But my innocence and faith were difficult to sustain in the face of the cruelty of humanity's constant warfare, social hypocrisy and religious intolerance.

My father was a lawyer and a politician. Even at my tender age, I'd already discovered the corruption and lies within the inner circle of most of the Establishment. I couldn't reconcile the asserted, altruistic principles of the world's political, religious and social institutions with the actual actions taken by those same bodies. To my young eyes, very little that our system proclaimed to be true turned out to be accurate. I could see why Native Americans lamented, "White man speaks with forked tongue." All my life I'd witnessed modern man saying one thing and doing another. I could see the duplicity in every branch of Western civilization. "I cannot fit into this culture," I grated aloud. "There's no place for me in this two-faced, deceptive society. My spirit won't permit it. My heart can't allow it."

As I drove away from the coliseum and the treacherous crime against life I'd witnessed, my heart slowed to its normal pace.

Back at my hotel, I contemplated what I'd discovered. Calming down, I moved from judgment to discernment, from subjective evaluation to objective observation. I simply saw the situation for what it was: I didn't belong. I realized that my particular spirit wasn't meant to fit into this particular civilization. This wasn't my culture; this wasn't my home. And I saw I needed to distance myself from the values of modern society.

Accepting this revelation without reservation triggered a fleeting, inner glimpse of my true nature and destiny. At the time, I wasn't able to identify or comprehend the full import of the vision. But somehow, in that moment, I knew that my spirit is here to express and evolve totally outside of the society in which I'd grown up. I'm destined to live *in* the culture, but not be *part of* it. I saw my true purpose and mission isn't to fit into this civilization, but to actually create a new culture. I'm to be part of a movement that will bring a whole new vein of original, fresh human expression on the Earth.

But what movement? With whom? And what should I do until I get more details? Suddenly, I felt a strong sense of impending danger. Feeling terribly alone in my newfound awareness, I recognized that I was in peril of being immersed in a society masquerading as a defender of life while, in reality, it was a killer of spirit. Fear washed over me. I panicked, *I'm not safe here. My soul is in danger!*

The next morning my eyes began to sting and burn. My vision was blurred. Within a few weeks, I was losing my sight in both eyes.

Increasingly unable to enjoy my travels, or even to drive safely, I cut my European trip short. Heading for my parents' house in Pennsylvania, I hoped to reconnoiter and get my bearings straight again. By the time I reached my childhood home in the U.S., my sight was totally gone in both eyes. The lights went out. I saw only darkness—inside and outside. My parents flew me around the country to eye specialists, seeking treatment for my mysterious affliction. No doctor could help my predicament or even diagnose the cause of the problem. The medical establishment told me I would have to "live with it." My lifetime dream was to make movies. My major in college and part-time professional vocation was filmmaking. Young, energetic, in the prime of my life and otherwise completely healthy, I was a filmmaker being told to live with total blindness!

Dylan Thomas' bold admonition reverberated in my head, "Do not go gentle into that good night. Rage, rage, against the dying of the light!" He was, of course, referring to fighting death. The doctors' advice to live with utter darkness was, to me, as a once vibrant visual artist, a virtual death sentence. For the first month of my blindness, I disappeared into comfortless despair. I wanted to die. I didn't want to live sightless and dependent on my parents for daily care. As a painter, sculptor, photographer and filmmaker, my primary connection to, and nourishment from, life had always come through my eyes. I felt lost on a bleak, black sea of fear, sadness and resentment. I could barely be civil with my parents who were so loving in their patience and tolerance in the face of my angry ranting and rancor.

I sank about as low as a human being can go, wallowing in self-pity and bitterness. After a month of despondency, I awoke one day with the idea of procuring a guitar to play. It felt as if the notion had been placed in my head somehow by someone or something outside myself. I'd never played a musical instrument, but I asked my mother to buy me an acoustical guitar. She was so ecstatic I was actually showing an interest in something, anything, that she readily complied. I taught myself how to play notes and chords. Although I had no conscious awareness of the traditional styles of jazz, I developed a natural, personal musical style similar to what might be called "jazz guitar."

The pure sounds of this simple stringed instrument helped me build a bridge to life again. I reached a point at which music was enough of a reason to get out of bed each morning and go through the difficulties of dealing with the world as a blind person. I still recall the feeling of the exact moment when I decided I wanted to live again. It's a point of reference and a source of power for me now when I get discouraged or negative about how my life is unfolding.

Fortified with the strength of my recent musical connection, I began the long road back to the level of openness and enthusiasm for living I once took for granted. I played to, and sang with, the birds outside my bedroom window. I slowly recharged my soul. Gradually, I pried my heart open again to feel and breathe in the joy of being alive. I restored my trust in myself. I reconnected with nourishment from the world outside myself.

As I reopened to the smells, tastes, touch and sounds of the physical universe, I spontaneously began to develop a *sixth* sense I never before noticed. I could "feel" where the furniture was located in my path as I walked through the house, steering successfully around chairs and through doorways. I could "sense" the presence of a person in the room before the person spoke or made a sound. I could even tell when someone was approaching our house and about to ring the doorbell.

Then, one day, I sensed an energy, a nonphysical Presence, in my bedroom. The sensation felt similar to how a person feels, yet distinctly different. The energy of the Presence was much more vibrant and penetrating than the presence of a human being. The phenomenon was even more dramatic and impactful than when my nonphysical friend St. Germain would come visit me. I'd felt such an energy before—when I was alone in nature and when I was in church. Instinctively, I began to converse with this Presence, asking who or what it was. I received an "answer" in the form of waves of loving, calming vibrations radiating from the location of the Presence in the room and, at the same time, from some innermost part of me! I felt these caring energies emanating simultaneously from outside—and inside—of my body.

Once comfortable with the vibration of the Presence—although not yet certain of its source or nature—I began to ask it questions out loud. "What happened to my sight? What can I do to see again?" Having recently gone blind, my concerns were very narrowly focused at the time!

At first, I simply felt waves of assurance that all was in order and proceeding along its proper course. These vibrational reassurances made no sense to me conceptually, yet I felt the intrinsic truth of their import. I was definitely put at ease by the power and perseverance of these energetic messages from the Presence.

At the time, I had a vague suspicion that the Presence was a mystical combination of Spirit, or God, and an aspect of myself, perhaps my higher self. My obsession over my lost eyesight completely overrode my curiosity or need to understand the nature of this healing Presence. I didn't pursue its precise identity to any extent. I was simply thankful for a friend of any kind in my prison of darkness.

Soothed into an authentic state of gratitude, I began to shed the mantle of despair and frustration I'd built up over the last two endless months of my stint in the darkness. I began to actually appreciate the time the blindness afforded me to relax, contemplate life's important issues and develop my newfound relationship to music, myself and this mysterious Presence. I even decided I could live the rest of my life blind if that was what was meant to be! My calm acceptance of this possible fate really surprised me at the time.

Even at my young age, I innately surmised that my blindness had something to do with a lesson or truth I needed to learn about life. I intuitively knew such a severe handicap had to be part of a larger scheme or purpose. I sensed this challenge of blindness was playing some sort of role in the unfolding of my personal spiritual game plan.

By diving into the depths of the soul in search of personal truth, I ascertained that receiving a helpful answer depends on asking the right questions. The focus of my queries to the Presence altered. I asked for illumination on the spiritual meaning and value of me going blind. I knew all too well the detrimental effect of my blindness, but I wanted to know the beneficial purpose of this limitation to my spirit.

As I pursued this new track of inquiry, I began to recognize why such a nightmare was happening to me. Simultaneously from within me *and* from the all-encompassing Presence came the insight I was seeking.

My intuitive understanding came on two levels: that of the personality and that of the soul. On the personality plane, I'd decided in the coliseum that it was crucial for me to find a way to diminish my exposure to public scrutiny and disclosure. I was afraid people would discover that I was seeing through society's cruel charade. My psychological strategy was to make myself appear powerless and innocuous so that I wouldn't be viewed by society as a threat. With the emotional logic of an ostrich burying its head in the sand, I was unconsciously trying to protect myself from being found out. If I couldn't see, I wouldn't be seen! If I couldn't see, society wouldn't know that I was seeing through its deceptive veneer of pretending to be a compassionate civilization. To stay safe, I felt I needed to become invisible to the culture. Then society wouldn't detect my personal revelations and judgments about its integrity. At the time, this tactic seemed completely reasonable to my scared personality.

On a more fundamental level of understanding, my blindness had inestimable value to my soul. Banished to dark solitude, I was forced to go within, and in doing so, discovered the existence of Spirit in the form of the Presence—and of my inner coach in the form of intuition. I felt very fortunate!

From my "dark night of the soul," I learned that I can use my intuition—rather than a physical handicap—to protect myself. I can use my inner sight to discern the truth of situations in order to react accurately and keep myself safe in the world. I can look (intuit) behind the appearances of situations until I find a deeper reality, a perspective more basic and authentic than what's showing up on the surface through the perception of my personality. With this intuitive approach, I can navigate more effectively and safely through the world of human affairs.

Also, I am extremely appreciative for the comfort and clarity of having forged a direct communication with Spirit—God. As is my newfound dialogue with my inner coach, my connection to Divine Presence is an eternal blessing that enriches every moment of my life.

Within hours of my realizations, events began to unfold that eventually brought back my full eyesight. In order to turn around the direction of my life, I changed my diet and lifestyle, as well as my attitude. I started to eat fresh, natural whole foods. I began to exercise daily again—even taking long walks outside guided only by my new friend, my sixth sense. I took up yoga and meditation. As I transformed from a fearful and resentful victim into a strong and grateful *source*-rer, my full eyesight gradually returned.

Viewing life with this fresh attitude and approach, I discovered that the root of people's callousness and cruelty to each other, animals and the Earth lies in people's fear of living life honestly and fully. Now I see how I can use my insights to help people dissolve this fear. Instead of hiding from life in blindness—or otherwise playing small, dumb or weak—I can use my powers of heightened perception and awareness to benefit humankind.

The curse of blindness turned out to be, in reality, a gift of power. Concerning any issue, I now go inside to consult my inner coach until I uncover the pure, undiluted stream of direct knowing flowing behind the scenes of every event on the planet. To embrace the soul expression that underlies all human affairs, I look beneath the surface manifestation of issues. I connect to the eternal beingness within each person and to the unity and grace behind all appearance of separation and conflict. I delve into the nature of disagreeable circumstances until I find a core reality that is more primary than what is showing up on the surface of human experience. I no longer accept any interpretation other than the truth of divine purpose creating every situation. This deeper meaning can heal and transform any circumstance.

To this day, I employ my inner coach to stay safe, play big and keep my vision clear. I use my outer power to assist others to transform the surface darkness of their lives into the inner light of true understanding.

Multidimensional Journeys
with Extraterrestrials

The breeze at dawn has secrets to tell you.
Don't go back to sleep.
You must ask for what you really want.
Don't go back to sleep.
People are going back and forth across the threshold
where two worlds touch.
The door is round and open.
Don't go back to sleep.

RUMI

In college, Thanksgiving was a great excuse for me to escape
from the pressures of schoolwork. The traditional rituals of the
holiday were secondary to my need to blow off steam and space
out watching the latest action flicks. I never suspected my soul
would cast me in an action movie of my own adventures featuring
extraterrestrials and *inner* space.

Lisa, Sylvia, Jacob, Chris and I were good friends and fellow
film students at the University of Michigan in Ann Arbor. We
were very thankful for the chance to skip town and reconnect with
living as normal human beings instead of college students. When
the holiday neared, we went our separate ways across the country
to spend time with our families and simply vegetate. As so often
occurred in my young sojourn on the planet, my inner coach had a
special, secret agenda for me on this particular holiday.

Returning to Ann Arbor after the school break, I discovered
my friends and I had independently latched onto the same idea for

a co-created film. Each of us came back to town wanting to do a documentary on "multidimensional travel."

As was my usual manner regarding spiritual breakthroughs, I backed into this one with no idea of what I was getting into. If I had suspected the divine disruption of my life lying ahead, I probably would have postponed this adventure another few lifetimes!

My friends and I didn't consider ourselves spiritually inclined people. We were an unlikely crew of metaphysical explorers. None of us had ever heard of multidimensional travel before. Nonetheless, in diverse ways in different parts of the country, we were each connected with the same esoteric topic at the same time.

One member of our group, Lisa, picked up a book on "astral projection." Jacob met a new acquaintance who shared her theories about "journeying to different levels of awareness." Chris was fascinated by a lecture on "past life regression." Sylvia came back from vacation bubbling with enthusiasm about "communicating with your Future Self," which she read about in a metaphysical magazine. I, personally, was riveted by a film documentary on "multidimensional realities." Reuniting after the holiday, we marveled at the synchronicity of our separate, independent discoveries and took it as a sure sign this subject was meant to be our next film project.

A few days later, I was hanging out with my rock musician friend Rhone who, in an intoxicated state, let slip that he had a relative in Montreal who was part of a very unusual organization. "My Uncle Gaston is the head honcho of a real mysterious group," he blurted out. "It's an international, secret spiritual society that teaches yoga and meditation publicly and more esoteric, mystical arts behind closed doors." Seizing the opportunity, I told Rhone about our documentary project.

"Uncle Gaston knows a lot about multidimensional travel," Rhone replied. "He refers to it as 'soul travel.' He even showed me how to do it. But it got too scary for me, man. Too weird. I stopped seeing him and quit answering his phone calls."

As much as I inquired, Rhone wouldn't share the details of his paranormal experiences with his uncle. In fact, the subject was closed by Rhone as quickly as it was opened by a few cans of Bud.

Undaunted by Rhone's fear, my friends and I wanted to contact Rhone's uncle in Montreal immediately. We weren't intimidated by the nature of the subject because our interest—so we believed at the time—was purely artistic and journalistic. It never occurred to us for one moment we would actually *do* any multidimensional travel. Intellectually intrigued and psyched, we simply wanted to make a film about the fascinating topic. Our standard journalistic modus operandi was to not get personally involved in any way with the subject of our investigation. We considered ourselves professionals. We would be objective observers, not participants. *Ah, the blind arrogance and naïveté of young journalists!*

After the shattering effects of his past tutelage with Uncle Gaston, Rhone was loath to contact him ever again. Finally, after much pleading on our part, he agreed to give us his uncle's telephone number. Since Rhone refused to call his uncle, I phoned the group leader in Montreal myself.

I rang Rhone's uncle at his home. As soon as I mentioned my name, Gaston instantly replied, "Yes, we've been expecting your call." Being certain that Rhone had not previously phoned him to tell him about us, I felt the Frenchman's super calm, knowing response was like an overused line from a cheap "B" horror flick.

Gaston added to the mystique of his reply by coupling it with an invitation that seemed overly hospitable to strangers. Before I had an opportunity to mention our connection with his nephew Rhone, or our interest in making a film, Gaston volunteered, "You can all come and stay at our house for as long as you like."

A red warning light went off within my suspicious personality. *Why such over-zealous hospitality?* Hiding my uneasiness, I responded to Gaston's offer with polite, professional decorum, "Great. My four friends and I would like to meet everyone in your group and film a documentary about your endeavors."

Jovially, Gaston agreed to us visiting over our Christmas vacation and staying at his sprawling home in the suburbs of Montreal. It seemed almost too easy.

Gaston's excessively gracious response should have been my first clue that my friends and I were getting involved in an adventure with greater implications for our future than the making of a documentary film. His words haunted me for days. Rhone confirmed he hadn't told his uncle about us. "Why such a generous offer of his home to people he's never met, before I even fully introduced myself and my motives for phoning?" I queried many close acquaintances. Nobody had an answer that quelled my uneasiness.

However, in keeping with my youthful innocence and inner trust, I ignored my personality's urging to investigate further before I proceeded. Had I hesitated or inquired more, I may not have undertaken that fateful, fortuitous journey to Montreal.

A few days after Christmas Day, we five intent filmmakers drove from Ann Arbor to Montreal to shoot a journalistic record of the teachings and operation of an esoteric spiritual society. About halfway there, I became violently ill with nausea, dizziness and diarrhea. I chalked it up to a combination of over-excitement and intestinal flu. In retrospect, I realize my condition had nothing to do with the flu. My body was reacting with trepidation to the prospect of the total life upheaval awaiting me in Montreal.

When we arrived, we were warmly greeted by Rhone's Uncle Gaston and Aunt Edith, who appeared to be a very unassuming, sweet, vibrant French couple. They could easily have passed for totally ordinary Quebecois. The two made a very cheery pair, alive with the Gaelic spirit and *joie de vivre*. They invited us into their typical suburban home, which we later discovered was called "the clubhouse," a meeting place for an international spiritual group of about two hundred people.

A short time after we arrived, it began to snow . . . and snow . . . and snow. It snowed heavily all night. When we opened the front door in the morning, we found six feet of snow had blanketed the city overnight. The powdery white fluff had drifted up above the opening of the front door. The storm was severe, even by Canadian standards. The whole city was at a standstill. It would take days for city plows to clear the streets. We were, in effect, shut in with the extraordinary subjects of our film.

My co-journalists and I reasoned it was the perfect opportunity to better know the people who were to be the focus of the documentary. Rhone's relatives, however, had other plans for us! Their intentions differed vastly from ours.

After a restful night's sleep, my friends and I eased into our first whole day with the congenial couple. We were still under the comforting illusion that we were there to make a film. After breakfast, Gaston and Edith calmly confided that they headed a secret international, or, as they described it more accurately, "intergalactic" spiritual society. "Our group meets and operates in secret," they shared, "because as an underground organization, we won't attract a lot of attention and can function more freely. Our membership consists of a wide spectrum of ordinary citizens comprised of all ages, races and backgrounds that includes doctors, lawyers, bankers, artists, truck drivers, post office workers, housewives, college professors and students. Most of our members feel it's best if their relatives, casual friends and work colleagues are unaware of their membership in such an extremely esoteric metaphysical society."

The talkative French pair elaborated on the inner workings of their society, and we were gathering a wealth of information for our film project. Listening politely, the five of us sent silent, bemused messages back and forth between us with our eyes. Their story had all the trappings of an old, classic mystery movie.

When Gaston offered to acquaint us with the group's spiritual practices, we quickly accepted his offer. After all, the more we knew about what these people were up to, the more thorough, accurate and affecting our documentary would be.

Having our complete attention, Gaston then informed us that he and Edith were not human! We five humans took a collective, lengthy breath. We remained silent. What could we say to that! In a casual tone, with a straight face, Gaston stated, "We have taken human form for the purpose of increasing the comfort level of the people with whom we interact. Our intentional guise of familiar human appearance makes communication so much easier, you see."

"Yes, of course," we agreed in stunned unison, attempting to hide the skepticism in our voices. My "flu" symptoms—read as "suppressed terror"—had been lessening up until I heard this mindblower. Now, my body as well as my mind was sent reeling! But, since the snowstorm had paralyzed travel in the city and trapped us inside with these folks for a few days, my friends and I felt we needed to reserve our opinions about the factual basis of these extraterrestrial revelations. Thus, we nodded diplomatically as Gaston began to unfold his version of the true history of Planet Earth and the cosmology of the universe. I was able to calm my nerves and nausea by reminding myself that I was only there to record and document. *As a professional, I shouldn't get personally involved,* I reminded myself.

The essence of Gaston's presentation was focused on the true nature and meaning of life. He declared, "All beings are, in essence, Spirit. As individualized aspects of the Oneness, people incarnate on Earth—and in other worlds and other dimensions—for the sole (soul) purpose of exploring creation. All beings leave the Unified Field of Consciousness, Oneness, by deliberately buying into the belief of separation and duality, the cosmic play of opposites: the polarities of right and wrong, good and bad, light and dark, up and down, and yin and yang.

"This deliberate forgetting of our connection to the unity of all things in Spirit allows people to create and play in a world of front and back, visible and invisible, and form and essence. The front—visible form—is the universe of physical matter, which you can see, touch, smell, hear and taste. The background—underlying invisible, essence reality—is made of nonphysical energy, which you can contact through multisensory perception.

"The majority of people have yet to open their senses to this more fundamental, causative aspect of life—the nonphysical, vibrational level of reality. This behind-the-scenes energy is primal life force, which is the creative power that animates all forms of life."

In elaborate detail, the lively Frenchman described Planet Earth's role in the cosmic unfolding of the Universal Plan or Game. He emphasized, "My explanation of the true nature of the universe will be heard and absorbed differently by each of you. Each person's perception will vary according to his or her individual personality with its unique belief filters and cultural conditioning. Every year or so, I will reiterate this same basic information to you, but in different terms and on a higher level of understanding. As each of you grow in wisdom and personal power, you will be able to absorb more truth. And I will be able to explain the workings of the cosmos in a more and more accurate way."

"However," he forewarned, "the account I, and other spiritual teachers, share with you at each successive, higher level will make the previous level of information seem to you, on the surface, like a lie. But each new, more accurate version of the human story will only *appear* to contradict the last version, because your understanding of the true nature of life will have changed so radically. You'll be in such a new place—a place of greater clarity and truth—that your old ways of understanding life will seem overly simple, naïve—even false. You will be seeing life through new eyes—a fresh, expanded perspective that will render your old points of view obsolete."

I will interrupt my tale for a moment to tell you that, since my time with Gaston, I have, in fact, been told and retold essentially the same cosmology in many different forms. Not by Gaston, but rather by other spiritual mentors: Indian guru Sai Baba, Ascended Master St. Germain, macrobiotic leader Michio Kushi, spiritual teacher Lester Levenson, and Hopi medicine man Medicine Cloud, among others. As Gaston had predicted, each new depiction of the truth of existence made the preceding rendition seem like fiction to me. That aside taken care of, I will continue with our experience with Uncle Gaston.

Gaston talked to us for a full day, breaking only for one meal. After hours of trying to integrate the incredible human adventure Gaston was positing, we were finally excused. We crashed for twelve hours of heavy slumber.

The next morning found the city of Montreal at a standstill, frozen in the grips of the blizzard. But not Gaston! He had a momentous journey in store for the five of us. When we awoke, the cheery, avowed extraterrestrial announced he was going to assist us in experiencing the full spectrum of our soul's cosmic existence. He was taking us "soul traveling," also referred to as "astral projection," "multidimensional awareness" or "exploring one's Akashic Record."

Having come to Montreal specifically to film a story about this fascinating procedure, we readily agreed to give it a shot. Mind you, none of us really believed the otherworldly technique was valid, or that it would work for us, so we were fairly cool and collected about such a weighty undertaking. Imagine our shock when, under the skilled direction of Gaston, we spent the next five days soul traveling through the multidimensional universe!

While lying fully clothed on a bed, each of us was cajoled into allowing our inner coach, or soul, to open to an awareness of various lifetimes on Earth, on other planets and in other dimensions. In some of the lifetimes, we didn't inhabit physical bodies as dense as our bodies on Earth; we had energy bodies that were translucent, very light and fluid.

Gradually over the next three days, the awareness dawned on us that we were no longer simply exploring our subject for objective investigative journalism. We were, in fact, undergoing a very subjective spiritual initiation and transformation. By the time we realized this, we were so thoroughly engrossed in the fantastic journey that it was too late to turn back, or to attempt to return to being solely objective, journalistic observers.

I was so absorbed in the adventure of it all that my physical and emotional discomfort almost completely vanished. The little bit of queasiness that remained actually assisted me to soul travel. Because being out of my body was so much more comfortable than being in it, I responded immediately to Gaston's suggestions to travel to other lifetimes and dimensions.

Each of us went on a dozen or so of these extra-dimensional awareness journeys. Whether we were truly experiencing actual other lifetimes was not important to us at the time because whatever we were doing was very real and inspirational for us. We experienced being physically in each body and lifetime with a level of concreteness equal to that of our everyday reality. We were aware of a small portion of our consciousness in a body lying on a bed back in Montreal on Earth in 1969, but most of our attention was riveted to very realistic, sensory, emotional and physical events in another time and place.

The experiential authenticity of these adventures was teaching us profound emotional and social life lessons. We didn't care if these other lifetimes were, in truth, *our own* previous or future existences, the lifetimes of someone else or something else altogether. The relevant wisdom and direct insights we were gaining from these explorations were so valuable, we gave little concern for the factual basis of our exploits. Our thoughts, feelings and sensations during the journeys were more pronounced and acute than those of our "normal" reality. This heightened awareness made our experiences during the soul travels even more genuine, engaging and enriching.

During each lifetime, Gaston would guide us through birth and death in that existence. The births were very visceral, tangible and emotional. The deaths were equally physical, palpable and dramatic. Over and over, we each experienced our soul coming into a physical body at birth and then leaving the corporal body at death.

We also connected with the interactions that generally take place for most people between lifetimes. We met with spiritual advisors, talked about what we learned during the last lifetime, and then chose our next lifetime. For the next round on Earth, we could elect to be a woman, man, farmer, artist, peasant or prince. The choices were as endless as the universe.

The cumulative effect of these realistic and fascinating journeys was immense. We were acutely aware that the purpose of each revisiting of a lifetime was for our soul to learn more about the true nature of life—the debilitating consequences of greed, selfishness, revenge, jealousy and dishonesty—as well as the nurturing influences of joy, innocence, humor and compassion. We'd stumbled into a treasure house of direct knowing about the most significant aspects of human existence.

Each lifetime allowed us to directly—and more consciously than in everyday life—absorb what happens when we stay overly focused on and obsessed with fame, power, money, sex or security for a whole lifetime. We saw firsthand how being stuck in a certain narrow point of view in one lifetime dominated and decimated our aliveness and humanity in that lifetime. We assimilated palpably the healing and liberating power of exchanging genuine kindness, intimacy and laughter with other people. The many soul journeys were explorations of all the various human strengths and frailties that exist on the planet—and in our personal past and future lives.

Every lifetime we visited also had significant, synchronistic relevance for the challenges we were, in fact, facing in our current life on Earth. Each of us intuitively chose issues to confront that were pertinent and timely for us to examine in terms of our weaknesses and strengths in our present daily lives. The lessons I learned were ones I've not forgotten. In fact, the revelations from those soul trips changed forever how I live my life.

After five days of soul travel, Gaston demonstrated how to open the chakra energy centers of the body. The chakras are an East Indian term for the specific areas of the body in which creative life force is stored. The vast inner reserve of natural vitality and raw aliveness released from these sessions was sublime. Each of us felt vibrant and open to the power and majesty of the universe in a way none of us had ever felt before in our lives.

As if the lifetime journeys and chakra revitalizations were not enough transformation for one week, Gaston then gave each of us an extensive, personal soul history. For hours, he candidly revealed to each of us who we really are as eternal spirits, what our souls have come to do on Earth this lifetime, and how well to date we were accomplishing our spiritual goals. Gaston did not pull any punches. He was blunt, direct and specific. He knew events in our lives none of us had ever told anyone before—not close relatives, not even our best friends. He spoke facts about our lives, and truths about our feelings, we hadn't even admitted to ourselves! It was quite shocking to all of us that anyone could know these extremely intimate details. This wasn't hit-and-miss fortunetelling. This was in-depth soul truth.

Gaston explained, "When the Oneness deliberately fragmented into separate aspects of consciousness, each individual being ended up embodying more of one aspect of consciousness than the other qualities of the Oneness. Some people mainly embody and emanate the vibration of love. Others radiate more the essences of strength, innocence, transformation or courage. We each carry all the different parts of the Totality, but express different aspects to varying degrees. We each have different jobs to do here."

My personal reading was most encouraging. The Gaelic seer told me I'm here on a multi-lifetime mission of peace. I'm here to observe humans and society to see how people behave and interact in a multitude of challenging, everyday human situations. "Then, when you've watched and learned enough, you're going to apply your observations to help people deal better with their regular, daily lives. Using various psychological therapies, you're destined to assist people to make peace with their inner demons, and in the process, with other people. You are also here to help develop successful approaches to conflict resolution in our society." Eventually, Gaston foretold I'll embody and radiate the vibration of peace to such a degree that if people who are arguing come within five hundred feet of me, they'll simply quit quarreling and move into a tranquil state. Gaston informed me that I was from a place, or timeless space, called Xeros, a planet of peace.

My closest friend in our group, Chris, also received a favorable reading. Gaston described to him in detail how he was progressing very well toward his life mission of sacred service. Chris' reading tied together many seemingly disparate events in his life into a cosmic mosaic of purposeful design. Soon after our collective adventure in Montreal, Chris' human journey would lead him to Findhorn, a spiritual community in Scotland. He went there initially to seek assistance in understanding the momentous events in Montreal. After integrating his radical tutelage with Gaston, Chris has been involved in spiritual healing and teaching in Great Britain ever since.

One particular aspect of Gaston's soul readings impressed me: the content of his life readings was not entirely complimentary. In fact, for three members of the group—Sylvia, Lisa and Jacob—the revelations of the frank Frenchman were very unflattering and disturbing. From my perspective, Gaston's appraisals of the soul expression of each of us were very loving and non-judgmental. However, my three friends felt they received very derogatory assessments of their lives.

Gaston was extremely honest and specific. My comrades weren't ready to hear reckonings as direct, accurate and detailed as he shared. He was quite explicit about each of them being "caught this lifetime in a very narrow band of egotistical self-interest." In retrospect, I feel his intention in his harsh delivery was to shake up and shock my friends so they'd look inward and refocus the direction of their lives. At the time, his stark truth telling had the opposite effect. All three of them became intensely angry and resistant toward Gaston and his suggestion they go within to intuitively review their present lives. They'd definitely had enough self-truth reflected to them by the candid extraterrestrial. After their life readings, the three were ready to revolt and bolt!

Chris and I were ready to split the scene as well. We'd reached the "outer limits" of our ability to absorb any further social or personal revelation. By then, Montreal's sturdy army of snowplows had cleared the streets of the city, and we could leave. As if of one intention, the five of us packed our belongings to return to Ann Arbor and familiar environs, both geographically and psychologically. It would be a gross understatement to say we felt completely overwhelmed by our experience with this secret, intergalactic society.

None of us had a way of adequately dealing mentally, emotionally or physiologically with the events of that week. What was left of our minds was blown into almost unrecognizable pieces. We were drained emotionally. Our bodies were reeling with the stress and strain of having our worlds rocked and exploded beyond recognition. Not having metaphysical backgrounds at the time, we'd never read or heard anything resembling the types of experiences we had just gone through. We had no frame of reference in which to fit our week of spiritual initiation. We'd totally forgotten our original plan to shoot a documentary film in Montreal. Our overriding desire was to put as much physical and psychological distance between us and the source of our overwhelming encounter as possible!

Driving the ten hours back to the good old USA, we had time to rehash the week's dramatic events in detail. And the privacy of a car allowed us to recount the traumatic ordeal with great emotion and depth. Together, the five of us considered at length every conceivable way to view the preceding week's extravaganza.

By the time we arrived back in Ann Arbor, Chris and I were awakening to a more compassionate and spiritual framework from which to view our life experience. However, the three who disliked their life reviews—Sylvia, Lisa and Jacob—reached a different point of view.

The three had concluded that Gaston and Edith were evil, or, at the very least, part of a cult that was very dangerous to their physical and spiritual safety. They reached a state of hysteria. Feeling they needed protection from the people in Montreal, they sought advice and defensive rituals from a "white witch." The day after our return to Ann Arbor, all three came over to the house where Chris and I lived. In a fervent frenzy, they sprinkled holy water and salt on our heads, and on every doorstep and doorsill in the house. They claimed being blessed by these sanctified natural elements would ward off the evil spirits connected with the "satanic" Montreal cult. They screamed and railed at Chris and me to awaken to the danger of the demonic spell cast on us by Gaston.

The frantic, bizarre scene unfolding in front of us resembled a skit from a cosmic, comic "Three Stooges" skit! Our three frightened friends had twisted every word of Gaston's presentation into a fanatical, ironclad indictment of the whole Montreal group and their motives. Chris and I didn't know whether to cry or laugh. Confused and bombarded by our friends' frenzy, we alternated between reacting with horror and humor. Certainly, it wasn't funny to witness our close friends in such a state of panic and terror. However, the extremely righteous and sanctimonious way they denounced the whole philosophy of the Montreal group verged on the absurd and ridiculous.

I might add here that throughout my subsequent decades of working with people undergoing spiritual initiations, I have discovered that the personality will often project an illusion of "evil" upon any person, event or source of information that rocks its boat, threatening its insulated, controlled world. I have also found that what people fear most is authentic love, which often comes in the form of radical truth telling.

Chris and I, conversely, were experiencing a spiritual healing and awakening from the initiation in Montreal. Our friends' fearful overreaction to the miraculous spiritual gifts of Gaston was challenging us to evaluate our experience even more thoroughly. Yes, Chris and I were also freaked out on a psychological level. However, we viewed our mental resistance as a normal, expected reaction to a mind-blowing experience. Our everyday paradigm was busted wide open by Gaston. The familiar security of our mainstream perceptual framework was shattered. Stretching our cultural envelope beyond its limits, we were thrust way outside our box of normal experience.

Contrary to our three hysterical friends, Chris and I were extremely grateful. We were unnerved, but not undone, by our expulsion from ordinary reality. The stark truth telling was freeing us. And we were thankful at being liberated from the prison of our old, rigid, narrow world. When our alarmed friends burst upon our home, Chris and I were celebrating our spiritual emancipation, not seeking a way to invalidate and reverse the effects of the Montreal encounter.

Naïvely, Chris and I tried to intellectually discuss our different point of view with our three fear-stricken friends. Unfortunately, they were long past the point of a philosophical resolution to their perceived predicament. They felt their very survival was at stake. They were afraid their souls were in danger from demonic forces.

There was nothing Chris and I could say or do to mollify their terror. Before our metaphysical adventure in Canada, we felt our three friends were fairly strong, stable individuals. However, the experience totally shook their grasp on a safe reality. All three eventually sought psychiatric counseling to help resolve the disruption of their worlds caused by the Montreal trip. They broke off communication with us. Unfortunately, I've lost track of all three of my former cinematic compatriots.

I've not had any further contact with Gaston either—that is, that I am aware of! On other levels of consciousness, I'm certain he's been assisting me. After my encounter with him, I needed an extensive period of time to absorb the expansive spiritual opening he afforded me—a pursuit that has become an ongoing project to this day. The only request Gaston made of us was to share what they revealed to us with whomever it felt intuitively right. As I integrate the wisdom and tools Gaston gave me in Montreal, I pass on these treasures through my workshops and personal coaching.

The central focus of the secret spiritual society in Montreal is the same purpose as that of my *Dream Workshops*. Our common goal is to bring people together as peers to assist them to awaken to their connection with the Infinite, and to empower them to use their natural spiritual powers for the good of humankind, as well as for their individual soul growth. The way Gaston helped us to open to direct communication and guidance from our inner coach laid the foundation for the intuitive soul journeys that are so valuable now for people in *The Dream Workshops* I facilitate across the country.

Freedom

In the land where "the sun always shines," the heavenly globe had not shone its bright face for many days. I drove into town during a torrential downpour. I had yet to see any golden, warming rays. In fact, three weeks had passed since I drove to Los Angeles from my graduation at the University of Michigan in Ann Arbor. It'd been pouring over since. I left the Midwest to escape the frigid, bleak days of rain, snow and clouds. This evening was especially ominous with pelting sheaths of wet and wind. It certainly wasn't a night to venture outside my rented room where I'd been holed up since my arrival! Yet my inner guidance was insisting I take a soggy, dreary walk to nowhere.

Spirit was telling me I needed to go out, to break free of the claustrophobic, gray walls of my cramped, matchbox of a room. I did not want to go! The dismal weather gave me a very socially acceptable reason to stay in my refuge because it was cold and clammy outside. However, fear was the real reason I was avoiding leaving my room and exploring my new hometown. Venturing outside would mean taking the next ominous step in my spiritual odyssey.

All day my inner coach was incessantly urging me to put myself out into the flow of the River of Life, so I could bump into my destiny. Spirit was not buying my lame excuse of inclement weather. To my real self, taking a walk during this tropical deluge was an excellent opportunity to experience life as a river, to allow the natural pulse and rhythm of life to pump some vitality back into my reluctant psyche. My personality argued nothing of any importance could possibly happen to me on such a raw, inhospitable night. No sane person would be afoot. There would be no one to encounter! But my inner guide would not be swayed from its objective. I *would* leave my isolated room.

I've learned to follow my intuition when it's demanding action as strongly as it was this particular evening. Reluctantly, I dressed myself against the drenching wind and left my safe haven for an unknown adventure in the "City of Angels." I'd driven across the country to get a fresh start. The foul weather delayed my plans and dampened my hopes, but I was still open to encountering some sort of messenger of God, angel or otherwise. I set out for my wet adventure, thinking to myself, *Perhaps my inner coach knows something about the city's namesake I haven't discovered yet.*

Or maybe not! After a brisk walk of a dozen, deserted city blocks in the bone-chilling rain, I was soaked to the core and ready to retreat from what was quickly turning into an ill-fated excursion. Turning, I began the trek back to my apartment when a glimmering light in the gutter caught my eye. The bright beam seemed to be shining *through* a soggy, mud-covered flyer lying in the street gutter. Naturally, I stopped to inspect the phenomenon more closely. Yes, there was definitely a glow shining through the paper. My curiosity peaked; I bent over to pick up the sheet. As soon as I touched the flyer, the mysterious luminescence behind it faded away.

Not only am I soaked and miserable, I'm starting to see things, I conjectured to myself. *Enough is enough! This crazy junket has come to an end. I'm going back to my nice, warm room.*

I wiped the worst of the dirt off the leaflet, stuffed it into my jacket pocket and started for home at a hurried pace. I had a souvenir of my soggy journey. At least, I wouldn't go home empty-handed!

Back in the cozy refuge of my toasty dry room, I carefully smoothed out the rain-swollen sheet of paper. I was very curious what the strange light was attracting my attention to. The shriveled notice was a public invitation to a home-cooked meal of natural foods. Hungry for nourishment from a source other than a tin can,

I was thrilled at the prospect of a homemade feast and some human companionship. And the cost was only five dollars! Little did I know at the time that I'd just taken the bait laid by my soul on that gusty, damp night.

The following Thursday evening, I enjoyed a sumptuous meal of creamy leek soup, organic brown rice, garden-fresh vegetables and something green called nori seaweed at the East-West Institute of Los Angeles. The Institute was a macrobiotic school and retreat of the international healer and teacher Michio Kushi, founder of the center and our host for the evening.

With my stomach full and my mind and body relaxed, I was totally unprepared for my inner coach's next outrageous move. Mr. Kushi asked the diners if there was a professional landscaper at the table. My hand shot up on its own!

What kind of adventure was my spirit getting me into this time? I sighed to myself. *I hate yard work! I've never planted a garden. I don't know the difference between a daffodil and a tulip. The only "landscaping" I've ever done was mowing the grass in our front yard when I was a kid. And I avoided that as much as possible. Besides, I've lived my whole life in a cool, northern climate. I'm totally ignorant of the subtropical foliage of Southern California. And I don't care to learn!*

"We've got several landscaped acres, including fruit trees, and flower, herb and vegetable gardens. Would you like to take over the duties of maintaining the estate's extensive grounds?" queried Mr. Kushi. I couldn't believe my mouth said, "Yes."

This outrageous phenomenon wasn't entirely new to me. I've been my spirit's pawn before when my inner coach usurped control of my speech and answered a question for me. I had a gut feeling my real self was about to take me for the ride of my young life. Events soon validated this premonition. My new job set my personal path on an interception course with my first extraordinary life mentor: Michio Kushi.

Japanese to the core, Michio was an enigmatic, beguiling, modern-day samurai. In his forties when we met, Michio's face was soft and pliable like a baby's, his gait spirited and assured. Although he was most often charming and charismatic, he could be fierce and demanding, especially with his students—like me!

Michio's domain was the Institute and the extensive grounds surrounding it. In the vibrant, romantic heyday of Hollywood, the magnificent estate had once been the home of jazz great Al Jolson and his paramour, film starlet Ruby Keeler. The manor house was a meandering forty-room Spanish villa with quaint French doors leading out to numerous patios and balconies overlooking the sprawling metropolis in the valley below. Avocado, banana, lemon, lime, grapefruit and orange groves; a rose garden; a grape arbor and a reflecting pool graced the hillside expanse. Antelope and deer frolicked through the pine forest in the surrounding acres. The estate's gatehouse was bigger than most people's homes.

I attracted Michio's attention and respect by successfully sculpting the property into a neat, trim and healthy Shangri-La. No, I didn't tap into an unknown gardening genius hidden within me. I discovered that the Greek and Italian groundskeepers for Hollywood stars met early every morning for espresso on nearby Sunset Boulevard. From these generous Old World gardeners, I learned how to care for my new horticultural charges. As their earthy wisdom had been ignored and unappreciated by their own sons, these talented landscapers were overjoyed to assist a young man interested in their broad knowledge of plant care. Before long, I was an expert in trimming and caring for bougainvillea bushes, carob trees, and every other common and exotic tropical plant.

Michio became a wonderful friend and mentor throughout the next ten years of my life. He helped me understand and integrate my first spiritual initiation in Montreal. Through him, I learned to view the world with a new perspective—one that was whole, vital and fresh. He soon promoted me to the position of director of the Institute, the person who coordinated all the diverse activities of the center. In addition to tending the grounds and gardens, I supervised the staff that provided the classes, meals and sleeping accommodations. At the facilities in Los Angeles and others around the world, Michio presented a fusion of Eastern and Western philosophy, psychology and applied practice that blended acupuncture, martial arts and macrobiotic, natural foods with pragmatic life coaching and community living.

This humble, yet very erudite healer had led a turbulent professional life. Considered a radical influence, Michio was forced in the late sixties by the American Medical Association to physically leave two of the most liberal communities in the country: Cambridge, Massachusetts, and Manhattan, New York.

Ironically, he was run out of town for espousing the same philosophy of health he now teaches at the most prestigious institutions in those same cities: Harvard and Columbia University Medical Schools. The medical establishment and the mainstream public currently accept and endorse what Michio expounded in the sixties! In the intervening decades, his simple, effective principles of harmonious, nourishing living have helped thousands of people throughout the world.

Despite long days of private counseling and lengthy evening lectures to hundreds of students, Michio always had time to meet with me and share his practical knowledge. The most valuable lessons I absorbed from him were not so much what I gleaned in the lecture hall, although I did take copious notes on his talks about everything under the sun in the realm of healing, cosmology and spiritual disciplines. The priceless wisdom I assimilated from this unassuming sage was on a more subtle and profound level. Michio presented his spiritual savior faire to me in a way that wasn't verbal or conceptual. He shared his world of wisdom in an existential, experiential way, through everyday actions and events. He was outwardly casual about his sharing, yet inwardly his way was very premeditated and deliberate. This was the knowledge that meant the most to me. We never discussed the life lessons he taught me. I simply absorbed them by being around him.

In Los Angeles and later in Boston, Michio and I would often sneak off together after his lectures to quiet, secluded French cafés where his fanatical disciples would never think to look for him. These quaint bistros served all the foods Michio warned against in his lectures, which focused primarily on how various foods affected one's health and spirituality. In his talks, he advised eating a main diet of natural whole grains, fruits and vegetables. He spoke adamantly about avoiding alcohol, drugs, coffee, sugar, dairy, animal fats, red meat, white flour, white rice and all chemicalized, processed foods.

Yet on these frequent outings, Michio ordered buttery French croissants, eclairs and every other sugary delight available. Traditionally, the Japanese love to eat and talk about food. He was always very intrigued about whether a particular pastry was made with orange or lemon peel, or if it contained a touch of vanilla, cinnamon, nutmeg or clove. In a ritual way similar to a Zen tea ceremony, he cut each pastry very carefully in half. Eating each piece slowly and delicately, we discussed what ingredients were used in creating the tastes and textures of the desserts, cleansing our palates between every bite with sips of strong, sweetened espresso.

On other evenings, we went to Italian eateries in Los Angeles and Boston. Consuming huge meals of white flour pasta with tomato sauce and meatballs, we'd sip red wine and enjoy sweet dessert cannolis—all foods on the absolute "Never Eat" list from Michio's lectures on macrobiotic philosophy.

Michio and I dined out like this for years. We never spoke to anyone about our excursions. And we never discussed between ourselves the seeming discrepancies between his words and his actions, between his recommended diet and his savored delicacies. Yet in his own experiential, paradoxical ways, he was teaching me the life lessons I needed to learn: the importance of enjoying food and celebrating life with gusto, flexibility, intuitiveness and, especially, freedom.

As we sat eating pastries, Michio would lean toward me and speak with great earnestness, "Keit, you must be free man." Very endearingly, he always pronounced "th" as a "t" in my name.

"You must be free to do anything you want. You must be free to eat anything you want. You must be free to be anything you want."

Michio's words felt good to me. At the time, I didn't have a conceptual sense of what he was conveying, but I did take in the spirit and energy of what he was sharing. I know now that in his presence, I was absorbing his vibration of being free and living intuitively.

Michio spoke to me about being "sovereign." He implored me to "never work for money. Never do anything you don't want to do to obtain money. If you work for money, you are no better than a slave!"

His words had a strong and penetrating effect on me because I knew in my heart they were true. Yet I didn't have a clue how to live this truth in my life. At the time, I couldn't imagine how a person could have money without working at a job. Since then, I've learned to attract the financial support of the universe by aligning my professional path with my soul passion and purpose.

Michio emphasized the joy of being a free individual. He taught that everyone is equally able to be free, intuitive and creative. He'd move close to me, speaking right into the ear of my soul, "You must be free to do anything you want. And you must be strong enough to do only what you want to do in life."

My mentor's words were very empowering and prophetic for me. I felt sublime love from him when he said, "You must, you will, go far beyond me. You must leave me behind. I teach what I do now, but you will teach something much bigger and yet much simpler." His words were foreshadowing *The Dream Workshops* I'd be facilitating twenty years hence. He foretold, "You will attract many people. They will come to learn something that is more pure, more basic and even more powerful than I teach now."

Michio's lectures focused on the exhaustive presentation of information, principles and universal laws concerning the best ways to eat and live. I asked him why he didn't emphasize the primacy of intuition in his lectures to the degree he did in our café discussions.

"Oh, but I do," he replied. "But not many people hear. At the very end of all my talks, I always say that to be happy and healthy, you must live intuitively. But few hear me."

Incredulous upon hearing his words, I began to investigate the enigma. I began to pay close attention at the end of his public seminars. Sure enough, Michio did talk about intuitive eating being the healthiest manner of eating and intuitive living being the most joyful form of living: "The most creative and effective level of living is to make all life decisions from consulting one's inner knowing. Pure, clear intuition supercedes all rules, concepts, principles and philosophies." He did accentuate the supremacy of intuition at the end of every talk. Yet I wasn't aware he made this concluding point until he brought it to my attention. I checked my friends' notes. None of the students had recorded Michio's views on the importance of intuition. I asked them if they'd ever heard him utter these ideas. They hadn't. In fact, my friends were very dubious. They didn't believe the macrobiotic leader ever spoke about intuitive eating or living! I even coached some of my friends on where to listen for the concept at the end of his lectures. They still didn't hear it. It was obviously not their time to hear this message.

As we sat together late at night, I'd often ask Michio why he was wasting his time with me. I considered myself just a hair above a snail in terms of my degree of conscious awareness. He always answered very simply, "Because you listen. Because you *hear*. And because you will pass this on some day." He certainly knew something I wasn't aware of at the time!

Often Michio touched me poignantly with his compassion. One night over pastries and cappuccino, he said, "Keit, you are very scared right now because of all the changes you're going through."

He was right. At his side, I was witnessing spontaneous, physical healings and spiritual breakthroughs almost daily. I was also experiencing miracles in my own affairs. My life was becoming very magical indeed. The boundaries of my small world were continually expanding—including the psychological borders that comfortably defined who I thought I was, and the intellectual frontiers of what I reasoned were possible according to the laws of physics and science.

He continued in a very intimate tone, "Sometimes you have great anxiety. But, you know, I am as afraid to take *my* next step on *my* journey as you are to take *your* next step on *your* journey. We are together in our fear. We are terror twins!"

Then he laughed and giggled as he offered me another sweet tart to celebrate our union in fear.

What Michio offered me in all our encounters was very difficult for me to accept emotionally at the time. He extended to me not only loving friendship, but also respectful equality— something I wasn't yet psychologically capable of receiving. He was inviting me to experience myself as his equal, to play and interact with him as a peer. This prospect was way beyond my self-image of my worth and substance. However, the vibration of peership did sneak in past my mental and emotional defenses. Michio did successfully plant the seed of equality deep within my being.

I'll never forget how it touched my heart to hear him proclaim our commonality in regard to the fear of change. In that one statement, he bridged the false separation I felt between us, and between me and all other people. He connected me with the truth of the common bond I share with all humanity on this decidedly exciting and terrifying human journey on Earth. He was preparing me to anchor my *Dream Workshops* as a "Gathering of Equals."

Foreverness

The Ancient Ones, the Real People,
don't look at your eyes when they look at you.
They look inside of your eyes.
They say it's the forever part of them
that speaks to the forever part of you.

MARLO MORGAN, *MUTANT MESSAGE DOWNUNDER*

In the course of our journey together, Michio Kushi blessed me with fresh ways to view the universe—and myself. Playing on the world's stage with him, I discovered doorways I didn't know existed—gateways to more harmony and fulfillment than I could ever imagine.

Above all else, Michio introduced me to my own eternalness. His gift to me was a flirting glimpse of the experience of timeless connection between souls, a tantalizing taste of foreverness. One evening, after finishing a particularly far-reaching metaphysical lecture, he suddenly shifted the wavelength on which he was broadcasting his voice and message. Only those listeners who could switch channels and tune into this new frequency continued to absorb what he was sharing.

Peering directly one by one into people's eyes, Michio spoke softly from a fathomless place within his being:

"Oh, it is so good to see you again. It is so good. Been so many millions of years. Been so, so long since we have been together. It is so good to see you again."

When his ageless gaze reached my eyes, I knew he was speaking to a part of me—and seeing and feeling a part of me—to which I was not yet awake. Nonetheless, he pierced the bubble of my forgetfulness, separation and limitation. He made a crack in my rigid, time-bound world. Within my being, that opening has since expanded gradually into a gateway of acceptance of my eternal real self.

His words that evening were very affecting. I'll never forget how his persona felt to me that night. I knew then I wanted to embrace for myself whatever state of being he was experiencing. I decided that night I would track down and capture that feeling for myself. I knew I wanted to live in that space permanently. The search for foreverness is the motivating theme of my Earth journey, the common thread that weaves through the tapestry of my adventures, and the river that runs through my heart and soul.

The Lost Art of Levitation

An old joke goes, "How do angels fly?"
The answer is, "They take themselves lightly."

One evening I uncovered the core of truth in this joke. Little did I imagine that all along the joke was being totally literal.

During a lecture, Michio Kushi became very frustrated with his Los Angeles audience of several hundred spiritual seekers. He was attempting to convey to us an understanding of the physics of life, the fundamental mechanism of creation and transformation in life processes. Sensing he wasn't getting his message across, Michio decided to get more simple and basic. He emphasized the fact that the core nature of all life is energy, declaring, "The world is all energy. Everything is energy. And if you understand that, you can understand the real dynamics behind how things happen the way they do in the 'so-called' physical universe."

The audience was comprised of bright, curious people of all ages and backgrounds. However, few of us were understanding Michio on the fundamental level he was trying to communicate. Exasperated, he switched to an experiential tack, announcing abruptly and emphatically, "All right. I'll demonstrate what I'm talking about."

Kneeling down on both knees in the traditional Japanese manner, Michio put his hands together in a prayer-like position, closed his eyes and sat very still. After several minutes, his body began to slowly lift off the ground to a height of about four feet. There he remained for ten minutes, suspended in the air several feet above the floor. Now he had my attention!

I was astonished, of course. Then I impulsively did something that, in retrospect, seems very irrational and even humorous. But, at the time, the maneuver made sense to me.

My mind's orderly framework of reality was being severely challenged by Michio's airborne body. I needed to do something to psychologically feel more in control. And if I was being forced to expand my belief in what is humanly possible on this Earth, I was going to make sure the phenomenon was genuine. I had to do something that would give the apparent impossibility I was witnessing some sense of validity.

With childlike logic, I felt the levitation would be more real for me if I knew firsthand that nothing was underneath his body. I was sitting in the front row of the audience. Reaching underneath Michio's hovering body, I pretended my only goal was to grab a notebook behind him. I discovered Michio was, indeed, floating in midair! There was only empty space underneath him. Inserting myself physically into the incomprehensible picture before me made the whole scene more concrete and authentic for me.

After about ten minutes, Michio's body gently descended to the floor. Opening his eyes, he shared offhandedly, "Levitation is very easy. It is a natural, simple process. You all can do it."

Then he proceeded to tell us how to levitate. He spoke casually, as if he were describing how to ride a bicycle, "You simply empty your mind and clear your consciousness. Eliminate yourself of ego and self-absorption. When you are completely purged of awareness of the small self, of identifying with the personality, you are free to move with the natural rhythm of the universe. You are no longer weighed down with self-concern and limiting beliefs. You are then able to utilize the electromagnetic wave energy that moves between the Earth and the sun, moon, planets and all the heavenly bodies in the universe."

Sensing that he was losing his audience again, he paused and then elaborated, "On a hot day, you can actually see the wave motion of this universal energy as it undulates the air over heated pavement. You can measure the powerful effect of this energy on the ocean. This invisible force causes the sea to rise and fall, creating the ocean tides. You can see this pattern of universal pulsation in the rolling of the ocean waves, the rhythm of rock strata in canyons and the formation of sand dunes in the desert. This universal, undulating motion creates all the spiral patterns you find in nature—from whirls in sea shells, twirling plant growth, twisted tree trunks and swirling ocean currents to water funnels going down the drain. The natural flow of life is an energy wave motion, up and down, in and out. All the wavelike patterns and spiral formations you find in nature exist because natural elements are fluid and flexible enough to flow with the inherent wave energy current of life. When you become light enough, free enough of ego-concern, you can let this wave energy move you as well. That's all levitation is."

Sensing his audience was close to grasping his meaning, Michio tossed out examples for them to identify with, "Observe children, dogs and wild animals tapping into this universally available energy source. To them, it's natural. Haven't you seen children and dogs in a park, or on a beach, as they run and jump all day without getting tired? If a child or dog feels especially happy and carefree, you'll see them jumping two or three times higher than they normally can. We all know wild animals have extraordinary abilities to jump and leap very high, as well as run fast and cover long distances. Indigenous, tribal natives who retain their childlike innocence and openness in adulthood can run 100 miles in a single day without being tired. This is because they are light and empty enough to flow with universal energy. They *allow* the natural energy pulsation between the Earth and other bodies to propel them. That is what the *Star Wars* screenwriter meant when he said, 'May the Force be with you.' His characters knew how to surf the Force. When you become fluid and malleable, *you* also can ride this energy and float."

Immediately after the lecture, I ran up to Michio, voicing my elation over what I witnessed. He turned and bestowed upon me one of those ethereal, accepting smiles I came to love.

"Most of the people will not remember the levitation, Keit."

I protested, exclaiming that, of course, they'd remember such a fantastic display of spiritual mastery, not to mention actual instructions on how anyone can do it. He simply shrugged his shoulders. "Maybe some. But very few."

Determined to prove him wrong, I joined the attendees milling about the lecture hall and questioned small pockets of people about what they witnessed. To my astonishment, the majority of the audience didn't see Michio levitate; they perceived him simply kneeling in meditation!

A minority of the audience did perceive the levitation. Yet questioning some of these people the next day, I was confronted with evidence of even more denial. Of the minority of people who originally stated that they saw Michio's body float, only a handful stuck by their statements the following day. The rest of the original witnesses could no longer remember having perceived Michio's body levitate!

I reminded these witnesses that they had admitted seeing the feat just the evening before. But they took back their words—and their experience. As one observer replied incredulously, "Oh, no. I never said that. I never saw that. All I saw was Michio kneeling on the floor." They changed their story and their memory by the next morning!

What an awakening for me! I was forced to recognize how strongly we humans hold onto familiar—therefore, comfortable—views of reality.

On three other occasions, I observed Michio suspend his body in midair for ten minutes in front of several hundred people. After each demonstration, I questioned people in the same way as I did after the first levitation. A few perceived Michio floating; most didn't. With those few people who acknowledged they saw the feat, the same pattern played out: admission on the day of the event followed by a retraction the next day! Seeing, then denying. When I followed up *the next day* with professed witnesses of the event, most of them changed their story. Overnight, the fact of a fascinating levitation was demoted to a memory of mere grounded meditation. Only a few of the witnesses retained their experience of the levitation from the evening it happened until the next morning!

Furthermore, with the passage of time, even the few people *who remembered the levitation the morning after* began to reinterpret, invalidate or completely forget they ever witnessed Michio float in the air. In other words, the further away in time the actual miracle occurred, the fewer people remembered seeing it.

The only witnesses who remembered over time that they perceived Michio levitate were people who saw him—or another gifted human being—levitate on more than one occasion.

What's going on here? I asked myself. *What a lesson in the filtering power of our programmed preconceptions. We only see what we're conditioned to see. We only perceive what we expect to perceive!*

Over the years, I've found this perceptual filtering often goes along with the witnessing of supernormal abilities. I call this perplexing phenomenon "spiritual amnesia." The mind works fast to cover up any evidence that contradicts its own rigid perimeters regarding what is possible in its world. This malady is like a 24-hour flu virus. It's easy to catch in our culture. The effects of the syndrome last just long enough to wipe out any memory of an unusual event that does not fit into our expected range of possibilities! By the next day, the extraordinary event is either made ordinary by the mind and memory—or forgotten altogether.

In my career as a journalist covering natural disasters and crisis situations, I've encountered the invalidating effect of spiritual amnesia after every major superhuman feat that was "out of the box"—beyond the envelope or scope of what most people believe is possible. A prime example is the seemingly extraordinary ability of people to lift and keep aloft heavy vehicles until a victim is rescued from danger. In the making of a documentary on the subject, I found out this act of extra-normal strength has occurred at least once in practically every community in the country! And, as with levitation, it's usually only those people who have witnessed this extraordinary human ability *more than once* who are able and willing to remember that it occurred at all.

Later that same year, I fell victim to the insidious power of spiritual amnesia in my own psyche. Until a friend at work mentioned levitation one day, I never considered attempting this skill myself. Recounting Michio's floating feat to my co-worker, I became so reinvigorated about the subject that I decided to try to levitate when I got home from work that very evening. I planned to use Michio's technique of tapping into universal wave energy. Yet by the time I got home that evening, I totally forgot about my intention to levitate!

It was months later that some reference in my environment again triggered my memory of wanting to levitate. Again, I forgot my plan by the time I was in a suitable situation to act on it. The same lapse of memory and carry-through concerning my notion to levitate occurred many times over the following years. I usually remembered my objective to levitate when I was at work during the day, only to forget again by the time I arrived home in the evening. It ultimately took writing down the levitation plan on paper during the day for me to remember it in the evening!

When the auspicious event finally occurred, it took me several hours to empty myself of self-absorption and quiet my mind enough to successfully tap into the electro-magnetic energy force field Michio mentioned in his lectures.

Finally, I felt very clear and calm. My kneeling body started to lift off the floor! I felt my body rising. I opened my eyes, looked down and saw I was a foot off the ground. As soon as I saw that startling reality, my whole body was immediately filled with the thunderous sound of "NNNOOOOO!!!!" This heavy, loud "NO!" filled every cell of my body, and I came crashing to the floor.

It took me years to recover psychologically from that "NO!" I felt very guilty, as if I had done something wrong or prohibited—as if I'd committed some crime against nature. Several years passed before I tried levitation again. The same thing happened. I started lifting off the floor. I noticed that I was having the thought, *I'm levitating. I'm rising.* And as soon as the reality of floating hit my awareness, again, immediately, this loud, forceful, heavy "NO!" pervaded my body. The command came from every cell in my body and from an unfathomed place within myself. I crashed to the floor.

Not being one to give up on something I really want, I tried levitation again years later. This time I attempted my experiment with two friends, Giana and Steve. During an evening of intimate, honest conversation, I told them the story of Michio's levitation. "Let's try it," they exclaimed in unison. Giana and Steve were the first people with whom I shared Michio's story who were motivated to try to levitate themselves.

With all our enthusiasm and expectation, it took hours of meditation for us to get quiet and calm our minds. When we finally did empty our minds, we all began to rise at the same time. I saw their bodies lifting off the floor. However, as soon as Giana and Steve noticed they were a foot above the floor, they came crashing down together. Watching their descent triggered me into *thinking*. I came right down after them!

Like me, Giana and Steve felt a strong sensation of shame and guilt—as if they'd done something forbidden. That night, we talked about our levitation experiment at length. But the next morning the "spiritual amnesia" had already set in and we all went off to work without mentioning the miraculous occurrence of the previous evening. And not one of us ever referred to that evening's adventure again in the following years of acquaintance. I have since lost touch with both friends.

I often wonder if I could have enticed Giana and Steve to remember the evening we explored the magic of surfing the waves of the universe. I also contemplate if I could entice myself to "fly" again. With considerable embarrassment, I must admit I haven't made another attempt to levitate since my exploits with Giana and Steve. I'm waiting for the right moment and situation. It hasn't yet felt intuitively right for me to again attempt flight. I haven't received the impetus or permission from my inner coach to undertake another experiment in expanding my known universe in this way.

My reluctance can be further explained by examining the inherent meaning of the word *experiment*. When we take a look at the Latin components, we discover the source of the word's meaning. *Ex:* to go out of, beyond. *Periment:* perimeter, boundary, border. *Experiment:* to go beyond the boundary. According to Webster's dictionary, another Latin root of the word *experiment* contributes to a deeper understanding. *Pericul:* danger, trial, test. Thus, *experiment* means literally "danger in going beyond the boundary"—which is what a lot of us feel when we test the borders of our known world.

The perils are considerable when barging ahead heedless of one's inner compass. Through much exploration, I've learned the wisdom of waiting for intuitive guidance as to when, how far and under what circumstances I venture into new, uncharted territory. Someday soon, I hope to receive the go-ahead from my inner coach that will tell me I am strong and clear enough to go again beyond my old, known borders to physically explore "the incredible lightness of being."

Talking Plants

Miracles do not happen in contradiction with nature,
but in contradiction with what we know about nature.

ST. AUGUSTINE

When I took over the landscaping duties at Michio Kushi's
East-West Institute in Los Angeles without any background in that
field, I viewed the challenge as an opportunity to expand my
appreciation of the Earth. Little did I suspect the job would also
expand my appreciation of Heaven.

Among my landscaping duties at my spiritual mentor's
teaching center was the responsibility to cultivate four large fields
of organic vegetables to feed our household. In addition to feeding
the thirty permanent residents daily, the Institute served two
gourmet, organic, vegetarian meals a week to the public. About
fifty guests dined at each meal. Hollywood stars who were into
organic food frequently graced our table for the evening, including
Gloria Swanson and Mia Farrow. These gardens also provided the
vegetables for the many organic and macrobiotic cooking classes
at the Institute.

All together, the four vegetable gardens covered an area about
half the size of a football field. That was a very large expanse to
water, fertilize and weed. When I complained to Michio about the
enormity of the task, he responded nonchalantly, "You know, you
don't really have to weed the fields. You can talk to the spirit of
the weeds and ask them to grow in balance and harmony with the
vegetables."

With this casual statement, Michio introduced me to the
possibility of going into conscious communication, communion

and cooperation with nature. At first, I was surprised and incredulous. *What a wild and bizarre concept,* I mused to myself. I really hated to weed. After contemplating the distinct advantages of adopting Michio's radical alternative to weeding, I decided, *Why not try it? Every other unusual practice I've tried of Michio's has worked. What do I have to lose?*

I began talking aloud to the weeds in the four fields about growing in harmony with the vegetables who shared the garden with them. In the course of speaking to the weeds every day, I expanded my conversations to address the vegetables as well, urging them to grow tall, strong and in harmony with their neighbors, the weeds. Sure enough, after a few weeks of conversing with the weeds and vegetables every day, I began to see a change. The weeds still grew, but not to such an extent they stifled the health of their neighbors, the vegetables.

Then, to my shock and delight, the vegetable and weed plants in the garden started talking back to me! I *heard* voices in my head definitely not my own. The messages were very clear and concise. The first revelation the plants laid on me was:

"You know, we don't need soil, water or air to grow. The truth is we are sentient, spiritual beings. We grow and thrive by consciousness. It's really not necessary for us to have physical nutrients. But you humans believe plants need these physical conditions to exist, so we go along with your belief system. It's part of the agreement we in the plant kingdom have with the human race."

I didn't yet have the conceptual framework of communicating telepathically with nature spirits and plant devas. I referred to this connection as simply "talking with plants." I enjoyed a natural innocence. I was very willing to believe the plants and I were conversing in some way. After all, I had irrefutable evidence from my communication with the weeds. The weeds were now growing harmoniously with the garden vegetables.

But depriving plants of water and fertilizer seemed too radical. The soil in the fields was very sandy and devoid of nutritional minerals. It needed organic compost and fertilizer to provide nutrients for the plants. I couldn't imagine plants surviving without water or food.

For weeks, the plants kept imploring me:

"Don't water us! We'll show you we don't need water. And don't use any more fertilizer. Just let us grow naturally. Come up to the fields and simply be with us. Talk to us. We grow because of your consciousness, because of your love and concern. Let us show you."

One day I became courageous enough to quit watering and fertilizing all four vegetable gardens. It hadn't rained for months. We had no neighbors near the fields, so the gardens weren't receiving water from someone else's irrigation system. In one of the most potent metaphysical demonstrations of my life, the vegetables proved their point to me by growing abundantly without water or fertilizer! One butternut squash plant produced over sixty large squashes in one season. Its central vine trailed out of the field for over a hundred yards, winding its way through the flower gardens and into the avocado grove.

The plants reminded me they needed to grow in accordance with the consciousness of the humans in their world—in this case, the residents of the Institute. This harmony is part of the plant kingdom's spirit agreement with humans. If people discovered the fields weren't being watered, the plants would have to die in order to conform to human belief. So, in accordance with the psychological strategy of the plants, I went to the fields each morning and laid in a hammock for three hours talking to the plants—the amount of time it used to take me to water all the fields. This ruse kept the illusion alive back at the main house that I did go up to the fields every day to water the vegetable gardens.

The spirit of the plants even went so far as to advise me to hide the monthly water bill from the rest of the household, so they wouldn't notice the sharp drop in water consumption and catch on to the truth. Since I wrote the Institute's checks, I paid the water invoice immediately each month so no one would see that our water charges had dropped by two-thirds! This documented water reduction was a very convincing, real-world confirmation for me that the plants weren't receiving water.

My second astounding lesson from the plants was in the form of a request. The vegetable plants asked me to create a special garden just for the insects, animals and other life forms regarded as pests by humans. This way, the plants explained, all life forms would be happy. Unmolested, the vegetables in the main fields could grow vital and healthy while the bugs, aphids, fungi, mold, snails, rabbits and deer would have their own vegetable garden to plunder.

Made sense to me! So I planted a new garden about ten feet square. It contained a few of every vegetable planted in the main fields. I told the elements of nature that loved to eat veggies that this was their garden to enjoy and to kindly leave the main fields alone.

Talk about ugly! Every form of hungry pest known in that climate ravaged the vegetables in the special garden. Yet the vegetables in the four main fields remained sound and robust, unscathed by blight or bites.

Michio knew what I was up to in the gardens. He would come by the fields and whisper surreptitiously into my ear, "You're not watering these fields, are you?" I would simply smile back. It was difficult for me to speak aloud to anyone about the extraordinary events unfolding in the gardens. Overwhelmed and a little superstitious, I didn't even talk to myself about the magic. Michio would simply laugh in response to my quiet smile and walk away.

Through playful dialogue with the plant kingdom, I allowed the means and methods of magic into my life. The plants offered me a portal to explore and understand the inner workings of nature and of all life. I learned that by communicating on the level of consciousness—by connecting directly to the spirit of each living thing—I can co-create harmony and happiness with all the elements of my world.

PART III

Finding the Way

Eye to Eye with a Whale

You didn't come into this world.
You came out of it.
Like a wave from the ocean,
you are not a stranger here.

ALAN WATTS

On a cold, dark, overcast afternoon thirty years ago, a ray of warmth and light shown into my world from a most unexpected source: the eye of a giant Humpback whale.

In my young twenties and already old with disillusionment at the state of the world, I was trying to escape my despair by spending an afternoon at sea on a small boat. Without much hope of success, I was asking "whoever might be listening" for a sign of something worth living for—some indication that there was light at the end of the tunnel in this struggle of a life I was barely enduring. That afternoon, my prayers were answered by none less than the largest living creature on the face of the Earth.

Lying despondent on the deck of the boat, disappearing into my mental malaise, I suddenly found myself staring into the eye of a being the size of a large office building. My gaze was locked into the penetrating gaze of this mammoth animal who surfaced from the depths just enough to peer over the bow of my boat right into my face.

Our eyes were only three feet apart. There was no distance between our hearts. Our souls were already one. I immediately dissolved into the depths of this being's essence—a vast inner sea of spacious emptiness, allowing anything and everything, embracing all that I was and so much more of life than I could ever intellectually comprehend. My mind went silent. My inner turmoil disappeared. I entered into a sanctuary of profound, gentle union with my own self in the form of a huge ocean creature.

In a very real sense, I've never left that sanctuary. I've carried with me to this day the feeling of fathomless total acceptance I received from the whale. That taste of the spaciousness of my true, natural state has inspired me to search for ways to incorporate that sense of allowing into every aspect of my life and being.

My dream in life is to become like the whale—a vast safe haven for weary hearts, a refuge from the slings and arrows of life where people can come to rest, reconnect and recharge.

Speaking Your Truth

Everyone wishes to have truth on his side,
But it is not everyone who sincerely wishes to be
on the side of truth.

ARCHBISHOP RICHARD WHATELY

I should have been enjoying the soothing caress of the playful breeze as it wafted its way through my hair on this balmy evening in the Hollywood Hills section of Los Angeles. Instead, I was too self-absorbed to notice the sweet, spicy fragrance of spring blossoms in the wind. I was brooding over what I should say in my speaking engagement due to commence in about ten minutes inside the East-West Institute meditation center. In a muted voice, I was practicing my speech out loud when I was startled by a shadow invading my private corner of the porch.

The sudden appearance of a tall, swarthy stranger looming over my anxious figure temporarily seduced me out of my self-indulgence. Obviously sensing my mood and malady, the lanky, dark-skinned man tried to coax me out of my funk in a soft, gentle, yet assured tone, "What's the matter, cat got your tongue? Didn't I hear you rehearsing some lines?"

"Yes, I'm preparing my presentation for this evening. I can't decide what to talk about. I don't know if people really want to hear what I have to say about the subject. Maybe I should just quote from the published research on the topic and let it go at that," I replied despondently.

"It's none of my business, but why don't you just speak from your heart what you've encountered personally?"

"Oh, that would be too easy!" I laughed. This bold, mysterious advisor had shifted me out of my doom and gloom. I was grateful for that. "Besides, people don't care what a twenty-year-old knows about healing. I'd better adhere to what the experts and professionals have to say."

"Suit yourself, but I've fared much better sticking to what I've discovered firsthand. May I tell you a story?"

I nodded agreement. I was thankful for any distraction at this point. A tale sounded like the perfect antidote to the seriousness that had overtaken me. Through a personal story, my candid friend offered the most precise and useful advice regarding communication I have ever received.

"Most of my early life growing up in Morocco, I was sickly," Michael began soberly. "After years of searching and experimenting in my quest for health, I came across a book by George Osawa, the originator of a philosophy of healthy living called macrobiotics. Encouraged by my discovery, I devoured all the books by Osawa I could find. By eating, thinking and living the macrobiotic way of life, I transformed the ailing youth I once was."

"I felt robust and alive again," Michael enthused. "My recovery was so miraculous and complete, I decided to devote my life to helping others in the same way George Osawa helped me. With great exuberance, I began to give public presentations about the macrobiotic system of eating and living. I described in detail how sickly I'd been. I expounded upon the vitality I now enjoy and how blessed I am. Hundreds of desperate North Africans were attracted to my talks—people seeking the restoration of fitness that I achieved."

Michael's poise and sincerity in recounting his tale to me explained his immediate popularity on the lecture circuit. His compassion and dedication was palpable in the cool night air.

"But as more and more people came to my talks and my reputation grew throughout the Arab world, I began to develop a severe throat problem," Michael continued. "At first, my throat would just itch. I coughed a lot during my speeches. As I continued to address larger and larger crowds, the tickle in my throat became an acute ache. My voice gradually became harsh and grating. I was stubborn and intent upon my holy mission to help others. I insisted on keeping up my hectic speaking schedule. Finally, in the middle of the evening lecturing to the largest audience I'd ever assembled, my throat started to bleed. Of course, in my arrogance, I attempted to keep going. Eventually I was coughing up so much blood, I had to stop talking for the evening."

As the tenacious stranger paused, I drew a quick, halting breath. I felt the need to bolster myself before he resumed. I was visibly rattled by the focus of his story. I was about to lecture on the same topic of macrobiotics to several hundred anguished souls also searching for help. The similarities were remarkable; the coincidence unnerving. My hands and legs were trembling. I grabbed the wooden railing of the stairs to stabilize myself. *Why was I reacting so strongly to his story?* I asked myself. I was afraid to know.

"After a frustrating week of saving my voice and waiting for my throat to heal, I began lecturing again," Michael carried on with his cautionary tale. "The same problem appeared after just ten minutes at the podium. This became a pattern for the next few months. I'd reluctantly take time off for my throat to heal. Then I'd return to my speaking schedule. Shortly into my next talk, I'd begin coughing up blood again and be forced to stop. It was extremely frustrating, to say the least!

"I consulted many medical doctors. No practitioner could find anything medically or physiologically abnormal with my throat. I saw I must to look elsewhere for relief. Needing to gain my own insight into the problem, I'd have to heal it myself.

"I became the lead detective on my own case. I noticed when I quit lecturing, my throat stopped bleeding and healed overnight. I also observed that my throat only acted up when I was giving a speech about macrobiotics. My throat functioned perfectly in everyday life. Since the only time my throat bled was during my lectures, I determined my soul and God must be trying to tell me something about my public speaking. After all, the problem brought my public talks to an abrupt and embarrassing halt every time! So, I began listening to myself in order to hear what I was saying up to the point at which my throat would begin bleeding."

At this juncture in Michael's biography, I was sweating profusely and about to faint. His tale was hitting much too close to home. I blurted out, "Please, Michael, tell me what happens— quick. I can't take the suspense!" My sudden outburst made me feel acutely embarrassed, but since the moral of his story was truthfulness, I was, at least, following the spirit of his sharing!

Sensing my distress, the lanky stranger reached over to gently, but firmly, grip my forearm with his right hand. It was a sensitive and reassuring gesture on his part. I was grateful for any assistance I could get at this point. I wanted to hear the rest of his adventure, but part of me was afraid to absorb any more of his lesson. I implored Michael to pick up where he left off and ignore my emotional reactions.

"The results of my self-observation didn't reveal any helpful clues," Michael admitted sheepishly. "I saw only that my talks consisted mostly of me quoting George Osawa and fervently admonishing people to eat and live according to Osawa's theories if they wanted to regain and retain their health.

"Confused and bewildered, I prayed to God, 'What's wrong with what I say? I'm just trying to help people.' God's answer was swift and explicit. That very night I was awakened from my sleep by two vivid visions. In the first, I saw myself in the present, stridently pointing my finger at a large audience, telling them how they needed to change the way they ate and lived. And then suddenly, I began to spew blood from my mouth. A crimson fountain gushed forth from my throat, soaking my lecture notes in bright red liquid.

"In the second tableau, I saw myself in the past when I first started to speak publicly. I was sharing calmly, compassionately— in my own words—how I'd healed myself by changing the way I ate, thought and lived. The group was small. The format was informal. My throat didn't bleed. My voice was strong and distinct. The audience was listening with rapt attention.

"Startled and shaken, I knew instantly the import of the two visions. When I spoke from my heart, my message was my own and it got delivered. I was sharing observations based solely on *my own personal* experience. And I wasn't trying to force my point of view down people's throats. When I taught *borrowed* wisdom from George Osawa—and bludgeoned the audience with warnings and admonitions—my own speaking mechanism rebelled. My throat bled, silencing my tirade. I realized that God was directing me to simply offer my own personal truth. If I stick to sharing my direct experience, I'll be heard. But when I preach secondhand information, I won't be heard."

Michael placed his arm around my shoulder as he exclaimed with the unbridled joy of a child, "From that day on, my throat has never bled again."

I was jolted back to the present by the sight of the watch on Michael's wrist in front of my face. It was time for my lecture inside the meditation hall. Despite the fears and resistance the story had triggered, I felt grateful for the co-conspiracy of Michael and my inner coach. This explicit and valuable guidance came just when I needed it. What timing!

Drawing strength from Michael's example of honesty and compassion, I spoke my own truth in my own words that evening. I didn't have to clear my throat once during the talk. I exposed my heart and soul to the audience that night and received profuse acknowledgement and appreciation in return.

During my long career as a public lecturer, my throat has never bled like Michael's did in his youth. But I have periodically encountered minor throat problems while speaking. Whenever my voice starts to become hoarse, raspy or blocked in any way, I remember Michael's story. I stop to reflect upon what I'm saying. Each time I find that I've strayed from my personal experience into quoting someone else's words or experience. Or, I discover I have shifted from simply *sharing* what I know into *preaching* to others what they should do. Then, as I return to sharing my own truth, my throat clears and I reconnect with the hearts of the audience.

I've learned for myself, what Michael discovered in his youth. When I speak what I know from direct experience, my body—and spirit—support me fully!

Choosing Innocence

Out beyond the ideas of right and wrong,
there is a field—
meet me there.

RUMI

Once in a while, I receive wisdom on the human condition from a specific aspect of nature. These direct transmissions have consistently helped me weather the changing tides of fortune and emotion in my life.

It was a crystalline winter afternoon. I was walking with my friend Ted through the snow seeking solace from the fatigue and despair we were feeling about the seemingly endless stream of challenges in our personal lives. Our walk ended with us lying on the snow in the center of a stand of young, bare birch trees. The sun was blinding, but soothingly balmy as it reflected off the stark white, tender bark of the saplings. The welcomed warmth eased us into a relaxed, receptive state. We asked the spirit of the slender fledglings for comfort and guidance to meet the hurdles placed before us.

The unaffected, fresh energy of the virgin trees shared a message about innocence:

> "If you return to a state of innocence, your life will be much easier. The majority of humans are born with natural innocence, openness and trust. For a few years you enjoy a period of grace during which life is simple, direct and pure. Later, as you gain experience in life, you encounter dishonesty, abuse and betrayal. You become wary, jaded and disheartened. But at one point in every human life, an opportunity to return to innocence is offered.
>
> "If you should choose to re-enter the state of innocence consciously from free will, this openness can never be lost or taken away—as was natural innocence. When chosen innocence is fully embraced, you are free of judgment, expectation, all conditioned beliefs and restrictions of the past. You have no limits whatsoever. Living in chosen innocence allows you to enjoy your real self, your true power and the only genuine reality—the present moment. The present moment is the space of magic, miracles, transformation and total supply. It is the path to enlightenment and peace."

Ted and I didn't believe the birch trees. On that emotionally woeful day, we couldn't imagine ever feeling good about life again, let alone being able to enter into a permanent state of innocence, openness and joy.

Some years later, I experienced a moment of striking clarity during which I remembered the tender message of the young birches. I realized I possessed the desire and the power within me to choose freedom from preconception and evaluation regarding every aspect of life. I reached a level of spiritual growth in which I was able to comprehend the great advantage in approaching each day—each encounter, each moment—with freshness, newness and innocence. On that day, I chose to be innocent again and live in the gift of the present. And as the young saplings promised, I've never lost that quality, that space, that grace.

Hot Tubbing with Angels

What lies before us and what lies behind us
are small matters compared to what lies within us.
And when we bring what is within out into the world,
miracles happen.

HENRY DAVID THOREAU

Twenty-five naked women and men lay between me and the exit. If I could have jumped across the collective mass of quivering skin, I would have bolted from that basement in a split second. As it turned out, I found myself inadvertently trapped in a situation that would lead me to astounding new levels of awareness and abundance.

My escapade began back in the '70s when a long-time, trusted friend in California wrote me about a versatile, vivacious woman named Alana. She was traveling from Los Angeles to Boston to present a seminar on a human potential method called "rebirthing." He felt I'd like to meet her and learn about this new and exciting approach to spiritual growth. I'd grown to trust my friend's keen, intuitive knowledge of my soul's agenda. My roommate Matt and I decided to attend Alana's program. We anticipated, at most, a captivating lecture on an unknown subject.

We joined a group of people in the quaint living room of a modest Victorian home located in Brookline, a close-by, unassuming Boston suburb. For some time, the room was filled with hushed conversation. Then Alana appeared. Wrapped in an exotic Indian sari, she commanded immediate attention with her long, jet-black hair parted just enough to reveal very large, piercing eyes.

After only the briefest introduction to the topic of the rebirthing process, Alana invited the assembled newcomers to proceed down a steep cascade of old, rickety stairs to the basement of the house. I dutifully followed the group, intrigued by Alana's description of rebirthing as a way to re-experience and release the emotional trauma of one's physical birth. In a cramped antechamber, she instructed us to take off every stitch of our clothing. Believe it or not, we all complied. Hey, she was from California. In Boston, this is what we expected from someone from California!

Then she shunted us into an even smaller room with a sunken hot tub in the corner. Quite suddenly, I realized I was trapped naked in the middle of a room, separated from the only door by twenty-five equally bare strangers. A mild panic began its journey up my spine.

Alana started to read aloud to us from a book called *Birth Without Violence* by Frederick LeBoyer. The book was the rebirthers' bible. LeBoyer described in unsettling, graphic detail how most humans come into this world. It was much more than I ever wanted to know about the birth process! With great feeling and drama, Alana read how most of us came out of our mother's womb into a freezing cold hospital room, are turned upside-down and then whacked on the butt until we cry. And, as if that's not shocking enough to newborn humans, a stinging medication is poured into our eyes to kill a certain type of bacteria.

The gut-wrenching description of a *normal* birth seemed to me to go on and on. As Alana read about the inhospitable, heartless conditions into which our souls arrive, my mild panic escalated into full-blown terror, spreading from my spine throughout my body. I held no conscious memory of my own birth. Yet listening to this literal, blow-by-blow description of the usual birth process was tortuous to me. Acute fear and stifling emotions were coming up. I was having trouble breathing. I felt trapped by her images and by the mass of nude bodies crammed into the tiny space. I didn't want to sit there and listen any longer. In search of a way to graciously flee all this raw nakedness and escalating emotional pain, I desperately scanned the room. I could find no avenue to freedom.

Then I heard Alana ask for a volunteer to become "rebirthed." In my terror, what I heard was "a way out!" I volunteered. Exactly what I was volunteering for, I didn't know. At the moment, I didn't care. Escape from the growing phobia of such a closed-in space and subject was all that was on my mind. Get me out of here!

Submerged in the sunken hot tub, breathing through a snorkel, I floated face down in the water, reassured and supported by Alana's gentle touch. The temperature of the water, like the surrounding air, was deliberately adjusted to match the temperature of my body. When the temperature of the water and the air touching the body is sensed as being the same as the body's temperature, people generally lose their discrimination of difference and separation between their body and their surroundings. This loss of skin sensation, coupled with silence and a feeling of weightlessness, stimulates abounding pleasure in the floater. The experience is similar to being immersed in a sensory deprivation or isolation tank. You feel as if you no longer have a body. You are a consciousness floating with complete comfort in a warm, womb-like environment. It is a life-changing, liberating interlude.

However, as is the intent of the rebirthing process, the experience is usually as ephemeral as it is ecstatic. The temporary rapture turns quickly into trauma. And so it was with me.

POW! There I was in the delivery room. I'd just come out of my mother. I re-experienced in full, living color and sensation all the torture of a typical clinical hospital birthing. My body tensed and my spirit recoiled.

Several assistants gently lifted me out of the tepid water onto a waiting bed of soft, warm cotton towels. A couple of hours of conscious deep breathing, loving massage and tender coaching by Alana were necessary for me to move through the memories and emotions of my violent birth. Old, dead energy of my birth struggle exited with each exhale. Fresh *prana* energy of new possibilities infused every cell of my body with each inhale. Pleasure replaced the pain. Euphoria replaced the agony. I entered into a state of full body orgasm. Every cell of my physical body felt fully alive and electric. I entered into an ethereal state of physical, emotional and spiritual bliss.

My roomie Matt went into the hot tub after me and had a similarly sublime experience—paradise, then trauma, followed by elation. After being shaken to our core, we didn't dare drive. We left our car at the house and practically floated the two-mile trek back to our home.

Both Matt and I awoke the next morning to find our living room filled with twenty to thirty full-winged angels! I had vague memories at the time of glimpsing angelic beings when I was a small child. However, I'd never before been in the presence of so many clearly visible and radiant heavenly beings. That I wasn't totally overwhelmed by the sight indicated how open I'd become from the rebirthing. My ability to embrace the love pouring forth from these heavenly messengers was also remarkable and spoke volumes of the power of the previous night's expansion. Matt was also able to accept and absorb the majesty of the moment. The incongruity of so many beings fitting into a small apartment living room never occurred to either of us.

This "impossibility" is a prime example of the phenomenon of physical space adapting to the spirit of the moment. Our intention determines our reality. The expansiveness and flexibility of the beliefs in our consciousness decide what can occur in our universe.

These golden messengers spent the next three weeks pouring golden light on, through and around Matt and me. We were filled with such serenity and bliss, we had neither the inclination nor the ability to go to work. Happy as larks, each day we called in to the natural foods business that employed us both to tell them we simply weren't yet capable of coming to work. Our spacey, euphoric tone and demeanor on the phone were more than enough to convince our boss we were correct in our assessment. Since the philosophical focus of our employer, Erewhon Natural Foods, was authentically spiritual in nature, the management gave us wide latitude and empathetic understanding.

In retrospect, I'd describe Matt and me as having been in a state of perpetual grace. We could barely talk coherently. We would fall silent in the middle of a sentence and then begin another, without noticing we failed to finish the previous thought. Yet we communicated. A meaningful exchange took place. We simply *knew* what the other was trying to convey. We conversed heart to heart, soul to soul, through direct transmission.

In this elated state, we were incapable of—or more accurately, disinterested in—even the simplest tasks, like preparing food. Friends from work dropped off meals for us. We attempted to

mouth words of thanks, but usually our friends would leave quickly, sensing we were in a special space that needed to be protected and honored. Spiritually, Matt and I grew tremendously from the rebirthing. Our worlds expanded to embrace the magical and the divine as an everyday possibility.

During those weeks of grace, Matt and I also underwent a release and renewal. Outmoded limitations and old, dead beliefs were purged and cleansed from our personalities. Fresh possibilities emerged from our revitalized souls. It was a miraculous period of divine alchemy, a transformation of our fundamental, core ground of being. Most of the healing and transmutation took place on an energetic, vibrational level. We had little conceptual sense of which old patterns were changing and leaving. Yet every so often I'd catch glimpses of a part of my current life, or a past life, that were being released—or, to put it more precisely, integrated into my being with a fuller understanding.

Finally, after about three weeks, Matt and I were capable of maintaining our physical balance and could walk about without collapsing. We left the apartment and sauntered across the street to a large city park. There, in a sizable playing field within the park, our limited personal world expanded even further. Crying tears of joy and gratitude, we gazed upon hundreds of angels, layered row upon row, reaching into the sky as far as we could see. We were granted a vivid, exalting vision of the Heavenly Host, complete with the magnificent, melodic sounds of celestial music. Basking in the beauty and blessing of the revelation until the coolness of dusk reminded us that we were still residing in human physical bodies, we retired to our home with a sense of all-prevailing peace. It's an inner serenity that's never left me.

The next morning, Matt and I awoke to a house void of angels, but filled with the energy of resurrection. Our youthful spirits of innocence, openness and enthusiasm for life replaced the disillusionment, withdrawal and despair we previously felt in our lives. We instinctively knew it was time to re-enter our everyday world.

Back at Erewhon Natural Foods, our regenerated exuberance for life and expectancy for goodness was evident to everyone. The remarkable changes in Matt and me inspired most of the company's two hundred employees to go through the rebirthing process. The reborn openness and playfulness of our staff proved to be infectious to our customers. Every natural and health food store in the Northeast wanted to buy from us because they loved the genuine warmth and thoughtfulness of our salespeople who called on them and of our truck drivers who delivered the goods. People ordered food from us because they wanted to interact with the energy of our employees in person and over the phone. The company's sales tripled. Matt and I continued to grow more honest and intimate with ourselves, each other and all our friends and relationships. It was a joyous spiritual opening for everybody in my life, both personally and professionally.

I am still expanding in my rebirth as you read this.

Possessed by a Spirit

For in and out, above, about, below,
'Tis nothing but a Magic Shadow Show,
Played in a Box whose Candle is the Sun,
Round which we Phantom Figures come and go.

OMAR KHAYYAM

The veil between life and death is very thin. When the veil dissolves, we can slip between time and space to discover people just like us looking for a place to call home.

My rebirthing teacher Alana was very comfortable exploring the dimensions of the hereafter beyond the veil of what we call death. In her spiritual work of rebirthing, she assisted people to travel consciously between physical and non-physical states. From her rebirthing exploits, she developed easy ways to pierce the veils between dimensions. Her dynamic opening process allowed people to extend their conscious awareness at will from their physical body to their subtle body, the spiritual state we're in when we're not in the physical realm. I didn't really understand the method, but, having learned to trust Alana, I was open to expanding my known universe a little further. Alana felt she knew the perfect place to expand my training in inter-dimensional travel.

In the dead of night, so to speak, Alana and I journeyed to Concord, Massachusetts, a small town outside Boston, where "the shot heard around the world" was fired. History tells us this skirmish ignited the Revolutionary War between the Colonies and Britain. Many young men on both sides were killed in the battle.

Alana was very curious to visit the battlefield to see if she could sense any lingering spirits of the dead soldiers who had fought there. If so, she felt it was an excellent opportunity for me to encounter life on the other side of a dimensional veil. We timed our visit to arrive at dawn to take advantage of the best conditions for connecting with the spirit world. At this hour, the battlefield would most likely be deserted. Also, the low-lying, early morning fog creeping through the valley would be perfect for seeing the vague shapes of etheric matter, the substance of ghosts. The fragile, shifting forms of spirits are often easier to discern in this earthly dimension when viewed through the extreme density of fog.

We were not disappointed. Through the heavy, early morning mist, we were able to clearly perceive the translucent subtle bodies of scores of soldiers who had died in that fateful battle.

Still in a state of shock from dying so quickly, unexpectedly and violently, the spirits of these American and British soldiers continued to hang around the site of their demise. Neither side of the conflict had anticipated exchanging gunfire that peaceful morning in Concord, let alone dying. The English soldiers were young and inexperienced. Most had never faced combat. They understandably anticipated what they had previously encountered in the Colonies: a compliant population. The Americans involved in the skirmish weren't even soldiers. They were farmers and townspeople hastily assembled to protest British soldiers coming to their hometown and enforcing new, restrictive laws.

Alana foresaw that the surprise and suddenness of the soldiers' deaths would severely traumatize the disembodied men, leaving them in a state of suspended animation or spiritual shock. Indeed, they looked and acted confused, bewildered and lost. The ghosts of these greenhorn English recruits and naïve American farmers were caught in a limbo between two worlds.

Alana spent the morning praying for the release of the nonphysical beings from their accidental purgatory. These men hadn't yet realized what had happened to them. They didn't know they were no longer among the living. She spoke out loud to them, explaining that they were shot unexpectedly and were now dead. She let them know it was time for them to move on. As each traumatized spirit comprehended her compassionate message, he began to dissolve and disappear from the discernable outer fringes of our world. One by one the disoriented recruits awoke to their fate and true condition. One by one, they chose to move on. Soon the killing fields began to take on a palpable feeling of calm and sacredness. I witnessed this merciful liberation with reverence, fascination and awe.

That evening, without any inkling of what was awaiting me in just a few hours, I invited Alana to one of my favorite Italian restaurants in Boston. In its quaint, quiet, intimate atmosphere, we discussed the profoundly moving events of that morning.

Suddenly, a brisk breeze blew out the candle on our table. Immediately, Alana and I both became very cold. I stood and checked the front and back entrances of the eatery to see if a door had been left open. All windows and doors were tightly shut.

Perplexed, I sat back down. Still experiencing an intensely frigid wind, we both draped our shoulders with our winter coats and looked around the small dining room to see how the other diners were dealing with the breeze and radical drop in temperature. To our puzzlement, all the candles on the other tables were burning bright and straight up with no sign of a disturbing current of air. No one appeared to be cold. Women in sleeveless dresses were dining comfortably. And there we sat, shivering in our down parkas!

I asked Alana if our inexplicable chill was some aftermath of the powerful rebirthing process we shared recently. "Well, rebirthing does open one to experience life more expansively," she replied thoughtfully. Then she added, "So does spending half a day freeing the souls of dead soldiers. This feels to me like the coldness that envelops me in the presence of a departed spirit."

Alana had no sooner uttered her reply to my question when, abruptly, the color in her face drained and her eyes widened. "It's my brother!" she exclaimed in a hoarse whisper. Haltingly, she explained that her young teenage brother James committed suicide just three weeks earlier. He'd killed himself mysteriously, without exhibiting any perceivable warning signs to her or the rest of the family. Alana intuitively knew his spirit must be experiencing a great deal of pain and fear. Still somewhat unnerved, she murmured, "I've been calling to him, trying to reach his spirit. I suspect this chill we feel might be him."

Spirit communication was still a fairly new subject to me. And I hadn't yet fully absorbed the import of the morning's events on the battlefield. Stunned by her hypothesis and frightened by the unexplainable, frigid breeze, I found myself utterly speechless.

"Keith, please help me contact my brother," Alana fervently implored, seemingly oblivious to my perplexed condition. "I just know this is James trying to reach me. The process of reaching out to him is very similar to what we did this morning in Concord with the soldiers. Please!"

In my bewildered state, I was amenable to any course of action that might lead me out of my confusion, especially when faced with the emotional force and conviction of Alana's words in that moment.

"Okay," I replied in my naïveté. I thought she was probably going to ask me to do something like pray with her. I could do that. However, Alana had something far more radical up her sleeve.

Emboldened with a sense of personal purpose and spiritual adventure, Alana whisked me out of the restaurant and up the street to the old, ramshackle Victorian house where she was currently staying. We rushed up to a tiny room on the third floor. She closed the door and lit a candle. Then she began calling out loud to her brother.

Once again, as in the restaurant, the air became very chilly. A howling wind started up *inside* the room—a small chamber with no open window or door. The candle flame blew out. Suddenly, the breeze stopped. The third-story attic room became deadly quiet. Alana asked me if she could talk to her brother *through* me. I didn't know what I was saying "yes" to, but I sincerely wanted to help.

As soon as I agreed, a very strange sensation began to fill my body. It was as if another being, or presence, was growing inside me. Indeed, a stranger, another entity's consciousness, was overtaking me. It was the oddest sensation I've ever felt. This awareness—who was not I—was occupying my head, legs and arms. Bizarre. The being continued expanding until the foreign sensation spread throughout my entire body. Then I could tell the invader consciousness was a person, a young male. I felt his emotions. He was sad and scared. And I experienced how he felt physically—cold and clammy. All these sensations were very uncomfortable and disconcerting.

Alana announced this presence was, indeed, her recently deceased brother James. He was inhabiting my body in order to communicate with Alana. She asked him questions: what was he feeling, seeing and thinking? He used my physical mouth to answer. The voice that came out of my mouth was not mine; it was the voice of a terrified, weeping, fifteen-year-old kid.

James related that ever since he'd killed himself, he'd been living in a sterile state of pitch blackness. He felt completely isolated and alone. Alana asked if he'd met or seen anyone else. He lamented, "No, I haven't met anyone. It's cold and dark and damp here. There's no one and nothing else around at all, not even walls. Just a terrible emptiness."

Her brother was so terrified, he could barely talk. He was stuttering. His teeth, my teeth, were chattering. As James described his condition to his sister, I reeled with the terror and trauma along with him. My predicament frightened me. Yet not knowing what to do, I did nothing. Alana continued talking to James. She was holding my body around the waist and shoulders, stroking my hand, but conversing with her deceased brother. Alana and her sibling were speaking heart to heart, soul to soul. After a half-hour of Alana consoling him, James began to talk about why he killed himself. It became obvious he felt the need for absolution.

"I'm so sorry, Alana. I didn't mean to hurt you and Mom and Dad. Honest! Can you forgive me? Do you think Mom and Dad can ever forgive me?"

James desperately wanted, needed, pardon for his deed. Very compassionately, Alana soothed his tortured soul. "Of course, I forgive you, James. And Mom and Dad forgive you. We all forgive you. We love you."

She urged him to allow himself to cry. I felt hot tears, James' tears, stream down my ice cold cheeks. Then a marked shift began to take place. As James cried, the extreme chill I was feeling lessened. My fingers and toes began to tingle with warmth. James exclaimed excitedly, "Alana, I sense some heat. I feel warmer. A strong force is pulling me. I see a glow in the distance."

"Go, James. Go toward the light," Alana urged.

James' agonized weeping transformed into tears of joy and relief. Through me, he exclaimed, "I'm going now. I can see Aunt Betty and Uncle Frank."

As soon as his words left my mouth, I began feeling alone again in my own body. I sighed instinctively. I was enormously relieved. Alana was ecstatic. She knew her brother was going to his spiritual home and would be greeted by familiar loved ones. She knew her brother was in good hands now.

I can still recall how it felt to have James' awareness slowly creep out of my physical body. Every one of my cells felt like something cold, sticky and thick was moving through and around it. I felt as if frigid mud or glue was inching up through and out of my body. Surprisingly, it took a while for me to get used to being by myself within my own carcass again.

Once James left, my body returned to its normal temperature. So did the air in the room. And the candle's flame sprang to life as though it had never been extinguished.

I had split the veil between life and death. A disincarnate spirit had possessed me. I was elated to have helped James move on. The evening was a very enlightening exploration for me, but not one I choose to ever repeat!

Guns and Gurus

A wise man chooses his battles.

CHINESE SAYING

"Treat death as an ally," the shamans advise.

I often wondered what Native American medicine men and shamans meant by this saying. One idyllic summer afternoon, I got my answer. The messenger was Indian—not from America, but from India!

His name was Muktananda. My friends in Boston wanted to visit this particular Indian guru they'd read about in books. I usually went along with my friends' spiritual adventures. We had a track record together of very good karma. Our intuitive guidance was almost always in sync. Whatever they were attracted to usually turned out to be something that was valuable for my spiritual unfoldment. We were what I call "karma buddies."

I agreed to go with them to visit this newfound sage. Leaving Boston Friday morning, we drove the length of Massachusetts, ending up at an ashram retreat in the middle of upstate New York for a weekend of communing with Muktananda. That evening, we attended our first *satsang*, a meditative, question-and-answer session of truth-telling with a spiritual teacher. *Satsang* is a term from India that means literally "abiding in truth."

As soon as I laid eyes on him, I liked Muktananda. Of short stature and dark complexion, he sported a closely cropped beard speckled with gray. His countenance radiated calm acceptance. He was friendly, jovial and humorous. Exuding a delightful spark, he spoke with penetrating wisdom. In front of several hundred, aspiring disciples, Muktananda talked for a brief period and then answered many detailed questions about spiritual practice and discipline. After countless, lengthy exchanges, we all meditated together in silence for a full hour.

My first encounter with this unassuming master had an unexpectedly dramatic effect on me. Muktananda's passion spoke directly to my soul, and, in so doing, stirred up uncomfortable, challenging issues for my personality. The meditation stimulated many disturbing memories and intense emotions within me. Wave after wave of energy releases rippled up and through my body. Overwhelmed, anxious and unnerved, I crashed out in my room immediately after the Friday evening *satsang*.

The next morning was one of those crisp, cloudless summer days that people in New England long for, but seldom get. I decided I'd rather take off, find a lake, go swimming and enjoy the sun, instead of staying cooped up inside with Muktananda and my emotional baggage. After all, my personality reasoned, I could meditate anytime, anywhere, in any weather. I felt an overpowering urge to take advantage of the day's extraordinary *external* conditions. In truth, the overpowering urge of my ego was to avoid the day's extraordinary *internal* conditions. Looking back, it should have been obvious to me how threatened my ego was that morning. I was antsy and fidgety at the breakfast table, and irritated with everybody and everything around me.

After breakfast, my friends went to Saturday morning *satsang*. I took off by myself in search of the perfect swimming hole, or, more accurately, in search of the perfect anywhere-but-here!

A thick evergreen forest surrounded the ashram property. Although there didn't appear to be any trails leading into the woods, a pair of railroad tracks cut a wide swath right through the trees. Deciding it was as good a path as any, I walked along the tracks into the quiet, cool cathedral of pines. Eventually, to my delight, I came upon a small, secluded, crystal clear lake encircled by dense green growth.

Since there was no sign of human presence in or around the lake, I stripped off all my clothes and pierced the serene, mirror-like surface of water. Totally enjoying the refreshing water and sense of complete freedom, I swam out to the middle of the lake and floated peacefully in my own slice of Heaven.

Suddenly, two rifle shots shattered my reverie. The bullets punctured the water within a foot from my head. I quickly hid all but my head below the water and looked around. It took only a few seconds to identify a boat about fifty yards away with two men in it, shooting a rifle—at me!

Where that boat came from I'll never know. As far as I could see, the pond was totally enclosed by a primeval wilderness. There were neither roads leading to the lake nor houses on shore. After they fired a third bullet in my direction, I darted beneath the water. Under water, I could hear more bullets whizzing within a few feet of my body. A sharp thrust of panic rippled through me. I had no idea why they were shooting at me, or why they felt they could get away with it. Then it struck me that this lake was so isolated and remote, I could be killed and no one would ever know what happened to me.

I felt very helpless, alone and scared. Every time I surfaced for air, a round of menacing shots encircled me. I couldn't stay under the water forever. Frustrated and desperate, I dove as far as I could into the dark recesses of the water and called out silently to God for help.

"Please get me out of this," I implored. "I'll go back to the ashram," I promised. "I'll go back to *satsang* where I'm supposed to be! Just get me out of danger."

Instinctively, I knew I should be at *satsang* with Muktananda instead of swimming in a lake. On some level, I was very aware that a soul morality play of sorts was unfolding here.

When I broke the surface of the lake again, a second motor boat had mysteriously appeared out of nowhere. I was positive the boat wasn't there before because I could easily see the whole shoreline of the small lake. There were no corners or inlets to hide a vessel. No docks or structures existed anywhere on the shore. But there it was, another boat. From its bow a man was yelling at the top of his lungs at the two shooters to stop their firing. When the newly arrived boat sped toward the riflemen, they turned on the motor and took off down the lake.

Well, that was enough excitement for me for one afternoon! I swam to shore, put my clothes on, and took off as quickly as I could down the railroad tracks to the ashram. As I ran, I thanked the good Lord for the intervention. God had sent me a crystal clear message in responding so quickly to my plea for help. I'd promised to go back to *satsang* if I got out of this predicament. I was going to keep my end of the deal. So, that's where I headed, posthaste! I was returning to *satsang* to open my connection to Spirit and my real self.

Scurrying down the railroad tracks leading to the ashram, I vaguely discerned a person way down the tracks in front of me. As I approached the figure, I saw it was another man with a rifle!

"Oh, my God!" I whispered to myself.

The man leveled his rifle and pointed it at me. I bolted off the tracks into the forest. I never heard a shot and didn't care at that point. I was gone. I ran through the thick timber as fast as my Nikes could go, heedlessly pushing low limbs and bushes out of my way. My skin was becoming laced with small nicks and scratches. The lacerations were not my primary concern. I'd already created being shot at once. I wasn't about to slow down and allow another opportunity for my inner coach to motivate me with a second round of bullets.

I ran through the woodland, stumbling and bleeding, all the way back to the ashram—just in time for the afternoon *satsang*! Entering the building, I collapsed in the back of the room, secure and peaceful for the first time since early that morning. I'd have to explain all the cuts, but I was safe from the materializations of my mind.

My suppressed fears have manifested physically before, but not in such a dramatic and extreme way as they did this bright summer morning. Needless to say, I received a lot of value from the meditation session that afternoon. I saw how scared my ego was of its own death. My mind and its rigidly structured world were being severely shaken and threatened by Muktananda. The wily Indian was inviting me to surrender my ego control, and allow God and my inner coach to direct my life. I saw that after the Friday evening *satsang,* I became afraid the raw force of my lifetime of repressed emotions would explode from within and kill me. I also realized I was afraid of the freedom and personal power waiting for me on the other side of resolving my emotions. Unconsciously, I held the belief that if I owned and shared my true wisdom and strength out in the world, I'd be killed. The fear of my suppressed emotions and the fear of my innate, vast potential had materialized in the form of a real physical threat. The gunmen were reflecting my paranoia for me in such an unavoidable way that I had to face it, feel it, own it—and then release it. What a blessing! Those fears needed to die. And they did die—that afternoon in *satsang*.

Muktananda was walking around the hall, selectively touching his meditating students lightly on the head or heart with his hand. When his fingers landed on my forehead, I felt a sharp shot of *shakti* holy energy shoot up my spine and out the top of my head. This ecstatic electrical charge activated an outpouring of divine bliss from the innermost recesses of my being, infusing my body with euphoria. I entered a state of oneness with All That Is. I allowed myself to be filled with the safety and serenity of my own spirit and of God's presence.

This fateful weekend, with a "gentle" nudge from my external environment, I surrendered to the care and comfort of my inner coach and my highest destiny. Hallelujah!

A Glimpse of Eternity

The Three in One is what I AM,
And Hell itself is but a dam
That I did put in my own stream
When in a nightmare, I did dream
That I was not the only One.
And thus by ME was doubt begun,
Which ran its course till I awoke
And found that I with ME did joke.

4,000 YEAR OLD EGYPTIAN INSCRIPTION

The sun was just coming up when I awoke in Boston on what was to become a very special day. Basking in the warmth shining on my face and body through the window, I sensed something was different on this particular morning. The sun was relaxing me in a way both familiar and yet intriguingly fresh. Rays of solar light cut like laser beams into the cold stiffness of my muscles, sending waves of electric impulses through every cell of my body. The welcome heat of the sun not only felt extraordinarily strong, but it seemed to pierce the very marrow of my bones. No, not my bones—my soul.

Although the view out the window was bright and sunny, there was an unusual, rarefied quality to the scene and a razor-sharp clarity to the air. It was as if I was looking *through* the vista before me, not *at* it, and so doing, touching another reality *behind* the solid steel skyline of the monolithic towers of downtown Boston.

I was acutely aware of feeling fully present in the moment. I saw rainbow-colored bands of energy radiating out from the center of my being and coalescing to become the physical world around me. I experienced my exact past and my specific future being created spontaneously from the core structure of my consciousness. With absolute certainty, I knew the true nature of reality, life and death—and my blueprint not only for this lifetime, but for my spirit's entire existence.

After a few, jolting waves of combined terror, joy and awe, I realized my soul had fully awakened within my body and my personality. Just as I became acutely aware of my true beingness, a gentle but firm voice from within spoke:

"This is enough for now. It is time for you to go back to sleep for a while longer. This brief glimpse will inspire and encourage you through the exploration that lies ahead."

On some level, I knew the truth of my soul's words. I then consciously, though reluctantly, *chose* to forget the revelation I had just experienced.

In a flash, the remarkable epiphany was a vague memory. Nestling under the covers, I immediately fell into a dreamless slumber. When I awoke for the second time that morning, I was simply a young man lying on a mattress on the floor of a tenement building wondering what to fix for breakfast.

I learned one very transforming truth from opening to that moment of total recall:

The eternal part of me has a divine purpose
to express this lifetime here on Earth.

This purpose is my destiny, my design, my dream—for this life and for my soul's timeless adventure. The script is self-chosen, self-ignited, self-nurtured and self-fulfilling. The plan is born in and emanates from, as the aborigines of Australia say, the "forever" part of me. And if I choose, I can know this scenario in as much detail as is right for me to know at any given moment. Realizing I can know whatever I need to know, whenever I need to know it, instills in me an inner calm and a great trust in the universe.

At various times in life, most people spontaneously and "accidentally" experience, as I did, moments in which they know the "whole score." They awaken to their true nature, their real self and their eternal purpose. In Zen, these flashes of clarity are called *satori* experiences. These awakenings are a sudden enlightenment, a brief glimpse of true reality.

Our personal divine blueprint often shows itself as a flash of brilliance, inspiration, talent, success, courage or wisdom. Sometimes our true design reveals itself as a freeing clarity cracking through clouds of doubt, despair and pain—or as a rush of intense energy surging through our being from the bowels of the Earth to reunite with Heaven. Often, such a breakthrough expresses itself as a miracle or a magical creation.

I've often asked my spirit why we lose track of who we are and why we are here on Earth. What is the spiritual purpose of "The Great Forgetting," as the Australian aborigines are fond of calling it? The answer I've received from my inner coach is that there are many unique and individual reasons why people forget, and that the reasons are particular to the intricacies of each person's distinct soul game plan. However, a common element of the schedule of most people's soul script is that it's simply not time to awaken fully and permanently. For these people, there's more exploration for the personality to do on the current level of consciousness. We don't remember our true mission because we've very deliberately chosen to forget glimpses of our true self. Forgetting is part of our own plan.

In my past, I've noticed that when acute self-awareness—radical clarity, personal power, true destiny—revealed itself in my life, I often became ill, busy or manic. Sometimes I'd quickly create an emergency, accident or crisis. I'd run away from the clarity into confusion, complication, chaos, or, as a last resort, total "spiritual amnesia!" Now, however, using focused observation and intuitive sensing, I keep a watch for the specific unconscious ways that I systematically cut short my awakened state. When I spot an automatic pattern starting to kick in, I make a conscious choice to override the emotional impulse to give up my power to the fear. I nip the self-sabotage in the bud. I refuse to let a knee-jerk, conditioned reaction rob me of the joy of heightened clarity. Once freed from the old programmed response, I can then follow my inner guidance and take fresh intuitive action to stay fully aware.

And there's encouraging news about this particular time in the evolution of human consciousness on Earth. It's finally time in most people's soul schedules to awaken to their greater destiny! Therefore, self-imposed blinders and limitations are no longer needed, useful or valuable. Thus, old patterns of forgetfulness and restriction now release easily.

One day I spent a few hours absorbing the essence of a giant desert tarantula spider from an intimate distance of a few inches. I never before allowed myself to hang out so close to this huge spider. I was very surprised and fascinated by the beauty of the intricate spiral formations of hair on its back, face, legs and pincers. The spirit of this wise reflection of my consciousness reminded me in a loving inner voice that:

"You are the weaver of your own web.
You are the designer of the reoccurring patterns in your life that comprise your prison—or your paradise.
And most importantly,
you can weave a new web any time you choose."

Calling the Bluff on Death

The warrior's approach is to say "Yes" to life—
"Yes" to it all.

JOSEPH CAMPBELL

"You don't begin to live until you have conquered your own Death," admonished don Juan Matus, the wise shaman in Carlos Castaneda's wild tales of spiritual adventure. I was always curious what don Juan meant by this declaration. One day I implored my inner coach to enlighten me as to what is entailed in "conquering one's Death." Spirit answered my request in a most definitive way when I found myself being stalked by Death in my own home.

My new roommate Rick and I were heavily involved in assisting people release their unconscious emotions and birth trauma by means of a personal growth practice named "rebirthing."

Rick took a week off work to assist the many people asking to be rebirthed. While his intentions were noble, he didn't take care to stay current with his own feelings during the many stimulating sessions throughout the week. When helping other people to process their birth trauma and suppressed emotions, it's imperative that rebirthing facilitators continually purge their own feelings as the process unfolds. If rebirthers ignore their own emotions, their energy can back up and get stuck. Very quickly, the backup creates new emotional and physical trauma for the very people trying to help others in the freeing process! Eventually, if the facilitators don't keep their own emotional energy moving, the whole rebirthing process comes to a screeching halt.

By the end of the week, Rick's feelings were extremely blocked. He didn't take the time to release his own emotions during and after each rebirthing session. A towering, lanky, ex-basketball star athlete in college, Rick was a stoic, tight-lipped, Gary Cooper double when it came to expressing his feelings. He always used his good looks and tough jock persona to plow under and avoid any uncomfortable situations in his life, choosing to sweep any emotionally charged issues under the rug rather than confront the feelings involved. Thus, he began the rebirthing purging process with quite a backlog of unresolved feelings. Then, day by day in the rebirthing sessions, as his own birth trauma, life disappointments and other emotionally charged issues were triggered, he resorted again to his life-long strategy of suppression. His stressful, negative feelings got really backlogged. Every day, he became more and more irritable, uptight, nervous and abrupt. Then he became fearful, angry and very paranoid. His fear eventually escalated to the point of terror.

As his roommate, I was the only person Rick saw for an entire week other than those people involved in the rebirthing sessions. My usually jovial housemate began to project his fear, anger and paranoia onto me. He began to see me as the personification of evil. One night, his paranoia climaxed. After hours of screaming that I was the devil himself, Rick left for keeps. In an unconscious effort to find some solace and safety, he moved back home with his parents, into the town and the house—and even the bedroom—that he'd grown up in. I've been out of touch with him since that night.

Denounced and deserted by my roommate and best friend, I found myself alone in the house. I recovered fairly well from his dramatic departure and continued assisting people to rebirth. However, working overtime every day at my job and facilitating rebirthings every night, I, like Rick, fell into the trap of not keeping current with my own past emotional traumas being triggered by each rebirthing. Like Rick, I became suspicious of people. The suspicion turned into fear, then paranoia.

Continuing with the overly stimulating regime, I began to have the feeling that something or someone was watching me around the house at night—as if I was not alone. I felt pursued, stalked, in my own home. I constantly checked the doors and windows to assure myself they were securely locked. My anxiety continued to grow. I turned on lights in all the rooms throughout the apartment to banish shadows where something or someone might lurk undetected. My fear approached panic. I had the distinct feeling something was about to snap my neck and snuff out my life. The vision of an ax, scythe or sword appearing out of thin air and slicing off my head tormented me. I was convinced I was being followed everywhere I went in the house. At any moment, I was certain that my physical life would be taken and my soul would be stolen. I wasn't just afraid of bodily extinction. I was also terrified for my soul!

Two weeks after Rick's departure, I reached my breaking point. Discovering all four tires on my car were slashed on the street right outside my house was all I could take. I screamed out loud, "That's it! I can't live this way." My body physically shook all the time. I barely ate. I barely slept. I was in perpetual terror. Intellectually, I knew my paranoia was psychological and imaginary. Yet I was incapable of doing anything about the emotional torment plaguing me.

That evening I paced about my apartment, too scared to sit quietly or lie down. My mind raced, trying to find a way to end the dread and apprehension. Then I remembered reading one of Carlos Castenada's stories about a particular teaching of his shaman teacher, don Juan. Carlos was told to intuitively find a specific spot in the desert that he knew was a personal "power spot" for him, a place where his soul was safe. It took Carlos a number of weeks to discover his personal place of power and safety. When Carlos found it, don Juan instructed him to invite Death to try to claim him there at that spot. The Death don Juan was suggesting Carlos confront was more than bodily demise; the threat included the annihilation of his soul. In his power spot, Carlos battled with Death: the fear that his soul could be permanently extinguished. After much anguish and drama, Carlos survived intact and triumphant.

I felt a profound empathy with Carlos and his fear of body and soul extinction. Instinctively, I knew I was being stalked by Death, by my fear of being snuffed out. I resolved not to run anymore from the dread. The terror of feeling tracked down was draining my energy and killing me slowly anyway.

I resolved to find, like Carlos, the spot in my environment where I felt the most courageous and strong, and then choose to face my Death. The center of my living room in front of a warm, roaring fire felt like the most supportive place for me to confront my fear. Lighting a fire in the hearth, I sat down on the floor—and waited. "Okay," I said out loud. "Here I am. Come and get me. Go ahead, show me what you've got! I'm not going to defend myself." I invited Death to reveal its true power. I surrendered to whatever might happen.

I was determined to allow this thing that was terrifying me to show itself. I decided not to fight it. I wasn't going to do anything to avoid my fate. There was definitely a healthy dose of courage and intuition at play in my action, but there was also a great degree of desperation, frustration and resignation. I urgently needed to be relieved of the fright and paranoia with which I was living.

As I sat there, the terror increased. I began to fill with the panic that was stalking me. I started shaking and perspiring heavily—a cold, clammy sweat. The longer I sat there, the more frigid my whole body became. Shivering from the chill, I was unable to still my chattering teeth. I no longer felt the heat from the fireplace. Seeing the roaring flames, I knew the room had to be warm and comfortable, yet I was freezing.

Then I noticed I couldn't hear any sounds. I could see car lights going by outside. I could see tree limbs banging against the window. But I couldn't hear the traffic or the scratching branches as I normally could. My world was enveloped in silence. For an interminable amount of subjective time—which was probably only about ten objective minutes—I sat in my "power spot" and awaited my Death. Anticipating my head being cut off and my soul being stolen, the muscles in my neck became as tight as steel.

I couldn't stand the suspense any longer. I surrendered my resistance to soul annihilation. I was so tired of running. I simply gave up. As my future spiritual friend Lester would say, I went "hootless." I didn't give a hoot anymore about my fate, about anything.

Nothing happened. Nothing moved. No more roving car lights. The tree branches appeared frozen in space. Silence. Then silence was swallowed by emptiness. I found myself in a kind of suspended animation.

After what seemed like an eternity, the recognition gradually dawned within me that nothing bad had happened to me. My neck wasn't severed. My soul wasn't snatched. I was still breathing. In fact, I could hear a sound: the soothing, short huffs of my own breath. I felt warmth slowly creep back into my body. I gradually sensed the heat radiating from the fireplace. The dance of car lights and tree shadows waltzed again on the wall. The reassuring sounds of cars passing by the house and trees scratching against the windowpane resumed their usual volume. Little by little, the room returned to normal.

My clamminess and shaking were gone. The anxiety for the safety of my soul had dissipated. Calm and clarity permeated my being. Soon I began examining the events leading up to and including this evening. Every facet of the emotions that had terrorized me was scrutinized. I took my time analyzing each feeling in turn. I remembered how Rick's paranoia and fear had begun. First was the irritability. Yes, I remembered becoming irritable. The nervousness, the abruptness. Yes, I'd followed the same path. Paranoia. Fear escalating into terror.

Then, as Carlos had done, I faced my enemy: my paranoia that Death would rip my soul away from me forever. I called its bluff. The truth was revealed: Death had no power over me. Rather than me, the threat was dead! I realized this threat I'd feared, not only for weeks but throughout my entire life, was not real. Death has no power of its own. I had given Death the power to terrorize me. I realized then that I determine the safety of my body and my soul—that I am the author of my own destiny.

Wave after wave of relief poured over me! Release turned into joy. I alternately cried and laughed. I was free of the threat of my body dying, free of the fear of my soul being extinguished! I have felt free of that terror ever since.

Hide and Seek with Nonphysical Guides

*You've got to have something to eat and
a little love in your life
before you can hold still for any damn body's sermon
on how to behave.*

BILLIE HOLIDAY

Are you familiar with Paul Harvey? A renowned journalist, he hosts a nationally syndicated radio show called "The Rest of the Story." On this program, Harvey relates stories about both new and well-known topics. His unique approach is to first emphasize what *appear* to be the obvious facts of the story. Then he presents the surprising "Rest of the Story," filling in the audience on hidden truths lying beneath the surface of the story. He gives his audience the "real scoop" behind the scenes, sharing unusual circumstances or unexpected consequences of the event. Paul Harvey covers a story more thoroughly than what the general media superficially report. He examines the human or spiritual side of events for us to consider before passing judgment.

I am an ardent fan of Paul Harvey. In my career as a journalist and therapist, I have observed the same phenomenon Harvey emphasizes on his show: what appears to be true or conclusive about a story is often, upon closer inspection, false or incomplete. A little additional digging usually exposes deeper social and spiritual meaning hiding below the surface appearance of human affairs.

In my mid-twenties, I became fascinated with this multi-layered nature of human experience. I prayed for more direct information on how this phenomenon actually works. I wanted firsthand

144 Inner Coach: Outer Power

exposure to how multidimensional reality plays out in everyday life. As usual, I soon received the personal evidence I longed for.

After ten years of flowing with easy rhythm from nurturing job to job, love to love and abode to abode in Boston, I hit a brick wall on all fronts. A fun job ended. No new employment adventure was showing up. I had lost out on a unique, spiritual teaching opportunity. My last romantic affair ran its course and I couldn't connect with a new soulmate. For the first time since I left college, I couldn't even land a suitable living arrangement. The message was evident and undeniable on all fronts and levels: "Move! This place is no longer right for you." The only problem was, I didn't have a clue as to where I should move.

Then, out of the blue, as they say, I received an offer to housesit a friend's empty home in Seattle for three months. Overriding my personality and its fears, my inner coach got me into my car and on the road to Seattle and my awaiting destiny. The drive across the country was leisurely and relaxing.

The pale autumn sun was calling it a day as I traversed a narrow country road threading a mountain pass through the serrated peaks of the Grand Teton Mountains of Wyoming. Even though the aspen were resplendent in their golden fall colors, there was no snow in the weather forecast. I checked my fuel gauge as I passed a sign that read "No gas or food for the next 100 miles." The tank was almost full. I wasn't hungry. I would be on the other side of the pass and near a town in time for a late dinner.

As I approached the alpine gap, it began to snow. At first the snowflakes were light, spiraling delicately to the ground and melting. I wasn't worried. Then the downy puffs descended faster. The ground was soon covered in white splendor. The snow became so heavy, my wipers could barely keep the windshield cleared enough to see the road. Very quickly, the pavement and roadside began to blur together. Finally, my little VW bug could no longer get enough traction on the slippery asphalt to continue up the peak. I pulled over, turned off the motor and watched the feathery pageant unfold. I'd spent my youth in the mountains of western Pennsylvania and driven in scores of snowstorms. *I'll just wait this out. No problem,* I concluded.

It didn't take long for me to realize I was caught in a bona fide blizzard. Thick sheets of sparkling crystals covered my windshield.

My option of driving to the nearest town was buried under three feet of fluffy powder. The road was obliterated. I knew if I waited much longer, I wouldn't even be able to open the car door. I'd be trapped inside and suffocate under the quickly mounting snow.

Snuggling my jacket around me, I forced the door open and started tromping through the drifts. Before I'd walked twenty feet, my car disappeared beneath a white blanket. By the time I shuffled another twenty feet, the mound demarcating my car was barely discernable. The entire landscape was one vast, wet, heavy expanse of whiteness. There were no signs of civilization. I felt extremely lost and alone.

Darkness fell. I no longer knew in what direction I was headed, or if the road was still under my feet. Looking for shelter where I could take refuge from the tempest, I trudged forward until the snow accumulated to such a degree I couldn't lift my legs. Exhausted, I collapsed. My tired mind decided it would be warm and cozy to curl up in a drift and let whatever happen . . . happen.

Just as I started to nod out and possibly fall asleep for keeps, I noticed a light. It was too bright to be a star. It appeared to be quite close. I mustered the energy for one last push. The snow was too thick and heavy to tread through, so I focused my eyes on the glow and crawled, pushing my body through the wet, white weight around me.

After what seemed an eternity, I reached the light. It was spilling from the window of what appeared to be a small hunting cabin. Pulling myself to a standing position, I tromped up the freshly swept stairs and knocked on the door. A little old lady—who was everybody's archetypal grandmother—opened it. She had gray hair, small, wire-rimmed glasses and a little apron tied over a frilly pink and blue dress. The faint fragrance of fresh roses scented the air around her. She smiled angelically and greeted me with a sincerely caring voice.

"Oh, we've been expecting you."

I stared at her. My cynical mind snipped to itself, *Oh, yeah, sure. In a blizzard!*

Yet her greeting sent chills up my spine. I'd heard a similar line before—from the people in Montreal who led me through the first spiritual initiation of my young life. In retrospect, this line should have been my first clue that something was fishy here—or shall I say, that something was occurring way beyond superficial appearances.

Graciously ignoring my silence, Grandma donned a shawl. "Come with me," she said sweetly, leading me through the snow.

I followed her to a one-room log cabin a scant twenty feet away. When she opened the door, I gazed upon a king-sized bed in the middle of the room with the sheets expectantly turned down. A lighted candle sat on the rustic nightstand. An inviting fire roared beneath the roughhewn beams of the fieldstone fireplace. The room was warm and welcoming. I walked through the portal. In front of the fire was a very comfortable, over-stuffed chair. A TV tray boasted a large plate containing my favorite meal, steaming roast beef and mashed potatoes smothered with gravy.

I mused to myself, *Wow, they really have their timing down here. She must have seen me crawling up to the cabin and sent someone over here to set everything up: the fire, the hot food, the prepared bed. I hadn't been standing on the steps of her cabin for more than a couple of minutes before she brought me to this cabin and opened the door for me. These people are pros. I'm impressed.* I turned and thanked her. She bade me to eat and have a good night's sleep. Then, patting my shoulder, she left, gently closing the door behind her.

Cold, starving and somewhat delirious, I immediately sat in the chair before the fire, wolfing down the delicious meal. With my stomach full and tingling warmth creeping through my veins, I peeled off my wet clothes, draped them over the chair to dry and climbed into bed. Pulling the plush, goose down comforter up to my neck, I instantly fell into a heavy, dreamless slumber.

The bright glow of morning beaming through the frosted windows woke me. The fire had burned itself out. The room was ice cold. I felt rested and revitalized. I quickly pulled on my clothes and walked outside. The storm was spent. Virgin snow sparkled like diamonds under the brilliant, cloudless sky. Walking over to the lodge where the elderly woman had so cordially greeted me the night before, I was anxious to pay my bill and respects, and be on my way.

Strange. The lodge was completely boarded up. Plywood sheets were nailed over the door and all the windows. Heavy, thick cobwebs and built-up dust lay on the windowpanes and behind the screen door. It was obvious the cabin had been closed up for a number of months, maybe even years. I walked around the deserted building, leaving a trail of footsteps in the pristine snow. There was no sign of the old lady, or any other human being. There was no indication of a car or a road that I could discern.

I was bewildered. I rushed back to the cabin I'd slept in to see if it was still in the state I'd left it minutes earlier. The cabin was, indeed, there as I'd experienced it all night: open, unboarded, clean and comfortable. I laughed out loud, "The maid hasn't changed the sheets yet!" I was determined to humor myself through this one. Otherwise, I might go nuts. Or realize I already was!

To keep myself from dropping immediately into a serious panic, I began to sputter aloud the tune of the old, familiar theme song of "The Twilight Zone" television show, the notes that played when the lead character began to realize that everything was not normal: do, do . . . do, do . . . do, do . . . do, do! This tactic gave me some breathing space to lighten up, reconnoiter and review my situation before my emotions spun out of control. I told myself I'd just gone through a very traumatic twenty-four hours. I'd been nearly buried alive in the snow. So, I deserved a little leeway until I got my bearings back. If I didn't cut myself some slack, I'd have to declare myself crazy right then and there! I wasn't willing to believe I'd lost my mind. Not yet, anyway!

I decided I was still a little dazed from my ordeal. As I cleared my head, the mystery would unravel and everything would start to make sense. Besides, being saved from the blizzard was definitely a miracle in my book. If my ordinary sense of reality needed to be rearranged a little for this magic to occur, so be it! Who am I to argue with the way God saves my skin?

Baffled by the enigma of the boarded cabin, I was suddenly desperate to find my car and locate civilization. I distinctly remembered the direction from which I'd come. I began walking, my rested legs breaking through the crusted powder easily. Within a mile, I heard a snow plow and followed the whirring sound to the road. The plow operator spotted me and stopped his noisy machine. I climbed into the toasty warm cab and told the obliging fellow where I sensed I'd left my car on the road.

"Where did you spend the night?" he asked immediately.

"In a cabin about a mile from here. Are you familiar with the place?" I answered.

"The only cabins I know of around here haven't been used for years. Hey, did you bust into a shack and use it? I'd certainly understand with the blizzard and all. You're one lucky son-of-gun!" He exclaimed.

Of course, I couldn't agree more. Seizing upon an easy way out of trying to explain my bizarre adventure at the cabins, I went along with his reasonable assumptions concerning the situation. In my perplexed state of mind, I didn't feel up to dealing with his reaction to my inexplicable encounter.

We found the mound of snow where my car sat buried. The plowman was generous enough to help me shovel the car out. He wouldn't take any money for the favor. What a good-hearted guy! I followed him as he plowed the rest of the road through the high mountain pass. Grateful to be alive and still in a daze, I drove off to Idaho and my next escapade.

Twenty years after the enigma of the cabin, I still wondered what really happened to me that night of the blinding blizzard. I hadn't found a satisfactory explanation for the appearance and disappearance of Grandma.

A nagging feeling indicated there was more to the story. I sensed that something additional happened to me that fateful evening than what I remembered. I realized I'd felt especially refreshed after spending the night at the cabin. A vibrant, inner radiance of well-being and focused purpose greeted me as I awoke.

I'd felt more recharged and re-inspired than merely a good night's sleep could provide. When the gnawing suspicion that something more had transpired at the cabin became extremely strong, I determined it was time to begin searching for "The Rest of the Story."

In my life explorations since the night of the blizzard, I've discovered a very valuable tool from shamanic and other powerful spiritual practices: a way to access a deeper level of personal experience and life events. In a meditative state, using a method of inner journeying, you can recall and re-experience more of the totality of what occurred during any event—a hidden meaning that you weren't aware of at the time, or that you buried in forgetful unconsciousness after the fact. Employing this technique, I traveled back to the night of the blizzard. What I found out blew my mind!

I discovered there was another person in the cabin while I was eating my meal and warming myself in front of the fireplace! This person served me a spiritual banquet for my soul as well as a sumptuous meal for my stomach. He was an older, white-haired gentleman who spoke telepathically directly to my inner coach. His words were gentle, but firm, as he described in detail my soul's blueprint and my life purpose. He advised me on various strategies and options open to me in the human adventures that awaited me along my path to come. Like a mentor, he was there to guide me in successfully navigating the challenges and pitfalls I was about to encounter in expressing my spirit out in the world.

The pragmatic sage counseled me about how to deal harmoniously with the people I would be meeting in Seattle and how to recognize a *kahuna* teacher with whom I would end up studying in Hawaii. He briefed me on the details of my destiny and made suggestions about how I could most adroitly handle each future situation. He gave me tips about how to most harmoniously deal with the diverse people I would be meeting— what to watch for, how to protect myself and how to reach mutual understandings. He encouraged me not to judge people and situations quickly or superficially, but rather to feel intuitively for the unrevealed soul dialogue and agenda that was occurring. In order to integrate every encounter into my life and being, he taught me to look past the form—and embrace the essence—of human interaction.

As I listened to the wisdom of my gentleman mentor speak within my shamanic vision, I felt the hairs stand up on my arms. Until I did this meditative process, I had no conscious memory of anyone else being in the cabin with me during the night of the blizzard. And I realized that everything he told me back then in the cabin had since come to pass, down to the smallest detail. From re-hearing our conversations, I could now see how I had known what to do and say in the midst of my wide-ranging exploits in Seattle and Hawaii that were to follow.

By journeying back and re-experiencing that long-ago evening during the blizzard, I discovered that a very far-reaching spiritual revelation had occurred in the cabin. It's obvious to me today that I wasn't ready at the time of the snowstorm to consciously accept the master who appeared to me that night. Nor was I ready to fully recall the teachings and spiritual initiations of our meeting. I needed to become stronger and wiser in order to fully appreciate and absorb their significance.

In my *Dream Workshops* now, I assist people through intuitive shamanic journeys to consciously re-experience buried levels of past events in their lives. Participants often discover that they also have had enlightening interactions with spiritual guides—especially during times of emergencies, crises, fever, illness, coma or other states of transition. Many folks recall talking with Jesus, Mother Mary, St. Germain, Krishna, Sai Baba, angels or other spiritual teachers. As with my gentleman in the cabin, these spiritual mentors imparted wise guidance and direction to people's souls during these meetings to assist them in the graceful expression of their unique life purposes.

Like Paul Harvey demonstrates on his radio show, I've discovered there is almost always something much deeper and more profound going on beneath the surface of seemingly obvious and ordinary life events. If we take the time and opportunity to look and feel beyond appearances, we can always uncover "The Rest of the Story." It's well worth it!

The Mind Creates Its Worst Fear

If you bring forth what is inside you,
what you bring forth will save you.
If you don't bring forth what is inside you,
what you don't bring forth will destroy you.

JESUS

On my sojourn across the country, a night spent camping in Idaho's mountain wilderness demonstrated to me the power of the human mind to create a *physical* reality from its deepest *emotional* fears.

A phone call in Boston foreshadowed the mystery to come. Half asleep, I picked up the receiver in my Boston apartment at 1 a.m. *Who could be calling at this hour?* It was my good buddy Gary in Boise, Idaho. He wanted me to come out to his neck of the woods and go hiking at 10,000 feet in the Rocky Mountains.

"You've got to come. It'll do you good. Fresh air, endless space, perfect quiet," my friend implored.

"Sounds like fun, but why are you calling me right now after three years of no contact?" I asked incredulously.

"I had a dream last night. You and I were on a most excellent adventure in some alpine mountains and we both had major spiritual awakenings," he explained breathlessly. "I want to find that dream."

I was already planning to drive right through Idaho on my way to the West Coast. On some level, Gary must have known I'd be ready and open to his proposal. The coincidence didn't really surprise me. Since the good old days when Gary and I hung out in Boston with our wild and beloved spiritual mentor Michio Kushi, we always had a synchronistic connection and a natural harmony of desires. For years, we'd get the same intuitive hit at the same time to travel to a specific place in the mountains or by the ocean, or to explore a particular new metaphysical topic or meditation method.

Besides, Gary knew I was not a person to pass on an adventure, especially a spiritual one. I had that feeling in my gut that demanded I say "yes." So I did. I was intrigued. The core of his invitation was thrilling: to deliberately go after a vision! To place oneself in the setting of a dream and welcome the substance of that vision to manifest. What a concept! I was "in!"

A new perspective on life was just what I needed at that time. The fact that the opportunity came through a dream vision of Gary's made the prospect all that much more exciting. I'd just lost my bid to be selected as the official instructor in Boston for the Release Technique, the human potential program of my current spiritual mentor of many years, Lester Levenson. This teachership had been my primary goal in life for the last five years. With the prize taken away, I felt lost and empty. I needed to fill myself again with new purpose and joy. The rugged, remote beauty and tranquillity of the Sawtooth Mountains of northern Idaho provided a most favorable environment to begin my search for the next focus of my Earth journey.

At the end of our first day hiking in the pristine wilderness, Gary and I discovered an inviting natural hot spring. We floated under the starry umbrella of the Milky Way for several hours. If you've ever soaked in a hot tub or hot spring, you know that not only does your body relax, but also your spirit, heart and emotions. In this open state, people often experience heightened awareness and direct connection with their inner coach. Often this opening also causes unconscious feelings to bubble up. In this state of extreme relaxation, some people spontaneously go into an innate rhythmic breathing that liberates extremely suppressed emotions.

In the soothing, warm waters of the alpine hot tub, Gary instinctively entered into this natural process of release. During the evening, Gary courageously encountered many childhood memories and adolescent traumas. Buried fears resurfaced from his past. He spent hours confronting, embracing and dissolving deep-seated anxieties he'd carried around since early youth. It was a poignant evening of intense feeling, letting go and cleansing in the hot spring. We crawled into our two-man pup tent later that night feeling light, open and vulnerable. After securely zipping up and sealing the tent at both ends, we finally drifted off to sleep.

About halfway through the night, Gary's fierce thrashing and screaming abruptly roused me from my tranquil slumber.

"It's got me! It's got me!" he was yelling.

Trying to calm him down, I reached over, gently massaged his shoulders, and said in a soothing voice, "You're only dreaming. It's okay. You're all right now."

Still asleep and trembling violently, Gary cried out, "This animal! Its teeth! It has me!"

I continued to murmur comforting words and softly nudge him. Gary gradually awakened from his nightmare. I asked him if he could remember what had frightened him.

"A wild animal grabbed my wrist and was gnawing at it. I was afraid I couldn't wrestle my hand free from the beast's iron grip."

Gary was shaking uncontrollably. It was obvious the nightmare still had a hold on him. I kept trying to calm him down, repeating that it was just a bad dream. Then I felt something wet on my hand. I reached behind me with my other hand, retrieved a flashlight and shone the light on Gary's wrist. It was bleeding profusely! There were sharp teeth marks across the whole back of his hand. His flesh was ripped open, exposing a few small wrist bones.

I quickly applied some antiseptic salve from my knapsack and wrapped his hand in a pillowcase.

"There has to be some creature here in the tent with us," Gary said in a strained, terrified whisper. "You probably spooked it when you sat up. It must have gotten scared when it realized there were two of us."

I concurred. We frantically started checking our securely zipped shelter for some sort of small wild animal. We searched every inch of the little pup tent. Both sleeping bags were turned inside out. Our knapsacks were cautiously emptied. No animal could be found. Then we searched for any tears or openings in the tent that a creature could have passed through. There weren't any openings.

Gary and I talked. We searched our worlds for a possible explanation. We couldn't find a plausible scenario, much as we wished it. But the conversation served to dispel some of our trepidation.

In the course of our exploration, I shone the flashlight on Gary's face and mouth to check for blood—or any other sign that he might have gnawed at his own hand. None. I even examined my own face and teeth, desperately searching for some rational source of the bites. Nothing.

Exhausted from the traumatic attack on his person and frustrated at the mystery of its origin, Gary eventually sought refuge from his ordeal in sleep. However, rest eluded me. I lay awake contemplating the enigma of my friend's chewed wrist, *Gary had been in the throes of a scary dream. In the nightmare, an animal had grabbed his wrist and chewed on it. It took me a long time to wake him from his horror. It was very real for him. But there were no animals in the tent. If any creature had been inside the shelter, it couldn't have escaped without leaving a rip or some sort of opening.*

I recalled how, just prior to our retiring, we spent a few hours in the relaxing hot spring. Gary confronted and resolved many fears in the therapeutic waters. I knew the mind was powerful. I knew fear was a potent force. I also knew dreams were symbolic.

Maybe, I pondered, *some entrenched anxieties arose in Gary that he hasn't consciously acknowledged or released. In my healing practice, I've witnessed many instances of unresolved emotions materializing into physical form. Ulcers are a prime proven and accepted example. Hives and rashes are two more. So,* I theorized, *when we have a fear and don't deal with it in some way to free the energy of the feeling, the fright can manifest in some physical form.*

Gary presented himself as a macho, rough-and-tumble, Wild West type of guy. He liked to be seen as a modern-day John Wayne, strong and stoic as a rock. He definitely suppressed and denied a lot of his emotions in life. Although he tried to hide it, I could tell from previous conversations that he was extremely worried—perhaps even terrified—that his life was falling apart. Recently his wife had threatened to leave him, taking with her the three children he adored. And his business was failing. In the hot spring, Gary liberated some of his bottled up tensions. But obviously, he only released a little steam from the top of the pressure cooker, just melting the tip of the iceberg of panic within him.

The more I reflected on the situation, the more enthused and intrigued I became. I didn't know exactly what unresolved fear was "eating away" at Gary, but I could hardly wait for morning to discuss it with him. I'd glimpsed the unleashing of Gary's mind and its power to manifest the energy of his dread. I'd witnessed how the mind can use emotions to create physical experiences in the physical realm. Once Gary isolated his anxieties and fully felt his feelings, he could resolve the nightmare. The wounds would lose their mystique. The power would be drained from the issue.

Lying there in the quiet of the night, I contemplated the personal import of the night's drama. I promised myself that from this day forward, I'd make a conscious effort to recognize and acknowledge the fears in my life. I'd open myself to feeling the energy created by each apprehension. I'd find a way to integrate and dissipate the energy and power of my feelings. I'd seek methods to handle my anxieties internally so that they wouldn't have to externalize in my physical universe.

Indeed, Gary and I had found his dream vision and opened to a most excellent spiritual breakthrough. I drifted off to sleep, thankful for the life lesson I learned, and looking forward to enlightening my friend at dawn.

Reading the Signs
the Inner Coach Gives Us

To look is one thing.
To see what you look at is another.
To understand what you see is a third.
To learn from what you understand is still something else.
But to act on what you learn is all that really matters!

NATIVE AMERICAN WISDOM

I've noticed that when we pay attention, life gives us messages. When we fail to get the message, life gives us a lesson. If we don't learn the lesson, life gives us a problem. If we don't deal with the problem, life gives us a crisis. If we don't handle the crisis, life quits giving!

In many Native American languages, the word for "to get the message" is the same word used for "my life has changed." In other words, if you don't *act* on the guiding signs presented by the Great Spirit, you didn't get the message. If you don't make the necessary changes in your behavior and attitude to alter the course of your destiny, you never really understood or absorbed the true import of the message.

For traditional Native Americans, there is no middle ground as there is for intellectual, modern Westerners. Instead of responding intuitively and immediately as would a traditional Native American, contemporary Americans typically *think* about the signs being given by the inner coach. Even after acknowledging spirit's sign, modern Americans may or may not make the indicated changes in their life. In allowing the thinking mind to enter into the equation, Westerners invite reinterpretation, discounting, invalidation and even denial of the message. And most often, the result of this mental intervention is inaction.

Being in intimate touch with the ebb and flow of the interconnectedness of life, indigenous and tribal peoples of all lands recognize life's *outer* signals as early warning signs. These outer signs are reflecting the inevitable course of our *inner* river of consciousness. Native peoples know the only way to have their life unfold harmoniously is to respond *immediately and intuitively* to the accurate signals life gives them.

I happened upon this helpful, built-in method of life counsel in my youth. I found when I acted from the outer signals Spirit sent me, my life unfolded in wondrous and magical ways. I noticed when I hesitated and questioned my external guidance, I often ended up not taking the suggested actions, which usually led to unfavorable and even disastrous outcomes.

One of my most fruitful adventures was a direct result of me accurately following the cues and clues that life presented along the way.

As I shared in previous stories, Spirit had unequivocally shown me through many signs that it was time for me to leave Boston. Once I was ready to move, I needed to know where I was meant to go. My first clue arrived in the form of an invitation to housesit for three months in Seattle. I arrived in the city by the Sound and settled into my friend Cheryl's house. However, once Cheryl had left town on her trip, it didn't take long for me to realize I felt truly alone in a strange city. I missed living in my familiar surroundings in Boston and interacting with my comfortable circle of friends whom I had come to think of as my spiritual family. I was beginning to believe I'd made a rash and unwise decision in moving across the country. Then, during a long, doubt-plagued stroll, a second clue appeared in the form of a circular pinned precariously to a tree. The flapping flyer grabbed my attention as I rushed by on my early morning jog. Cutting back to check, I found the notice promoted a group called the Aquarian Foundation. From the wording of the piece, the folks sounded like kindred spirits. Their next meeting was the following evening.

As I entered the room, the loneliness of my solitary existence in Seattle lifted. The group's leader channeled—served as a human mouthpiece for—various Ascended Masters such as St. Germain, Mother Mary, Katumi and Jesus. There were also several trance mediums at their meetings who appeared to manifest jewels out of their mouths while in an intimate connection with a disembodied spirit. For a number of months, I attended the organization's meetings because I enjoyed the wisdom of the Ascended Master channeling. However, I really didn't resonate with the members of the group, especially the trance mediums. I felt very uncomfortable around them. This dichotomy was a definite recurring pattern in my life. I was philosophically attracted to the wisdom of a group's teachings, but intuitively put off by the people and the organization that sponsor the teachings. Even though I liked the channeling sessions, I acted on my gut warnings and quit going to the Foundation's meetings. At least, in Seattle.

While waiting for my friend Cheryl to return and relieve me of my house-sitting duties, I learned my way around the picturesque city nestled between snow-capped mountains and the pure blue waters of the Puget Sound. By the time Cheryl arrived, I decided to rent an apartment and stay in Seattle for a spell to explore the forests and islands surrounding what turned out to be a gem of a town.

However, just as happened in Boston prior to Seattle, every time I attempted to rent even the most modest apartment, I was denied. I had good references and enough money for a security deposit. It made no sense. Also, although I'd made some casual acquaintances, I wasn't meeting the soul friends I usually encounter with ease in a new locale. I hadn't made any heart connections at all. Nor was I attracting a fun, exciting way to make a living in Seattle. As in Boston, the universe was sending a message. I accepted the telltale signs of guidance to move on. But again—to where?

My inner coach often uses public advertising to reach me, as with my flyer cues to explore Michio's East-West Institute and the Aquarian Foundation. As my financial resources dwindled to the crisis stage, I began to take extraordinary notice of the billboards, posted placards, newspaper items, and radio and television ads, looking for a clue as to my next soul destination. All forms of media in Seattle were promoting a special $250 roundtrip airfare to Hawaii. Not having the extra cash to take advantage of such an offer, I subdued my strong attraction and exhilaration whenever I saw or heard one of the ads. While living on the East Coast, I deliberately suppressed my desire to actually visit what sounded like paradise, because the trip felt so out of reach. However, since my early youth, I was fascinated with Hawaii. Now I knew intuitively I was being drawn and guided to the Islands, but the dream still felt impossible financially.

Spending my last five dollars, I savored my final West Coast Mexican meal of chicken enchiladas and planned how to borrow enough money for gas to drive back to Boston the next day. When I left the restaurant, I discovered a business card neatly tucked under the windshield wiper of my Volkswagen. A very honest man had hit my car in the parking lot while I was in the restaurant. He left his card with the name of his insurance company for me to call about covering the damages to my car.

I phoned the insurance company the next morning. They informed me that I could either take a $250 cash settlement or have them fix my car. A light went on inside my head! I could easily pound out the small dent in my car. The money was obviously an allowance from the universe for my next soul adventure. East or West, young man?

When I noticed a travel agency right next to the insurance office where I picked up my windfall, I began to suspect my soul had already made the decision where I should go. When I spotted the now familiar Hawaii airfare special in the agency window, I knew. Hawaii, here I come!

On the plane ride to Honolulu, I read the travel agency's brochure with intense interest. The guide claimed—because of the unique evolution of natural life due to geographical isolation—the Hawaiian Islands contained no plants or animals hazardous to humans. There were no poisonous snakes or spiders, dangerous wild beasts, or nasty poison ivy or oak. Amazing! Years later I found out this claim was not entirely accurate. However, the required seed of external safety was sown in my consciousness so that my next awakening would sprout in this tropical paradise.

I spent the first few weeks on the main Hawaiian island of Oahu without money for lodging or food. I slept on the beach and ate wild fruit from public trees. Then one day I came under the influence of a strong pull to visit the north shore of the island where surfers rode monster waves. The sheer might of those great waves intrigued me. I'd seen the daring Hawaiian surf riders in movies and on television. Those images had fed my longing to visit the Islands since I was a little boy.

I assumed my childhood dream was the reason I was riding a rickety, old local bus to the north shore that particular morning. However, my inner coach again had a different agenda. About halfway up the coast, a very short, older native man stood up, walked very slowly and deliberately down the central aisle, and got off the bus in the middle of nowhere. As if lifted by some external irresistible force, I rose and followed him. At the time I wasn't aware why I got off the bus. As I mentioned in the previous story, I later discovered in a meditation that the mystery mentor in the Wyoming cabin had coached me to recognize and pursue this old Hawaiian.

I found myself standing half dazed by the roadside in the middle of a rain forest with no visible signs of civilization. Way, way down the road I saw the diminutive Hawaiian wave for me to come in his direction. For lack of any other pull or purpose, I followed him.

This vintage Hawaiian was more spry and quick than I would have guessed. Staying a good hundred yards ahead of me all the time, he took me along narrow, overgrown paths, up and down steep hills, and through streams and dense jungle. Finally, we arrived at his thatched hut on a secluded beach. The squat shelter was so low inside that I couldn't stand up straight. When he pointed to a grass mat by the door, I immediately accepted his silent invitation to sit.

The old man turned out to be a very wise *kahuna*, the name given to the medicine men by the ancient Hawaiians. He stated he had a vision I was coming and that he was to accept me as a student. For the next several days, he taught me the Huna way of living, breathing, and attracting what one wants with the conscious mastery of attention. In essence, his teaching was:

"Wherever your attention flows, so flows your life."

This fundamental approach to manifesting later became one of the first vital pieces of my own teachings in my *Dream Workshops*. When the *kahuna* knew I'd absorbed as much of his wisdom as I could at the time, he shooed me from his hut and left me to figure out how to get back to civilization!

I hitched my way back to the south side of the island and Honolulu only to find I was now inexplicably drawn to the interior of the isle where verdant hills lifted their noble heads above low-lying clouds. The desire to explore the island's heights continued to grow until, one misty morning at dawn, I headed to a nearby peak in a section of the island preserved as a National Forest. I began hiking upward. It just happened to be Thanksgiving Day.

About halfway up the ridge, I found myself thirsty and hungry. A pure mountain spring bubbled up refreshment from the forest floor. Papayas, bananas, and other less familiar tropical fruits offered nourishment from nearly every tree. I was surrounded by an almost inexhaustible profusion of food and water. While I'd become familiar with the abundance of fruit trees down on the coast of the island, I never imagined fruit-bearing trees would grow at such an elevation. I grew up in the rugged, cold mountains of the Northeast mainland where very little human nutrition was naturally available.

Gradually it dawned on me that I could stay in this place and do nothing, absolutely nothing, and *survive*. I certainly would not go hungry! I was within eyeshot of enough fruit to keep me alive for a year. The year-round subtropical climate of Hawaii made shelter unnecessary for sleeping outside. Rain wasn't a danger to my health. Even with daily rain showers, I dried off and warmed up within minutes. Wind wasn't a threat to my safety. The winds were balmy. I didn't have to protect my body from snow, rain, wind or cold temperatures. I read that no poisonous animals or plants existed to endanger me. And, I was sitting on public property, National Forest land, from which no one was going to order me to leave if I didn't set up a permanent camp.

I suddenly understood that all the protective psychological and physical armor I'd developed since birth to assure my safety was not necessary in this situation. All the subconscious safeguarding attention, alertness and awareness was superfluous. Here I no longer needed to focus on watching for threats to my well-being. In the northern mountains of the mainland where I grew up, a freezing rain or snowstorm could come up out of nowhere, even on a beautiful summer's day. One had to be ever vigilant to stay alive and well. This was not the case here. I didn't have to keep a constant watchful eye to keep myself safe and healthy.

As the liberating implications of this new concept continued to hit me on my innermost levels, sheaths of tension began lifting off my body. Layer after layer of tightness disbanded. The need to be ever alert eased. Lifelong ways of holding my body and maintaining my psychological defenses immediately abated. All my fearful programmed buffers and defensive shields began to dissolve. I realized, *I'm safe. I don't have to protect myself. I don't need to be constantly vigilant, ever-scanning for dangers.*

For hours my body and spirit freed themselves naturally and spontaneously from obsolete, overly cautious tension and readiness. Wave after wave of anxious watchfulness sloughed off my body, just as old, dead skin peels off a snake. I never recognized what an immense amount of my personal energy and attention had been wrapped up in the worrisome safeguarding of the physical well-being of my body. As each stratum of outmoded belief and emotion released, my body and spirit relaxed in a profound way. It was a liberating, exhilarating feeling to know I could stay right where I was, do absolutely nothing the rest of my life, and I would be fine.

I entered into a state I'd never experienced before in this lifetime. I *knew* I would always be safe. I *knew* I would always be taken care of, not just here on a hillside in Hawaii, but anywhere and everywhere. There was nothing for me to do but trust in the universe and just simply be. As I entered into this newfound peace, my body and spirit rested, healed and recharged.

As I sensed the dimming light bringing this miraculous day to a close, I climbed the remaining distance to the top of the ridge. I was immediately struck by the view. I was overlooking Pearl Harbor. Right in the center of the panorama was the battleship memorial commemorating the infamous act that started a world war. It seemed ironic to be contemplating such a massive deadly attack on my fellow human beings, as I sat there in my state of grace, feeling so free from the fear of any kind of physical threat ever again. I felt so blessed.

My intense feelings of gratitude reminded me that the day was Thanksgiving. I concentrated on expressing my appreciation for the discoveries I'd made this day. I let my gratitude flow out into the universe. Then my attention turned inward and I reviewed all the good fortune I've received throughout my life.

My spiritual family back in Boston suddenly felt very close. Right then an internal message board lit up. I remembered that I made a vow to connect with my spiritual buddies on Thanksgiving Day wherever I might be in the world. As an experiment, we agreed to take a few moments at noon on Thanksgiving to meditate and reach out to each other telepathically to see if we could connect and sense each other's energy and love. My friends planned to be together this Thanksgiving. Before dinner, they were going to focus as a group to try to contact me. I looked at my watch and calculated the time difference. I'd missed my Boston noon appointment by ten hours! I laughed and promised myself I'd call my compatriots when I returned to Honolulu.

Dusk was close at hand. Although I was reluctant to leave my marvelous place of revelation, I knew the lessons would go with me. I traversed the narrow path down the slope with a newfound sense of being eternally cared for. I noticed even my manner of hiking was different. I was more relaxed and carefree. I walked with the gait of a person knowing he was safe and he would always be safe.

That evening, I placed a call to my spiritual family. It turns out they also totally forgot about our noon experiment. The fourteen of them ate a huge Thanksgiving meal and then watched a movie on television. For conversation's sake, I asked them what movie they viewed. They enjoyed an old World War II film. It was about the bombing of Pearl Harbor!

I laughed out loud, realizing that unbeknownst to my friends and me, we had connected. I was watching Pearl Harbor just as they were watching Pearl Harbor. We had met in consciousness— not in the form, but in the spirit we had intended!

I felt very good inside. Without doubt, I knew that a force— with a highly developed sense of humor—is always watching over us all—keeping us safe, taking care of us, connecting us. I realized then that a natural, behind-the-scenes synchronicity is built into all our lives. And this orchestrating force, this divine choreography, gives us guiding signs throughout our lives to help us live harmoniously.

I felt very complete about my first soul sojourn to Hawaii. It was time to return to Seattle and then Boston to put into everyday practice what I had learned from the Islands. Then, just to ensure that I didn't forget the lessons of the *kahuna,* the bountiful hillside and Pearl Harbor, the universe gave me one final reminder of the certainty of divine coordination and care before I departed Hawaii.

Again, by special soul delivery, a small notice in a newspaper grabbed my gaze at the café where I was having breakfast. A local Hawaiian chapter of the Seattle Aquarian Foundation was holding their weekly Sunday morning meeting at a hotel just a few blocks from where I was eating.

My plane wasn't due to leave for several hours. Later that day, I was flying from Hawaii back to Seattle to pick up my car and drive to Boston. Curious to see if I would find the Hawaiian Aquarian members more agreeable than the folks at the Foundation in Seattle, I was thrilled with the opportunity to check out the people at this local chapter. I wanted so much to belong to some group, but I could never find an organization within which I felt comfortable. I was grateful my inner coach realized I still wanted to explore this group. Off I went to give the Aquarian Foundation a second chance, and possibly find out that my first impression of the association was inaccurate.

I didn't have to wait long for my first sign. As I was crossing a wide boulevard walking toward the hotel where the group met, two policemen shouted fiercely at me to stop. They ordered me to return to the side of the street from which I'd come. Pretending I didn't know they were yelling at me, I proceeded straight ahead. To my horror, I almost stumbled over a ghostly gray dead man lying perfectly perpendicular to the crosswalk. An ambulance attendant was laying a white sheet over the deceased's face when I pulled back to prevent myself from tripping over the corpse.

Again, with even more urgency, the police commanded me to return to the curb. Emotionally shaken, I retraced my steps to the sidewalk. My connection to my intuition was blocked by the shock of seeing the corpse. Stubbornly, I recommitted myself to pursuing my original purpose of attending the Foundation's meeting.

Ignoring the obvious message to abort my plans, I rushed to the next intersection, crossed the wide boulevard and headed back up the street to my original destination, the hotel.

Although I was upset at being ten minutes late for the start of the morning's meeting, my irritation turned out to be for naught. The speaker was also late arriving. As I caught my breath, I overheard group members discussing how their leader had never been tardy for a lecture in the twenty years he'd been the head of the organization. A half hour passed. A young woman announced to the patient audience that the staff was still unable to reach the speaker by phone. They'd called everyone who might know where he was. No one had a clue where he could be. Another half hour elapsed. Finally, I recovered enough personal attention from my unsettling encounter with the corpse to remember to consult my intuition. In checking with my inner coach, I came to understand that the lecture was being postponed for my spiritual benefit. I left the hotel. The import of the dead man and the late speaker was now obvious to me. I wasn't meant to attend this or any other meeting of the Aquarian Foundation!

Once I'd walked off my frustration, I laughed at my obstinate arrogance in trying once again to ram through the petty plans of my ego personality in the face of intuitive stop signs. I gave quiet thanks for the gentle, persistent guidance of my spirit.

Boarding my plane on that memorable Sunday afternoon, I was extremely thankful for the lessons I learned in Hawaii.

After years of painful personal experimentation with ignoring and denying the early warning signs life constantly gives me, I've now decided to always heed Spirit's messages—without hesitation or analysis!

E.T. to the Rescue

*Children understand adventure.
It's intuitive to a child what adventure is . . .
out playing, living for the moment, discovering things,
approaching the unknown without fear.*

WILL STEGER, ARCTIC EXPLORER

"Ouch!" reverberated from the kitchen as Leslie opened her front door. I arrived to pick up my friend and her seven-year-old daughter Kriya to go to the movies. Kriya just burned herself quite

severely on a toaster. She came running from the scene of the crime to her mother. The blistered skin on her finger was white, swollen and already beginning to peel off her finger. Kriya was wailing and obviously in great pain. Her mom applied medicated ointment to her finger, but it wasn't relieving the sting of the burn.

"Keith, can you help us out?" Leslie knew I recently completed a course in a healing method called Reiki, a technique involving the laying on of hands. As a caring mother, she pleaded, "Would you do some Reiki on Kriya's finger?"

Without waiting for my response, Leslie turned to Kriya and told her, "Keith has done this healing class, honey. He knows how to cure burns and take all the pain away."

Of course, I wanted to help if I could. However, I'd finished the workshop days earlier and had yet to use my new skill in a real-life situation. Buying time to think of a strategy, I softly asked Kriya to let me see her burn. Still sobbing, she hesitantly held the hurt finger up for my inspection. "I'm going to put my hands over your finger," I said gently, still stalling until I could come up with some strategy. Kriya shook her head and pulled her injured hand away from me. *Help!* I instinctively implored whoever was listening above. Silently asking how I could assist her, my heart and intuition clicked in. I knew Kriya had recently seen the movie "E.T." My inner advisor said, "Tell her it's just like E.T." I had no idea of where I was going to go from there, but I followed my inner instructions.

Kriya's tears stopped flowing. She smiled and asked, "Oh, you mean when E.T. takes his finger and fixes the boy?"

Scrambling mentally to follow her lead, I blurted out, "Yes, it's just like when E.T. points his finger and the finger starts to glow."

"Oh, okay," Kriya nodded, offering the injured finger to me with the trust only a child can give so completely.

Since Kriya wouldn't let me lay my hands on the affected area, I asked silently, *What would E.T. do in this situation?* Of course, I knew. Very delicately, I extended my index finger to oh-so-lightly touch her outstretched, wounded finger. I whispered softly, "We're going to do just like E.T."

Her face glowed with anticipation. She relaxed and sighed sweetly, "Oh . . . E.T."

Kriya, Leslie and I sat together in silence for several minutes. After a timeless interval, Kriya withdrew her finger from our intimate contact. Not only was the pain gone, but also the white, blistered, burned skin had disappeared. Her finger was completely healed. Kriya examined her finger closely just to make sure, rubbing it up and down with wonder.

Meanwhile, I sat there in total awe, listening to Kriya as she whispered faintly to herself, "E.T. . . . . E.T." The tragedy and pain over, she started playing with some marbles, content in her innocence that I fixed her finger just like E.T. would have done.

A Cult Classic

*The higher goal of spiritual living is
not to amass a wealth of information,
but to face sacred moments.*

RABBI ABRAHAM HESCHEL

The first time I saw Joe was the night he ripped a door off its hinges and stalked into a spiritual gathering uninvited. Twenty longtime friends and I met on Sunday evenings to study Native American meditation, herbs and healing. For several months the focus had been on learning to communicate with the Great Spirit. However, tonight was about to prove itself a distinctly different sort of get together.

We all knew the leader Quey was psychic. He began the evening by stating that he sensed unwelcome guests were about to visit us. He bolted the door to the meeting house. "When the intruders come, be cool. Act as calm and normal as you can," Quey implored us. "Don't do anything to provoke them, okay?"

The party crashers were quick in making their presence felt when the locked door flew open to reveal two hefty construction workers, Joe and his friend Michael. Joe, a husky Nordic football tackle, was hell-bent on saving his sister Joan from being brainwashed by what he perceived to be a cult. A barred door meant nothing to a brawny, determined young stud on a divine mission to retrieve his sibling from the clutches of a hippie demon. In one quick motion, Joe effortlessly thrust the door open and flung it aside. Wordlessly, he and Michael lumbered across the room and sat down in our circle, sandwiching me uneasily between them as they sized up the situation for their righteous rescue.

As I later grew to expect from my ancient soul buddy, Joe's sense of timing was exquisite. Joe arrived on the scene just as Quey was about to make his boldest, most alluring move to date. Joe's sense of intuition was also finely tuned. He was right on the mark in his assessment of the true colors of the spiritual gathering. However, until this evening, I didn't realize our innocent, friendly group was subtly evolving into a classic controlling cult.

For several months, Quey had been teaching us how to open ourselves to direct personal guidance from the Great Spirit. Tonight, however, an opening of a different nature was coming my way. In an act of seeming unification, Quey declared, "Now that we've become one body, one mind and one soul, I am the Voice of our one being." Unfolding his deception, he continued, "I am the sole one designated to receive the messages from the Great Spirit, and, as our Voice, I alone speak Spirit's guidance to you."

Under the cover of "Oneness," Quey had quite covertly made a radical 180-degree shift from what he'd been teaching us for months. No longer was the official plan to empower each of us to communicate directly with Spirit. Suddenly, it was Quey who would be the spokesperson and intermediary between us and God.

A red flag immediately went up in my mind as I caught the sinister switch. My gut began to knot. As my world slowly turned upside down, I resisted absorbing the full ramifications of his ploy. In my heart, I knew Quey's action meant the end of my spiritual comradeship with my friends in the circle. I could see in their glazed-over eyes that they were under his spell. They were going along with his about-face. On a break in the meeting, I tried talking with them, but couldn't reach their hearts. These friends with whom I had shared a mutual spiritual path for years informed me I was simply afraid of taking my next "natural" step into Oneness with the group. The knot in my stomach tightened. I was scared. I knew my next step would be to walk out of the lives of those I had considered my spiritual family for a decade.

Joe realized his sister was also totally under the guru's enchantment. After hearing Quey's pronouncement, he turned to me and emphatically shouted in my ear, "This is bullshit!"

Joe's blunt assessment was all that was needed to ignite me into action. I was on the cusp between social approval and personal integrity, between the illusion of collective security and the reality of spiritual freedom. My inner coach performed an instant computer analysis of the situation. Joe's reaction was added to lifetimes of input from all my experiences with groups and leaders throughout my many sojourns on Earth. Scenes of similar incidents flashed in my mind. Adrenaline pumped through my arteries. A sharp stab of déjà vu gripped my heart. I'd been here before. This was not a new predicament. It was so familiar. It was, indeed, a sacred moment, requiring me to marshal all the wisdom and courage I could from every corner of my universe.

Once I shifted all my attention to my inner coach, the choice was totally obvious. I'd made this decision many times before on my spirit's ancient quest for integrity and harmonious expression.

I left the room and the group right then—forever.

Joe, in effect, saved *me* instead of his sister from a seduction of the soul. She is to this day still a member of Quey's cult. Joe's gift of salvation was only the first of many blessings from my ancient soul buddy. Our first meeting had set the stage well for our next adventure together, which swiftly catapulted me from the spiritual backwaters into the forefront of heart magic.

The Seven Sacred Pools

The winds of grace blow all the time.
All we need to do is set our sails.

RAMAKRISHNA

"What's it like being a spiritual person?" Joe persisted.

Pulling in more wind than the boat could balance, I purposely tipped over the catamaran to avoid the question. I was determined to dampen my friend's insistence that I was somehow different from other people. Yet despite my avoidance maneuvers, I sailed smack into my destiny that afternoon.

After my narrow escape from the cult, Joe had invited me to go sailing on a sparkling pure body of water called Newfound Lake in New Hampshire. At the time, I didn't realize the prophetic import of the lake's name. Surrounded by the vibrant green of sturdy pinewoods and the steel-blue of soaring granite peaks, the lake filled me with a sense of awe and peace. The calm gave no warning of the changing life currents Joe was about to innocently introduce into my life.

A very unusual exposure molded Joe as a child. He attended one of the few remaining schools in the United States—Boston Latin—that still taught the Ancient Greek language, as opposed to the modern version of the language. Joe read the *Iliad*, *Odyssey* and other important Greek writings in the original language in which they were written. He lived and breathed the Greek myths in their primal power without the loss of intended meaning from multiple translations. He possessed a vast warehouse of wisdom of direct transmission from the Greeks. These writers expressed very subtle states of mind and being, especially concerning diverse shades of reality, truth, love, relationships and human nature. The ancient Greeks had terms and concepts for which we have no words or adequate translation in English. He also devoured all the writings—in their original Latin—on Roman gods and myths. As a result, Joe had a rare archaic and archetypal window through which to view the world.

From his line of questioning, I realized Joe was wrestling with understanding his own spiritual quest. He was trying to come to grips with how to begin his own inner journey. He felt he needed someone to help him step onto the path. We met at a spiritual gathering, so he decided I was the person to help him sort everything out.

All day on the boat, he kept asking me what it was like to be a "spiritual" person. I was trying to stay incognito at the time, revealing my metaphysical side only to my closest friends—and only when severely pressed. I had all kinds of philosophical reasons why I was reluctant to call myself "spiritual." All my reasons were actually rationalizations—frantic, futile attempts to cover up and postpone the true majesty and mystery of my own divine destiny. I was afraid of my soul's purpose and power. Like many people, I was concerned about my perceived consequences of living an *openly* spiritual life. Among my fears was that I'd lose friends if I revealed my inner knowing and strength. I felt I'd scare them away with too much truth. I'd be too intense, too unsettling.

Trying to maintain my cover as just-one-of-the-guys, I skillfully dodged Joe's probing questions all afternoon. Each time he honed in on aspects of my life I didn't want to discuss, I'd deliberately tip the boat over to divert attention away from the focus of his inquiries. We'd right the boat. Then, without missing a beat, Joe would come back to the same question he'd asked before we went flying into the water. When he started in on me again, I used the scorching heat as an excuse to dive off the boat for a quick, refreshing dip. I simply wanted to enjoy the wind, water and sun. Unwavering in following his inner urgings, Joe had a totally different scenario in mind—or rather, in his heart.

Joe was very curious about my daily lifestyle. He felt that I, as a "spiritual" person, must be living a completely different way of life than most people. He was, of course, right on the mark. But I didn't want to admit to myself the full extent of my distance from normality, let alone confess it to others. Up to that point in my life, I'd observed that abnormal behavior attracts attention in society that isn't always welcome or benign. So, I kept my wild side secret. Eventually, however, Joe wore me down. I threw in the towel. Even though we'd only recently become acquainted, I decided to relate to Joe as if he were an old trusted buddy. I responded spontaneously and honestly to his unrelenting barrage of inquires. He asked about my friendships, finances, sex life, and eating and sleeping habits. Over the course of his persistent Neo-inquisition, I revealed miraculous events and magical encounters that I'd forgotten—or, more accurately stated, I'd been hiding from myself.

On the way home, we drove to a nearby gorge for a quick, late afternoon dip. The locals called it Sculptured Rocks because of the dramatic, serrated beauty carved by ancient glaciers. Pure water tanks had formed as a river cut down through the mountain. As tiered droplets, the river gifted the gorge with seven deep pools, which flowed into each other successively through waterfalls and flutes. Native Americans referred to this powerful spot as the Seven Sacred Pools. They used the pure waters for initiation rites in ritual ceremonies many moons in the past.

Initiation, however, was the furthest thing from my mind as I dove into the pure, cold water. My intention was to swim, relax and cool off after being out on a boat all afternoon exposed to the sun—and to Joe's impassioned, personal questioning.

I was floating in the largest pool when I spotted Joe on a high cliff about fifty feet above me. Tall, sturdy, blonde and resplendent in a shaft of sunlight, Joe resembled a reincarnated Viking. I'd seen local kids jump safely from that height in the past and could tell he was contemplating the plunge. But Joe was hesitating, and appeared lost in serious inner concentration. Later he told me he'd been reviewing his Greek mythology and comparing it to the concepts he learned from me that afternoon.

Suddenly, Joe pointed down to me, shouting, "You're one of those teachers, aren't you? You're one of those spiritual teachers who gets people to jump off cliffs."

He'd been riding me all day to come out with my true identity and power. Still reluctant and clinging to my old protection of playing dumb, I shouted back, "I don't know what the hell you're talking about."

Joe ignored my protestations of ignorance. "I know what you're doing. You're trying to get me to leap off this cliff . . . to trust God and Spirit and leave my old world!"

From the heights of the precipice, Joe explained how the Greek myths taught that for a person to receive a gift, they have to give a gift. Then he said, "I know for me to jump off this cliff and receive the gift that's here for me—the gift of opening to a whole new spiritual life—I need to first give a gift."

Joe gave the gift of trust: trusting the universe, Spirit and his inner coach. As he hit the water, his weighty body thrust sharply into the pool. After an eternity of seconds, Joe's left hand popped up above the surface of the water. The skin on his wrist was torn open. I could see two stark white bones sticking out through bleeding flesh. Joe's hand had hit a hidden tree trunk submerged under the water, fracturing his wrist in two places.

Distraught, I helped Joe climb out of the pool to solid ground. His hand swelled to about three times its normal size, the color of his skin changing very quickly from pale white to a sickening spectrum of yellow-green, then olive, blue, and, finally, black.

Joe wailed in confusion and betrayal, waving his broken wrist at the gods. "Is this the gift?" he bemoaned. "You know, I trusted. I gave my trust . . . and this is the gift I get back?" Turning to me, he insisted, "There must be another gift."

I was in shock and resistance, trying to avoid dealing with the whole crisis. Joe walked over to me, holding his now grotesquely deformed hand and wrist. "You just did some sort of healing class awhile ago, didn't you?"

I nodded. I recently attended a Reiki training. I went mainly, I told myself, to meet some new friends. True to form, I was keeping myself in the dark as to the real reason my spirit pushed me to explore something new. The soul purpose of my learning Reiki was to re-ignite my natural healing abilities, and in doing so, open me to a whole, new world of public, spiritual expression.

Joe persisted, "Reiki teaches you to heal things, right?" And, in his innocence and trust, he demanded, "Well, heal my wrist."

The Reiki class taught me how to send a warm, gentle vibration through a person's body. The treatments eased the pain of headaches and other minor ailments. And I'd used it once since the class to assist my young friend Kriya to heal a small burn on her finger. But Joe was asking for a healing on a much more profound level. Lord, help me!

Joe sat down next to me and placed his wrist on my lap. "Okay, heal it," he commanded.

Upset, tired and frustrated by Joe's tenacious will, I felt I had little choice and nothing to lose. So I put one hand underneath his wrist and the other hand on top. I allowed Reiki energy, or Universal Life Force, to flow freely through me to Joe's wrist. My concern and focus were on trying to get out of the situation and save some face. I also didn't want to completely destroy Joe's illusion of the "spiritual" nature of his new buddy.

Without warning, the palms of both my hands became hot— really hot! I'd sensed a little warmth when I'd done Reiki before, but now my palms felt as if they were literally on fire. Just as I was freaking out at the intense heat in my palms, I heard a strong, lucid voice rising from the depths of my being. It was the voice of my soul. I'd heard it a few times before in my life, but only as a faint whisper. The authoritative voice cut right through my fear and denial:

> "Keith, if you want to have this level of transformation in your life, you have to relax your grip on everything."

I knew the voice was referring to a level of power that could heal a wrist broken in two places. My inner coach repeated:

> "If you want this level of alchemy, magic and healing in your life, you have to loosen your grip on all your beliefs about the world and everything else you're so tightly holding on to."

Not only the events of that day, but of my whole life, passed by my mind's eye. I could see how I was trying to hold my old, familiar world together. I felt the strain of all the effort and work I invested each moment into trying to maintain my narrow view of the universe and my limited image of myself. I knew the voice was correct. I knew I wanted and needed transformation in my life. The voice continued:

> "When you ease the grip and allow this magnitude of transmutation to occur, not everything will change radically. Some aspects of your life will only change a tiny bit. But other aspects will shift a lot. You cannot control which aspects will shift a lot, or which will shift a little. You simply need to

loosen your grip on the whole thing and allow everything to move, rearrange and realign however it needs to. Do you allow this?"

Realizing the folly of resisting my soul's plan for natural healing and harmony, I eased up on my grip. The part of me that was resisting my inevitable fate was exhausted. I surrendered into agreement with my inner wisdom. In this exquisite abandon, I experienced extreme relaxation and calm. The searing heat in my hands subsided completely.

Very timidly, I took my hands off Joe's wrist. The wrist was whole! The skin wasn't scarred, scratched or disfigured in any way. The color was a good, healthy pink. The hand was back to its normal size.

Joe and I stared at the wrist. We both started to massage the hand to see if any pain remained and to check if the healing was complete. Joe rotated the wrist to make sure it turned normally. The wrist moved easily and painlessly.

My mind was racing in an attempt to explain what had happened, *Did we hallucinate this whole thing? Did we have too much sun today? Did the icy cold water get to us?*

Then we were blessed by a fortuitous confirmation of the miracle. Just as my mind began to question, reinterpret and discount the healing, we heard shouting from above us. From the rim of the gorge, about a dozen, very exhilarated bikers were hollering and waving at us. They had seen Joe come up out of the water with his broken wrist and had witnessed the transformation. As they streamed down the path to reach us, they yelled, "Hey man, how'd you do that?" Each biker placed his hands on Joe's wrist. One after another, every guy insisted on touching Joe's hand and moving his wrist back and forth. One gnarly guy mumbled, "What kind of people are you?"

In a fascinating gesture, harking back to the olden days of jousting, the bikers handed Joe a large, staff-like tree limb and asked him to twirl it. They wanted to see if his wrist was truly healed and strong. So Joe spun a big, heavy stick in the air for several minutes until everyone was satisfied. The ancient Viking warrior was back!

The bikers were an added gift that day. Their acknowledgement of the healing gave Joe and me valuable external evidence that we didn't hallucinate the whole incident. Joe had broken his wrist. And it was miraculously healed. By Joe. By me. By Spirit. We had witnesses. Very impartial witnesses. A dozen strangers had watched Joe come out of the pool with white, broken bones jutting through the bleeding flesh of his wrist. The objective observers kept repeating, "I saw your wrist. There was blood on it. We saw the bone sticking out," as much for us to hear, as for themselves. They saw Joe lay the swollen hand on my lap. They watched me cradle the wrist between my hands. A dozen people, their presence unknown to us, observed the healing that afternoon by the sacred pools. They validated the event for us and helped us fight back our minds' desperate attempts to discredit and deny the magic.

After a while, the bikers drifted away. In a state of amazement and awe, Joe and I were left sitting there to fully absorb the wonder of the day. Not only did I participate in a miracle, I learned from my inner coach a useful nuance in the skill of letting go.

For many people, "letting go" initially triggers fear and reluctance. The mind tells us we'll lose something valuable if we simply let go. So we hold on, tightly grasping our worldview, controlling the way we think things need to be to keep us safe. It's a death grip on a predictable world that leaves little room for miracles.

Now, instead of asking myself and others to "let go," I ask myself and others to "relax the grip" on tightly held beliefs, so that everything can shift that needs to shift for real transformation to occur. The difference in the question being asked is subtle, but profound. With this approach, we don't give up the opportunity to re-tighten our grip on old viewpoints if we feel the necessity to *feel* in control again. We are much more willing and able to *ease our grip* on something familiar and precious than we are to *let it go altogether*. Loosening our grip a little allows the elements in our life to rearrange for our benefit, helping us to shift more easily out of undesirable situations.

"Relaxing the grip" also allows the wisdom of our inner guidance to come into play. In setting our sails toward newfound horizons and inviting the currents of change to take us to fresh ports of call, our inner navigator can offer crucial shifts in direction that can greatly ease our journey.

Saved by Neptune

The great sea has set me in motion, set me adrift,
moving me as the reed moves in a river.
The arch of sky and mightiness of storms
have moved the spirit within me,
till I am carried away
trembling with joy.

UVAVNUK, ESKIMO SHAMANESS

In my youthful, glib, mainstream naïveté, I considered all mythological gods to be creations of very active human imagination, conceived in a time long ago when formal education was rare and gullibility plentiful. Even as metaphor, these ancient beings and their wild exploits had little impact on my modern, pragmatic personal world—until the night I met Neptune, Lord of the Depths.

My friend Joe was by nature a very courageous, trusting and adventurous fellow. Seduced by his innocent enthusiasm for life, I constantly found myself involved in situations beyond my control or comfort zone. One steamy, stormy summer night, Joe had an itch to go swimming in the ocean. It was past midnight. There was no moon for light. But physical limitations were not a consideration for Joe. After a quick pitstop at Dunkin' Donuts for caffeine and chocolate, we rumbled away in Joe's rusty, rattling truck to an isolated, rocky peninsula north of Boston called Marblehead Point.

Even when the waters surrounding Marblehead Point are calm, the jutting peninsula is a perilous place to swim. There's no beach. The shoreline is a gauntlet of jagged rocks. Quite invisible to the uninitiated, sharp, knifelike boulders and a treacherous undertow conspire to lure unsuspecting bathers into their snare. The sheer power of the wind, water and rock seem to magnetically draw their victims under their spell. Even if one survives the crushing might of the waves and the spiked edges of the granite, the razor-sharp barnacles covering each stone slash human skin to the bone. It's not a hospitable place to frolic.

The water was not calm this night. A North Atlantic tempest was brewing. Fierce, monstrous surges over twelve feet high smashed against the craggy coast. I looked at the scene before me with growing trepidation. Joe wanted to jump off the highest cliff right into the surging sea. I didn't see how we could possibly leap over the jutting granite and land safely in the ocean. And, even if we successfully cleared the serrated stones, the violent waves would pummel us back against the rocks.

Joe, bless his virgin heart, gently persisted, "I know it looks dangerous. But I know we're safe. I'm being called by Neptune, the Spirit of the Sea."

In an earlier story, I related that Joe was raised reading Greek and Roman myths as they were originally written in Ancient Greek and Latin. Neptune was not a mythical god to Joe. He was a living, conscious being with whom one can communicate and physically interact.

To me, Neptune was no more than a vague concept from a high school mythology lesson. I'd just begun to re-open my ability to perceive entities beyond my programmed five senses—be they nature spirits or mythological gods. I wanted to trust that these nonphysical beings were real.

I did trust Joe. He taught me through example that one has to *leap into the Possibility* before one can *enter into the Reality*. So, I allowed myself to be caught up in Joe's spirit of adventure and anticipation. With total assurance, he proclaimed, "I know it's the right thing to do. I can feel it. If we jump, we'll be caught. We'll be cradled. I trust my friend Neptune. You'll see!"

Together, we took the fateful plunge that night. Leaping into the shadowy darkness, somehow sailing over the grasping, seductive rocks, we landed in the momentary safety of a lull between breakers. "Lord, have mercy on me!" I whispered under my breath.

Then the first big swell scooped us up and hurled us in the direction of the jagged cliffs. I should have been terrified. But, even as my body seemed to race toward the rocks and certain death, I felt a warm, tingling sensation surging up from below the tempestuous water's surface, spreading throughout my entire being. The wave itself started to glow with an emerald-green phosphorescence. The feeling was one of total acceptance and support. I've felt it before. A rush of recognition swept over me. The serenity of grace was very familiar. I relaxed and surrendered my body to the pulsating, comforting aqua presence.

While I saw only bright, blue-green foam swirling around, infusing me with a sense of boisterous, yet serene joy, Joe could see and feel an energy form he knew personally as Neptune. As giant swells crashed against the serrated cliffs, Joe and I flowed in and out with the waves, miraculously safeguarded within the pounding surf. We never once touched the jutting stones. We were gently cradled, as a parent rocks a child, in the protective arms of the King of the Sea.

Then Joe and I heard the strong, booming voice of Neptune bellow words of wisdom and wonder into the core of our being. Neptune suggested we tap into the many useful, natural qualities of water. While describing the unique characteristics of water, the Spirit of the Sea physically demonstrated each attribute until we understood the message being conveyed to us.

Neptune spoke of the fluidity and malleability of water and how it flows with, not against, the strongest force. The God of the Ocean exemplified his point with an aquatic whirlpool that engulfed us. The spiraling vortex intensified to such a degree that we were forced to totally abandon ourselves to the power and direction of its force.

Elaborating, Neptune discussed the astuteness of water in harmonizing with its surroundings. The spirit explained how water is flexible, rather than maintaining a rigid structure. The liquid whirl we were in suddenly reversed itself, shifting its direction 180 degrees, compelling us to choose cooperation. My mind flashed back to the numerous stories I'd heard about drunks so relaxed they tumbled down stairs unharmed.

Our education lasted for several human hours and an eternity of spirit time. Joe and I continued to be protected from the craggy cliffs, as we were gently imbued with the vibration and compassionate power of Neptune. The Spirit of the Water shared its essence and alchemy with us. I internalized the practical wisdom of choosing to allow, accept, integrate and embrace the flow of life, rather than resisting the ever-changing course of events in life.

The lesson over, Joe and I were delicately deposited on a small bed of sand high above the rocky shore and crashing surf. Rays emanating from the rising sun warmed our drenched bodies. We rose and began our trek back to Joe's truck.

I'll never forget my stirring adventure with Neptune. I took many new abilities home with me from my encounter with the Sea God. I've since integrated these practical tools for living an easier, fuller life into my everyday world. I rediscovered within myself the knack of how to surf the affairs of the world and to go with the tide of events. I've learned to go into a storm, argument or upheaval and surrender to its dynamics, confident I'll come out the other side unscathed—or, at least, intact. I now know that by going with the flow of the forces I usually fear—chaos, confusion, and calamity—I can ride, and even be supported by, those same energies. What a night! What a gift!

PART IV

Following the Inner Coach

The Magic of Synchronicity

In the depths of your hopes and desires
lies your silent knowledge of the beyond;
and like seeds dreaming beneath the snow,
your heart dreams of spring.
Trust the dreams,
for in them is hidden the gate to eternity.

KAHLIL GIBRAN

If we pay attention, life gives us many clues to the future of our destiny path. But often it's not until years afterward we realize that the seeds of our destiny were being planted right under our noses. Such was the case with my move to the state of Arizona. If only we had eyes to see clearly along the road!

Signs prepare the way by triggering the supportive changes in attitude and behavior necessary for our future design to unfold.

For twenty years my spirit planted the seeds of synchronicity for my eventual growth into my new *state of being*. What appeared on the surface to be an abrupt change of *geographical* residence later revealed itself as a deliberate, soul-driven journey to an eternal and very familiar *spiritual* domain.

The portents were visible at each stage, but not for me to perceive at my level of awareness at the time. Until I arrived, I couldn't conceive of my living in such a state of boundary-less free fall—let alone enjoying it!

Visiting the Folks in Hell

*You are led through your lifetime
by the inner learning creature,
the playful spiritual being that is your real self.
Don't turn away from possible futures
before you're certain
you don't have anything to learn from them.*

RICHARD BACH

My world was Boston, referred to as "the Athens of America," a refined, cultivated center of urbane sophistication, history and charm. I enjoyed a successful acupuncture healing practice, an eclectic circle of friends who shared my diverse interests, and a comfortable, old house I called home.

Boston filled me with the romance and spirit of great writers. I frequently had afternoon tea in a parlor where I sat in the same chairs once occupied by Mark Twain, Emerson, Thoreau and Longfellow. Handwritten letters from these early American seers, framed and mounted on the wall, served to make their presence in the room all but tangible. I could almost see and hear them conversing about the philosophical intricacies of their day.

The richness of the past is very present in Boston. The house I lived in was nearly three hundred years old. Original gas lanterns lit the cobblestone lane outside. Their flickering glows reflected off polished bronze and copper roofs and door plates. My Boston was a place steadfast in time and tradition. On a crisp winter's morning when a late-night snow had made the steep, narrow byways of the city impassable by car, I awakened to the ageless clamor of the hooves of police horses on cobblestone, a sound I could have been hearing on the morning of Paul Revere's ride. I loved my hometown.

Until my parents moved to Arizona, I had zero interest in that state in the vast desert. Ever since I could remember, my mother longed to move away from the perpetual cold, clouds and gloom of the mountains of western Pennsylvania where I grew up. After a lifetime of tromping through snow, Mom was ready to thaw out. Campaigning relentlessly for thirty years, she finally persuaded my reluctant father to retire and move to Phoenix in 1975. In her defense, by the time she won the battle, the move was not only just for her. She was confident my father would enjoy a warm climate and more relaxed style of living after working so hard for so many years.

After several postcards and telephone calls from my mother, I finally agreed to visit my parents' new habitat. The plane circled the black-topped cross of pavement and a two-story control tower the Phoenicians called an airport. I disembarked the plane via steps wheeled across the runway and placed against the exit door. Stepping onto the searing asphalt, I waited in the blistering heat for my luggage to be pulled from the underbelly of the airplane. My trepidation about the visit leapt to new heights. I felt myself recoil from the dry, dusty, desolate emptiness surrounding me. Only a couple of lonely palm trees wilting in the relentless sun against the brilliant blue sky broke the bleak, forsaken landscape. I felt as if I had landed in a remote Saharan outpost somewhere in North Africa!

My mother was thrilled to see me. She chattered away about her and Dad's fabulous new life as we began the long trek to their desert digs. When I mentioned the broiling sun, Mom only laughed, "You don't have to shovel sunshine, honey!" Extolling the wonderful amenities of their retirement center: the activities hall, the swimming pools (yes, there were five!) and the gorgeous golf courses, Mom was finally in her element. On the other hand, Dad was pretty silent, only nodding when my mother would chirp, "Isn't that right, dear?" Eventually we entered Sun City, a shiny new retirement community built in the midst of the stark desert vastness. I watched vacantly as we passed street after street of single story, all-white homes with cute, little front yards boasting cacti, small citrus trees and colored gravel instead of grass, until, finally, Dad pulled into a driveway identical to all the others with a cheerful "We're home!"

My father and I spent most of my visit sniping at each other. His favorite line was, "What the hell's wrong with you?" He couldn't understand why I wasn't getting "with the program." To his mind, I had everything going for me: good looks, health, brains, education, social standing and financial support. Why couldn't I be like my brother the lawyer? Why in the world wasn't I happy to become a doctor or an attorney (my assigned spectrum of two career choices), get a wife and house, and settle down to replicate to the penny my dad's lifestyle?

"Well," I would shoot back, "What the hell's wrong with you?" I felt it was obvious I needed to follow my own drumbeat, but my father felt otherwise. We'd go off on a good, three-hour tear of gibes, quips and other nasty forms of disparagement. We'd both mumble a lot of our barbs under our breath. It would have been quite comical, actually, if it weren't so sad. My poor mother always felt caught in the middle of "her men."

I would love to have communicated more directly with my father; but in my youth, I wasn't skilled or confident enough to find an opening to even approach honest dialogue. I found the man totally inaccessible. Dad was a short, bald and bespeckled autocrat. To me, he was cut from the mold of the "archetypal banker," concerned mainly with bureaucratic proprieties and social status. From my viewpoint, his manner was stuffy, stodgy and stifling.

He kept me on my toes, though, dodging his rolled-up Time magazine—his weapon of choice when he got angry and felt like lashing out at the world, i.e., his youngest son. His rare and unpredictable rage was the only emotion I ever witnessed him expressing. In retrospect, I can see he did make faint-hearted, inept overtures to bridge the gulf between us; but at my age, I couldn't recognize his actions as such. I stayed in the inferno as short a time as a good son could and then returned to my beloved city of Boston.

Nine months after my first, dismal visit, I went back to the harshness of the Arizona desert to bury my father and to bring my mother back East. My father the lawyer, after just a few months of separation from the mania of legal wrangling and village meetings in his old life in small town Pennsylvania, decided to lie down after dinner one evening and leave Earth for good.

Uncharacteristically, he didn't have the public decorum to have a heart attack, or some other socially acceptable excuse to check out. He died of boredom and disinterest, official cover-ups for his smoldering anger and desperation.

Little did I know those two short trips were my first steps into the *state* I would someday call home.

A Medicine Man's Warning

In the fire of His ecstasy I melted like a candle;
his flames rushed at me from all sides,
and I saw only God.
When I looked with my own eyes I saw only myself.
When I came to look with God's eyes,
I saw only God.
I was annihilated by Love and vanished into Nowhere—
suddenly, I was the All-living one,
and saw only God.

BABA KUHI OF SHIRAZ

Many years after burying my father in the bleak desert, I received the second portent of my eventual migration to Arizona and a new awareness of life. I was barely surviving a very lonely and bewildering period of my life. Throughout my twenties, I evolved personally and spiritually with a group of friends I came to think of as my "spiritual family." As I shared earlier, our intuitions were always naturally aligned until we joined a metaphysical group led by a teacher named Quey. My inner coach told me to leave the group if I valued the health of my soul. I shared my intuition's warning with my buddies. Unfortunately, my "family" did not heed my guide's foreboding. Totally controlled by Quey, they obeyed his orders to break off all contact with me. I lost my closest friends with whom I'd shared every facet of my life for a decade.

Yearning to find new compatriots and a spiritual practice that felt nurturing to me, I attended a training to learn Reiki healing. Afterwards, during a meditation, I received an explicit vision instructing me to add Reiki energy channeling to the acupuncture treatments in my healing practice. Very quickly, I found out why I was led in this direction.

The first time I went into the Reiki healing space with an acupuncture patient, I met my new shaman friend Medicine Cloud, a Hopi Medicine man. He appeared in spirit form as a translucent body standing beside me as I delivered Reiki energy to my client on the treatment table. His potent message to me was short and blunt:

"Keith, you and your friends have gotten really good at getting rid of and releasing feelings, traumas and blocks. But you are lousy at *letting in*. If you continue letting go without balancing the process by receiving, you will enter into such terror that you will quit progressing altogether. In fact, you will experience quite a setback. You see, if you only release old energies without filling back up with new energies, you'll begin to experience letting go as dropping into a total nothingness, emptiness, the Abyss, the Void. This one-way approach to clearing brings great fear and eventually paralysis. However, if you let the old and dead go while simultaneously letting in the new and alive vibrations of the Great Spirit—grace, love and universal supply—you'll experience the whole process as a nurturing celebration. By letting in *as you let go*, you open to enjoying the true nature of life—the never-ending circle: emptying and filling, ebb and flow, death and rebirth. You'll no longer be letting go into a void, but into the richness of life, into the bounty of life, into the truth of life—into Fullness."

For the next four years, Medicine Cloud taught me how to receive energy, power and wisdom directly from the Spirit of the Earth through all the energy centers of my body—particularly through the legs, the soles of the feet and the base chakra. He also taught me to see and consult with people's spirit animals. These power animals would tell me what was really creating a person's ailment. I saw how all people's problems arise from where they're giving away their power to someone or something—how they're allowing their energy to be drained by another person or situation. Medicine Cloud and people's animal spirits showed me how to effectively treat this true causative syndrome, rather than what people *thought* was to blame or what *appeared* to be at fault on the surface. My patients began to heal at a very accelerated rate.

Then, after four years of intimate, daily instruction, my shaman mentor casually announced with no hint of importance, "I will no longer be appearing by your side at your acupuncture healings. You've learned well to hear and follow the advice of spirit animals and intuition. I'll see you in the desert."

I was saddened by the loss of my close advisor and friend. And I didn't understand what he meant by his reference to the desert. I felt he might have been speaking metaphorically of the vast, empty plains of the hereafter. At the time, I didn't realize he was referring to the actual physical desert of Arizona where I was to meet up with him in his physical form years later.

The Prophecy of the Great Spirit

The real voyage of discovery consists not in seeking
new landscapes but in having new eyes.

MARCEL PROUST

In 1980, Lester, my spiritual mentor on the East Coast, moved to Arizona. At the time, I considered Arizona to be a great uncharted, sweltering inferno, fit only for snakes, scorpions and people looking for a quiet place to bake their bones during the waning years of their lives as they awaited death.

I was bereft at losing the personal tutelage of Lester. And to forfeit him to that inhospitable state seemed to double the pain. Yet when he announced he'd be continuing his teaching in Sedona, I immediately booked a flight to Phoenix to take part. It was during my first visit with Lester in Arizona that I received the most profound and straightforward clue to the next stage of my geographical and spiritual odyssey.

I was standing on a vast mesa in the high desert country south of Sedona, surrounded by immense crimson cliffs and lavender peaks. Dusk was falling. Suddenly, I felt an energy move up from the mesa and through my legs and mid-section like the tentacles of a mighty serpent. The grip of this Presence was awesome, but not scary. A mighty, resounding voice from the depths of my soul proclaimed in no uncertain terms:

"You belong here! This is your home!"

The thundering force and strong resonance of the words reverberated through my body and being for what seemed an eternity. I stood motionless and stunned for an hour in the swirling evening breeze. I tried to shake off the dramatic effect of the voice, but I couldn't. I felt different, changed. Another destiny seed had been successfully implanted within me. I was about to be transformed into a new being. All the seed needed now was the right environment and nutrients to sprout, grow and eventually blossom. These requirements were not long in coming.

It's Never Too Late to Say I Love You

I am holding a key
and so are you.
I can open the padlock into your circle
and you can open mine.
Let us keep opening padlocks
that have been long forgotten.

GEORGINA MURATA, age 9

Lester's first Arizona seminar was very dynamic. As always, I learned a great deal. But I left the workshop filled with sadness, frustration and regret. During the conference, many people, especially men, expressed their recent joy and gratefulness in reconnecting with their estranged fathers. They shared with us how fulfilling it was to tell their fathers they loved them, and, in many cases, to even have the expression of affection returned. Since my father was long dead, I felt I'd blown my chance to experience an exchange of love with him. Throughout my life, I often remarked to friends that it would take an act of God, a miracle, to reconcile my father and me. And that is exactly what it took.

After the final session of the seminar, I shuffled off to my motel room, packed my bags for an early morning flight, and hit the sack. However, sleep eluded me. I kept seeing the happy faces of those fortunate men who reconciled with their dads. I could still hear their joyous laughter as they compared stories with each other and the group.

Memories of my father and our countless arguments played over and over in my mind. My dad and I never spoke much about anything, let alone affection or feelings. In anger and arrogance, the last words I spoke to him while he was alive were "You'll find out!" Some send-off I gave him!

And his last words to me were the same: "You'll find out!" That one phrase was our central conversation. For twenty years, our main communication to each other was that the other one would find out he was wrong—about whatever topic we disagreed, about life in general, about everything! I winced at our voices of anger reverberating through my mind and then cut off by the abrupt slam of a door—his death. Yes, it was too late for me. Finally, unable to shake the feeling of hopelessness and self-judgment to find solace in sleep, I dressed and left my motel room for a late night walk.

Shoulders hunched, eyes staring at the pavement below my feet, I took a sorry stroll through dark and empty streets. I'd been wandering aimlessly for some time when, through my self-absorbed despair, I noticed a faint, yet definite glow of golden light around the manhole covers I'd been passing over. I examined each lid I came upon, but could not discover the source of the soft, vague radiance.

In my understanding of the world, abnormalities—such as this faint shimmer—in my "normal environment" are never an accident. These irregularities in the "expected picture" are usually my spirit's way of trying to get my attention. This signal means my inner coach has a message for me and wants me to listen up. It's like "You've got mail!" on the computer. This particular sign of a soft glow is familiar to me. A faint radiance has been one of my soul's principal devices to attract my attention and get me to go inside to check in with my intuition concerning the situation.

So, when I got back to the quiet of my motel room, I did a quick meditation to see what message was waiting for me. My inner voice answered immediately, "Look more closely at the manhole covers." I recalled the metal lids in my mind. After concentrating for a few moments, I saw they were all engraved with the same large words. The inscriptions read: "Salt River Project." This is the utility company in which my father had left a sizable trust for my brother and me. As I contemplated this connection to my father and his generous gift to us, I detected another muted, golden glow emanating from the corner of the bedroom.

I turned to face the light and gasped. Standing by the wall stood my father in spirit form! The apparition was so real I almost evoked the courage to reach out and touch his hand. Twenty years of intense, backed-up emotion rushed like an express train through my being. I was relieved when he began to speak:

"Son, I'm sorry I wasn't able to help you with emotional or spiritual affairs while we were together on Earth. I couldn't assist you with those aspects of life, because I couldn't help myself in those areas when I was alive. I did share with you everything I knew of the material, financial, political and social worlds. That was all I'd mastered. Please forgive me for not helping you with your feelings or spirituality. I am moving on now, Keith. I came to say good-bye and tell you this man Lester is in your life to assist you with your emotional and soul concerns. Trust him. Spend time with him. Open to him in the way we could never open to each other on Earth. I love you, Son. Good-bye."

Sobbing with joy and relief, I blurted out, "Thank you, Dad. I love you. I understand. I love you."

I was graced with the opportunity to tell my father that I loved him fervently. I also asked him to forgive me for being such a rebellious, ungrateful son. By the time he said his final farewell, we each knew the other was very sorry. We also totally forgave ourselves, as well as each other. In the end, I recognized there was nothing to forgive for either of us. We gave to each other all we had available at the time to give. I slept more peacefully and fulfilled that night than I'd ever slept before in my life.

In retrospect, I now laugh at the universe's sense of humor. The sharp, attacking words my father and I so loved to throw at each other were more accurate and prophetic than we could ever have imagined. "You'll find out!" had a hidden soul message for both of us. We each did eventually "find out!" Even though neither of us was consciously aware of it, we were both foretelling our eventual spiritual understanding of life and our true connection with each other.

I also found out—to my eternal delight—that it's never too late to say, "I love you."

The morning after my father's hearty recommendation of Lester, I had breakfast with my mentor before flying back to Boston. I vividly remember sitting across from him thinking how impossible it felt to imagine myself living in that physical and cultural wasteland called Arizona—despite the prophetic words of Medicine Cloud, the Sedona mesa and my father. Interrupting my thoughts, Lester looked up from his newspaper and asked a seemingly casual question.

"Do you know why acupuncture really works?"

I'd hung out with Lester and other metaphysical teachers long enough to know this was not an innocent query. I'd experienced, and observed with others, the *deva*-stating effect of Lester's simple answers to simple questions. I wasn't sure I wanted to hear his answer. But I concluded, *What the hell! It's okay to hear his response. I'm out of here in a few minutes, and within hours I'll be safely back in Boston thousands of miles away.*

Yes, I was going back to my nice, neat, organized, safe world in Boston. *Intellectually*, on the surface of it, Lester's question didn't faze me at all. On many occasions, my acupuncture colleagues and I talked *philosophically* about how acupuncture worked because people *believed* it worked.

Lester was going to say what he intended to say, to have the impact he intended, no matter how I responded. This was a teaching query, not an idle question. And I'd learned there was a certain inevitability about teaching sessions with Lester. So, I gave him the answer he was seeking from me, "It works because people believe it works."

He replied, "That's right. People believe it. Therefore, it works. It's in their consciousness. It's their belief that it will work." With his characteristic leprechaun twinkle in his eye, Lester stated quietly, "That's the only reason that it works."

He paused for a moment to emphasize his last statement. Then he launched into a protracted story about scientifically designed studies with double-blind control groups he carried out with medical doctors to test the primacy of belief in healing situations.

Through these experiments, Lester demonstrated it wasn't really the medicine healing the doctors' patients; it was the patients' belief in the medicine and in their doctor that caused the healing. Actual patients with almost identical medical conditions were given two kinds of treatment. Half the patients were given the appropriate, clinical medicine for their condition. The other half were given a placebo, a sugar pill or a fake medication with no medical value. Patients in both groups experienced the same rate and degree of improvement.

I breathed a heavy sigh of relief. I'd survived another in a long line of "guru tests!" I already knew and accepted Lester's answer on an *intellectual* level. I'd read about similar studies of the placebo effect. My acupuncture colleagues and I often joked about how it didn't really matter what we did with patients because it was the patients' belief in us and in acupuncture that created the healing.

I flew back to Boston confident in the delusion I had a solid handle on that particular truth and had nothing to fear from its power. However, Lester had managed to poke a little hole in my secure fortress back East. And he knew the hole would grow larger and larger until all the air and life seeped out of my insular bubble of a world in Boston.

Soul Seed No. 5

A Cure for Cancer

*Past the seeker as he prayed, came the cripple
and the beggar and the beaten.
And seeing them, he cried,
"Great God, how is it that a loving creator can see such things
and yet do nothing about them?"
God said, "I did do something. I made you."*

SUFI TEACHING

A few years after my breakfast acupuncture talk with Lester, I went through a transformation with my brother that took Lester's prophetic words from the world of *theory* into the realm of directly experienced *reality.*

One evening in 1985, the telephone rang. It was my brother John who lived in Washington, D.C. A call from my elder sibling was highly unusual. A year my senior, John hadn't connected with me for several years. It wasn't that we disliked each other; we loved one another. We simply didn't have much in common and, therefore, little to talk about. He was a big city, government lawyer, married with a family. I was an ex-hippie acupuncturist living the single life in Boston.

When I answered the telephone, it took me a moment to recognize my brother's voice. John was crying profusely, his voice conveying a feeling of terror and extreme loss. I'd never heard my brother in this condition. He was ordinarily a bastion of macho strength and bravado.

"John? What's wrong? What's happened? The boys? Sharon? Did something happen to Mom?"

"I'm dying, Keith," John choked out between sobs.

My brother had developed a cancerous tumor the size of a golf ball in the center of his brain stem. Most of the left side of his body was already paralyzed. Within a few weeks doctors said the paralysis would reach his heart. At that point, he'd die.

I was stunned. "Can't they operate or something? Did you get a second opinion?"

The answer was no, they couldn't operate because of the size and location of the tumor. Yes, he'd seen a slew of doctors. All the cancer specialists he consulted concurred: because of the location and size of the tumor, his condition was beyond help through surgery, radiation or chemotherapy. There was nothing medical science could do. My brother had approximately three weeks to live. John had been sent home to die. His wife Sharon and our mother were immobilized with grief and anxiety.

"What can I do, John?"

"Nothing, Keith. I just need to talk to someone. I've tried to talk to Sharon and Mom. Every time I do, they just break down and cry. The doctors can't help me, so they don't want any further contact with me. My friends, well, they don't know what to say, so they avoid me. I just need someone to talk to, Keith. Will you talk to me?"

John had never asked me for any kind of assistance our whole lives. He was the big brother who always had everything together. I was the younger brother, the nonconformist who espoused strange philosophies, made weird career choices and had all the societal problems. *Talk to him? Of course I would talk to him!* I was willing to do anything I could for him. I immediately offered to catch the next plane to Washington.

"No, that's not what I need, Keith. There's nothing you can do for me here. I just want to talk to someone."

"Okay, John," I answered.

We conversed for over two hours the first night. I quickly realized that despite my accumulation of so many varied, alternative healing techniques, nothing in my bag of tricks could help my brother. It was too late to try acupuncture, macrobiotics, yoga or rebirthing. The cancer was too far advanced. He was paralyzed. He was being fed intravenously. It was too late to change his diet or lifestyle. I'd never felt so helpless.

What use is all my healing knowledge, I asked myself, *if I can't help my own brother in a life and death crisis?*

Again, I offered to fly to Washington. Again, he refused. He simply wanted someone to listen to him and be with him right where he was—in pain, fear and despair. He didn't want to be alone in his terror. Death was stealthily approaching, and my brother had surrendered to the inevitable. He asked me to make sure his two young sons had a strong male presence to support them as they grew up. Although barely staying afloat in the ocean of life's emotional challenges myself, I assured him I'd be there as a caring and reliable father figure for his sons. When we hung up, I was emotionally drained.

John called the next evening and, within minutes, again began crying and expressing his fears. I listened helplessly, offering suggestions based on my beliefs and experience as honestly as I could without causing him even more pain. After he spent himself and broke off the connection, I meditated late into the night searching for some way to help this man who was such an integral part of me. The answer I received didn't seem appropriate, but I was determined to trust my inner coach. It had never let me down before.

When the telephone rang the next evening, I listened to his already familiar litany of tears and angry tirades. Finally, taking a quivering breath, I put to him the question my inner coach had suggested, "John, do you want to die?"

"No, damn it!" he yelled into the receiver. "What a stupid question! What the hell's wrong with you! Of course, I don't want to die!"

Drawing on my abiding faith in my spirit, I responded with total assurance, "Well, you don't have to. You can decide to live."

I told him about people who'd been diagnosed with terminal cancer. Many I knew personally and some I'd heard of. Like him, the medical profession had abandoned them. Like him, they were sent home to die.

"But they refused to accept the verdict of death, John. They healed themselves."

There was a long pause on the other end of the line. Finally, he asked, "What kind of cancer?"

"All kinds," I answered. "Through the power of meditation and the personal power of intention, the disease went into remission. The cancers simply disappeared without any medical explanation."

I knew the concept was hard for my brother to accept. The notion of self-healing was difficult for John to understand when he was healthy, let alone while looking death in the face. Meditation, spirit guides, angels, other dimensions—those things didn't really exist for John. He loved me. I knew that as fact. But he felt I was a kook. I asked him to think about it. He said he would. The conversation ended shortly thereafter. I worried that he would dismiss me and not call again.

The next evening, I hung around the telephone. It was getting late. It was past the hour my brother usually went to sleep. I was getting up my courage to call him when the phone rang. It was John. We talked about the practical and physical worries that had preyed on his mind throughout the day. Would there be enough life insurance money for his family? Would his early demise emotionally scar his sons? He cried. The paralysis had spread. He didn't think he had much more time.

Once again I was prodded intuitively to ask, "John, do you want to die?

Again, his anger crackled across the telephone line. No, he did not want to die. How could I even ask such a ridiculous question? This tumor in his brain wasn't something he wished for!

As before, I told him he didn't have to die. He could decide to live. I listened to him rant on about my irrational beliefs and eccentric lifestyle. I held my tongue.

"Do you *know* anyone who has beaten terminal cancer?" he demanded angrily. "*Personally*, Keith! Do you *personally* know anybody who's survived advanced cancer after the doctors gave up on them?"

Pausing first to fortify myself, I then began sharing the stories of every acquaintance I knew personally who had cured themselves of terminal cancer. Like many people facing a medical death sentence, my brother didn't want to hear about any secondhand examples of cures. He was only interested in those case histories in which I personally witnessed people with tangible, visible complications directly linked to medically diagnosed cancer. In addition, the examples were only valid for John if the people had gone into remission and been cancer-free for at least a year after the healing. John basically eliminated every story I had in my arsenal except for five people. But that was enough. He was listening.

Fortunately, *in regard to my story telling,* John's memory was slipping fast. So, I could get away with repeating the same five case histories over and over again!

I even got him to meditate with me over the phone. Together, we asked for assistance from—as John put it—"whoever was listening." After two months of nightly, intensely emotional talking marathons, John awoke one morning to find his paralysis gone! He could move his whole body. His wife rushed him to the hospital for a magnetic resonance imaging test. The tumor had completely disappeared! Within weeks, John's health returned to normal.

My brother decided to live. He cured himself. John is alive and kicking today. And he's now decidedly more open to possibilities beyond the limitations of the tribal collective consciousness—the arbitrary societal beliefs he took on from his family, friends, school and society.

In fact, he's begun his own exploration outside the boundaries of mainstream cultural conditioning. John is enjoying being a "househusband," driving the kids to soccer practice and music lessons while his wife Sharon gallivants around the globe lecturing as a tenured professor.

Appointment with Destiny

If you think that the truth can be known from words,
If you think the Sun and the Ocean
Can pass through that tiny opening called the mouth,
O someone should start laughing!
Someone should start wildly laughing—
Now!

HAFIZ

During the weeks of talking with my brother, I had moved my acupuncture offices into a very classy but drafty Victorian mansion in a Boston suburb. The treatment rooms were elegant, professional—and very chilly. My patients constantly complained how cold they were whenever they had to remove any of their clothes for their acupuncture treatments. We had yet to figure out a way to seal the cracks in the windows to block out the brutal New England winter winds. Consequently, I was forever apologizing and turning up the heat another notch to warm my patients. And every time I had to raise the heat in order to use the proper, traditional acupuncture points on people's bare legs, arms and torso, I heard Lester's proclamation in my mind: "Why does acupuncture work? Because people believe it works."

Out of necessity and curiosity, I began to play with the potential implications of Lester's theory on healing. Fresh from the miracle of my brother's escape from death, I questioned some of my sacred beliefs about the ancient art of acupuncture. Then I made a simple, practical decision. I decided to put acupuncture needles only in people's hands, feet and head. By treating only those areas already exposed on the body, people wouldn't have to take off any clothing. They'd stay warm, be able to relax and wouldn't complain.

This point selection meant I was giving all patients the same treatment regardless of their ailment or diagnosis. With thousands of potential acupuncture points to choose from and six thousand years of precise Chinese Medical theory, this one-treatment-fits-all system was the height of heresy. This approach was the equivalent of a Western medical doctor giving everyone who came in the door the same medicine. I was acutely aware of this blasphemy. But every time I went to treat a patient, all I could hear was Lester's mischievous voice chiming, "It's only their belief healing them. They're healing themselves. It's not your diagnosis, your treatment or your selection of points."

Encouraging me in this traitorous direction was the fact that my patients were getting better much faster than in the past, when I had treated them with the traditional, personally tailored, individualized diagnostic procedure of needles all over the body. With this new approach, instead of a successful treatment taking thirty sessions, it took three!

Also, I did realize I was adding to the therapeutic mix my recent breakthrough involving my brother's cancer. I walked into the office every morning radiating the confidence and power I felt from participating in the grace of my brother's self-healing.

Quickly I acquired quite a reputation around town as a very effective and powerful healer. I developed a waiting list of people wanting to secure an appointment with me—a prospective patient list that grew longer and longer with each day of success.

One fateful morning, I could no longer go through the pretense of claiming acupuncture was the main ingredient in helping my patients. My inner coach had taken charge of my destiny. From a place of total clarity, I instructed my secretary to cancel all my appointments for the rest of the day.

I informed the receptionist I was leaving the office for the afternoon, but I knew in my heart I was leaving my acupuncture career for good. My old world was coming to an end, and with it, my ability to perpetuate a myth. Acupuncture doesn't heal people. People's *belief* in acupuncture does. People's deep faith in the reputation of Chinese Medicine and in the doctor persona of the healer does the trick. People cure themselves. The patient's own belief is the causative factor. A person's will to heal is the ultimate power. I'd witnessed my brother heal himself. I could no longer spout half-truths about the real source of the magic.

I drove to my house in a state of wondrous awe. My emotions and spirit were swirling around and through me. I arrived home with no idea whatsoever of my next step in life. I did what I had to do at that moment. I harbored no doubts about my actions. I knew I could no longer practice any approach to healing—or to life in general—based on beliefs that give power away to an outside cause. I felt empty of thought and intention, yet full of energy and momentum.

As I opened the door to my home, the telephone rang. It was Lester calling from that *other state*. In his uniquely impish, nonchalant way, he casually inquired, "You want to come out *here*? Come help me assist people to release their limiting beliefs and create the reality of their dreams?"

The wily shaman was asking me to join him in Arizona and help people change their lives by changing the beliefs in their consciousness. Lester hadn't contacted me for years—not since our infamous breakfast discussion on the subject of acupuncture. Somehow he knew I was ready to come out. His timing was intentional and very intuitive.

I laughed out loud, "Yes!"

Already there in spirit, I said I'd be in Arizona physically in six days. On that very day, I put my beloved house up for sale. It was time for me to move to Arizona, to move to a different state, geographically and spiritually. It was time for me to work directly with the real power behind all creation: intention and Spirit.

I was in transit physically—and psychologically. Synchronicity had adroitly planted the six seeds of my destiny in a specific pattern—from the first soul seed of visiting my folks in Sun City to the last soul sign of quitting my career in Boston. Those seeds had taken root and grown until they could no longer be ignored. I was traveling to my new physical home, and more importantly, to my new spiritual home.

PART V

Living in the Outer Power

Cops and Robbers of Time

The whole Earth is in jail and
we're plotting this incredible jailbreak.

WAVY GRAVY

In an episode reminiscent of the Keystone Cops, I'm reminded once more that our universe has a wonderful sense of humor. While enjoying pie and coffee in a funky diner in Phoenix with a friend, I was shown just how malleable time and space can be. On that day, the Phoenix Police Department and the universe conspired to rid me of any remaining rigid notions of a set reality and open my mind to unlimited possibilities.

My buddy Anthony was visiting from San Diego. Anthony was a lean, confident, self-made Hispanic businessman with jet-black hair combed straight back, as if it was being flattened by the wind as he sped along. And he was always speeding—to catch the next opportunity, out race the other guy and make a bundle of money. Anthony was what you call "hungry." He was hungry for challenge, success, recognition, and, at the time of his visit, meaning. Upon achieving a degree of success and the "good life," he was beginning to question his one-sided materialistic lifestyle and open to affairs of the spirit. He'd been barraging me with metaphysical questions for days.

One morning, I took him to McDonald's to meet Lester, my friend and spiritual mentor. I affectionately dubbed my teacher "Lester, the Mind Molester." Lester's main focus with his students was to expand their horizons as much as he could on any given occasion. He had a penchant for planting time bombs of outrageous possibilities in people's minds—or, as he put it, "assisting people to expand their envelope of what's possible in life." Everything Lester did around his students was to make a spiritual point, including holding court at a local fast-food restaurant. The pedestrian venue itself brought the judgmental attitudes of us "spiritual seekers" to the surface so we could see the arrogance of our intolerance toward the "less enlightened" masses—and, perhaps, make some changes in our attitude. What a radical thought!

Upon greeting Anthony, Lester launched immediately into his fundamental teaching that "people only perceive and experience what is in their own consciousness." He related several real-life stories to demonstrate his favorite "secret to understanding life." The key, according to Lester, is to realize that our conscious and *unconscious* thoughts and feelings determine what we perceive, and, therefore, what we experience in any situation. He emphasized that it is *the beliefs we're not aware we hold* that most limit our perception. "People's unconscious, emotional beliefs act as a filter, screening out events that don't jive with these beliefs," Lester concluded.

Anthony couldn't quite decide if Lester was a genius spouting philosophies beyond Anthony's ability to comprehend or simply an entertaining crackpot. Relishing the fact that the California greenhorn was teetering on the edge of his ability to absorb more expansion, Lester decided to take the point to the extreme. "If a nuclear bomb went off in the parking lot right outside of this McDonald's, and you had no fear of a nuclear bomb within you, you would not be affected by the explosion," Lester explained. "You would either not perceive the blast at all, or see it and not be harmed by it. If you had no concept of harm by nuclear explosion in your consciousness, no fear in your emotional programming of danger from an outside source, you would not be hurt."

Lester knew his assertion was a lot to swallow, even for me— and I'd been listening to his speculations for a long time. He explained that what determines our experiences in all situations are the actual beliefs we hold on an innermost, emotional, programmed level, not what we think conceptually and theoretically. And so, if we rid our total awareness—unconscious and conscious—of fear of outside harm, we will be free of harm from anything.

New to the scene, Anthony didn't know the best way to react to Lester's radical notions was to not respond immediately. Lester's students have learned the wisdom of taking some time alone to contemplate all the various aspects of his seemingly outlandish ideas. Instead, Anthony took Lester's bait and argued for an hour about the absurdity of Lester's conjecture. He was still ranting as

Lester slipped out the back door with one final tease, "Look, if you don't have fear within you, nothing can harm you!"

Anthony's view of the universe was seriously challenged. While his logical mind rejected Lester's philosophy immediately, some parts of Lester's worldview were intriguing and even seemed conceivable. Anthony sorely needed to talk some more about the ramifications of what he'd just heard. After taking a brisk, agitated walk, we headed into a diner for some soothing hot apple pie, caffeine and conversation.

For three hours, Anthony and I sat in a booth discussing the plausibility of Lester's theorems. Both of us recalled many instances in which people saw only what they thought or believed was possible, perceiving only what fit into their preconceived picture of reality. We shared personal experiences of how, once we had a certain presumption in our head, our experience then flowed from that expectation.

"It's like people who decide their keys are lost," I said. "They don't see them in plain sight under their nose." In her job as a court reporter, my mother often encountered legal cases where witnesses perceived very different versions of the same event. The story I remember most was about three people seeing a truck cause an accident and two other observers not seeing a truck at the scene at all! How could you not see a truck that is right in front of you? You could if you had a preconceived notion that a truck isn't present.

Anthony and I developed theories about the physics of the universe that would explain this phenomenon of selective personal perception. The existence of simultaneous, parallel personal realities would allow two people to have two different perceptions of one mutually experienced event. We expanded the envelope of our personal belief systems through validation from our own direct life experiences of selective perception. Each of us recalled instances where someone didn't see something that was in plain sight, or did see something that wasn't in fact there. Anthony realized that Lester's view of a flexible personal reality was not as implausible as he had felt earlier. In fact, by the time we finished talking, Lester's nuclear bomb scenario had actually become a theoretical possibility for both of us.

We finished off our now cold pie and coffee and stood, finally ready to leave the diner. Looking around for our server and our check, we were startled to see an empty restaurant with the cash register and lunch counter covered with white sheets.

We had been so completely absorbed in our conversation, re-arranging our emotional belief systems and integrating radical, new information that we'd been totally unaware of our surroundings for three hours.

Just then, a police officer came around a corner. From his expression and body language, we knew our presence took him by surprise. Glaring at us suspiciously, he barked, "Who the hell are you? What are you doing here? Where were you hiding?" As we explained our situation to the officer and attempted to calm him down, a remarkable scenario of events revealed itself to us through our conversation with the agitated policeman.

Anthony and I were embroiled in our conversation about the flexibility of reality, wherein people only see what they believe is possible, thereby creating their own reality. During this time—we learned from the officer—the diner had been robbed! Two masked men came in with guns and forced every server and customer to lie on the floor while the thieves cleaned out the register. Then they robbed several customers of their jewelry and cash, and left.

When the police arrived, they covered the register and counter with sheets to preserve fingerprints as evidence. The customers and staff of the diner had to give their names and phone numbers before they were allowed to leave. The police wanted to be able to reach them later as possible witnesses. Then the authorities searched the entire restaurant, including the bathrooms and closets, to make sure no one remained in the diner who hadn't been interviewed. Throughout the whole investigation, the officers didn't see Anthony and me until we stood up to get our check. And *we* were never once conscious of anything unusual occurring around us!

The officer suspected that the two of us had something to do with the robbery. He felt we successfully hid somewhere to avoid arrest. He asked several other officers who searched the building if they'd seen us. No one had. It took me over a half hour of fast talking to convince the officer we weren't involved in the burglary, didn't hide and should be allowed to leave. Whew! Once released, Anthony and I hustled down the street, relieved and happy to be free.

It wasn't until later in the day that it dawned on Anthony and me what had actually occurred in the diner. We had created for ourselves *direct physical evidence* of exactly what we'd come to accept *hypothetically* in our lengthy discussion: that people experience life according to what is in their own consciousness. The universe, working through the Phoenix Police and a couple of hoodlums, had given us proof of the veracity of Lester's proposition. In our total absorption of focus on the *possibility* of parallel universes, Anthony and I created the *reality* we were focused on: different worlds co-existing in the same time and place.

And, as Lester proclaimed, because of our newfound beliefs, Anthony and I were naturally protected from harm from the dangerous parallel world of cops and robbers!

Playing in Parallel Realities

Life is the movie you see through your own eyes.
It makes little difference what's happening out there.
It's how you take it that counts.

DENIS WAITLEY

Consciously playing with parallel universes is a fun and effective way to manage challenging situations in life. After accidentally stumbling upon the miraculous flexibility of time and space with "Cops and Robbers," I attracted several more intriguing encounters with this useful phenomenon. As I learned how to invoke this special aspect of the universe, I began to *intentionally* employ this versatile feature to serve my own needs in regard to facilitating space and time.

One spring in Phoenix, I was conducting a workshop of twenty people in the poolside clubhouse of an apartment complex. To keep us cool indoors, we had the door open to the pool area. If the poolside had been full of sunbathers, our proximity would have been a diplomacy problem. The seminar's interactive exercises—which I no longer use in my workshops—were, by their nature, extremely loud and boisterous. Fortunately, however, the weather during the first few days of the seminar was still too cool for swimming, and no community residents were using the pool area.

Uncharacteristically, the temperature began to soar on this particular morning. The air conditioning in the clubhouse hadn't yet been turned on for the summer season, and the room began to heat up. Since the pool area remained deserted, I felt safe moving the class outside when the temperature in the room began to get unbearable.

At that point, the participatory exercises the class was doing were especially noisy and raucous. People were instructed to sit opposite each other and voice their feelings in a deliberately loud and exaggerated way. This method of releasing emotions was extremely energetic and often involved a lot of cursing and crude, foul language. For the process to be natural and authentic enough to be effective, people needed to feel safe to speak freely and spontaneously. Obviously, we usually did this technique in a closed, private room; but it was just too hot this day to stay inside.

We'd been alone by the pool all morning. As the temperature rose into the nineties, residents of the apartment complex began to come out to enjoy the first warm pool day of the season. Adults brought their kids with beach balls in tow. They soon filled the empty lounge chairs in between and around my students who continued the shrill, vulgar emoting of the course exercise.

I panicked! The situation was destined to become a disaster. How could the residents relax in the sun and water when, a few feet away, my people were swearing and screaming bloody murder at each other? Frantically, I searched a mental inventory of locations in Phoenix to which we could immediately relocate the workshop. Where could twenty people go and vocally express their inner demons without disturbing anyone? My living room at home wasn't large enough. The apartments I knew weren't private enough.

As I frenetically scoured my mind for a solution, I noticed some children playing with their beach balls, bouncing them between two workshop participants doing their evocative processing. I reasoned, *My students have paid a lot of money for this course, and they're not going to appreciate some kids bouncing balls between them. And they're not going to feel safe to verbalize their innermost feelings with all these strangers nearby. They'll feel inhibited and then shut down. Meanwhile, the residents lounging around the pool are going to get upset at the intrusion of the students. What can I do?*

I felt I needed to separate the two groups. I couldn't take my class back inside the stifling hot clubhouse. And I still hadn't come up with another site for the course. As I continued to rack my brain seeking a solution, it suddenly dawned on me that none of my students had complained yet. No one had quit doing the exercise. All of the participants were still emoting and screaming at each other, going through the process and enjoying it. I also realized none of the sunbathers had complained either. They were lying about peacefully soaking in the sun. Neither group had even noticed the other. This harmonious juxtaposition was as fascinating as it was perplexing.

I mused to myself, *Maybe we don't have to go anywhere—at least not until someone complains!*

Entranced with the *absence* of conflict where there *should* have been some, I waited and watched. I knew something extraordinary was going on here. There were two diametrically opposed activities overlapping in the same place, and none of the people engaged in either of the activities were aware of the other.

Some boys started playing a very rowdy game of tennis in the court next to the pool. At times the tennis ball would roll between students doing the exercise. The boys ran between the pair to retrieve the ball. Still, my people weren't distracted or interrupted!

The "impossible" compatibility between the groups continued all afternoon. I sat there in utter amazement. My mind was blown. It didn't fit my past experience of what was possible or my beliefs of what was plausible.

By evening, the temperature had cooled down. The participants congregated in the clubhouse to wrap up the day. As we were discussing everyone's experience of the exercise, one of the students suddenly shrieked, "Oh, my God!" Startled by her impromptu outburst, everyone turned and stared at her. She blurted out, "We weren't alone out there today! There were other people and kids a few feet away all afternoon." She'd just realized there'd been a dozen strangers sunbathing around her while she was sharing the most secret aspects of her life.

A surge of recognition swept over the circle of faces. Startled expressions and raised eyebrows flowed from person to person much like the movement of "The Wave" of uplifted hands flowing through the stands at a sporting event. One collective thought: "Yes, we were baring our souls before an audience of strangers all afternoon!"

Then a long period of total silence while the deeper reality sunk in.

A second round of recognition and surprise careened through the group. The shared realization: "Yes, and we didn't see them, and they didn't notice us!"

We sat quietly for ten more minutes as the reality of the day's mystery slowly dawned within each person's awareness.

Soon we were talking the enigma to death—or, shall I say more accurately, to life! Each person's words tumbled over the previous speaker. People presented various theories about how it could be possible to have two conflicting universes co-existing harmoniously. No one could explain what we had communally experienced.

Nonetheless, two opposing worlds had existed simultaneously in our shared experience. Together we had witnessed a lot more malleability in our reality than we usually allow ourselves to notice or enjoy.

Having several weeks to absorb the reality of this collective phenomenon, I began to appreciate how practical this special characteristic of the universe could be if invoked deliberately. Excited by the possible benefits of this newly discovered feature, I looked for an opportunity to play more consciously and creatively with the flexibility of the physical universe.

A month later, I was leading another workshop in the same venue. Being summer, the air-conditioning was turned on for the season. We were happily doing our thing in the clubhouse when I found myself again smack dab in the middle of another uncomfortable juxtaposition of opposing forces. Normally, I would undertake some active leadership strategy to harmonize the conflicting parties in an effort to diffuse the conflict. This time, I decided to experiment with a new approach. I chose to explore the power of my intention to resolve the friction through deliberately invoking the phenomenon of peaceful co-existence of opposing realities.

The Phoenix Suns, our local pro basketball team, were playing a crucial playoff game that day. Along the side of the pool right in front of the clubhouse, apartment residents hooked up a television set so they could watch the game while they swam and drank beer. Fortunately, due to the sound of the air conditioner, my students couldn't hear the blaring television from inside the clubhouse when the door was shut. We were involved in a very quiet segment of the seminar in which people were lying on their backs on the floor in quiet meditative states.

At the first commercial break of the basketball game, I heard a loud knock at the door. One of the basketball enthusiasts poked his head inside to ask if he and his friends could use our refrigerator to keep their beer cold. I could have answered "no." However, since the complex manager let me use their clubhouse for free, I wanted to cultivate a harmonious relationship with the residents. Without fully considering the consequences of my consent, I responded, "Sure, that's fine."

Two exuberant young men tumbled in with four six-packs each. To reach the refrigerator on the other side of the room, they had to tiptoe carefully around twelve workshop participants lying on their backs spread out on the floor. One of the bewildered youths realized they were disturbing some sort of strange, purposeful activity, mumbling "Oh, we're sorry. Excuse us." under his breath as he wove his way to and from the refrigerator.

At the next break in the court action, a third fellow came in for a beer, excusing himself throughout his journey to and from the refrigerator. I was praying to God, requesting that the guys would come in and out without speaking at all. But every time one of the basketball fans came in for a beer, he apologized very vocally.

As the day wore on, the sun got hotter, the Suns got hotter, the game got closer, the fans got drunker—and more boisterous! Now every time the avid sportsmen came in for their beers, they excused themselves even more loudly and often. The combination of excessive alcohol and intense sun had a decidedly debilitating effect on the intruders. The revelers had an increasingly difficult time navigating their way through the maze of prone bodies to the refrigerator.

I felt strongly that I needed to put a stop to the increasingly frequent and noisy disruptions. My class certainly required a quiet place to do their introspection and meditation. Or did they? I recalled the enigma earlier in the year outside by the pool in front of this very clubhouse. The residents talking and playing in the midst of their serious workshop exercises had not bothered my students. I pondered, *Could that harmonious co-existence happen again if, as before, I took no overt action?*

I decided this would be the perfect opportunity to test my power in creating my own reality by invoking a dual reality to satisfy all parties. Besides, I couldn't think of an alternative strategy!

I resolved to hold the intention: "Everybody involved in the situation is harmonious and content. Using our refrigerator, the residents revel in their game and beer, and my students enjoy a conducive space to practice their meditation." I focused on the intent and sat back, allowing the scene to play out without my intervention.

Tipsy basketball zealots continually maneuvered in and out of the maze of prone bodies to get at their brew for the balance of the afternoon. At one point, a guy dropped and smashed a bottle of beer, scattering glass everywhere. While he awkwardly cleaned up the mess, he cut his foot, making even more noise and commotion.

As the visitations increased in volume and frequency, I began to feel very guilty. I berated myself for not handling the situation in a normal, efficient leadership manner. *I should have taken action and spoken to the revelers,* I scolded myself. *I'm not being considerate to my students to experiment with harmonizing parallel realities when the situation so directly involves their need for quiet and safety.*

The old belief program running in my mind said this noise had to be experienced by my students as a disruption. My emotional conditioning was certain my students would be very angry with me for not doing my job of giving them a peaceful workshop space. I had quite a nerve-racking few minutes before stopping the old mental tapes and renewing my resolve to hold my intention of harmony.

To my delight, and, I must admit, surprise, the same magical phenomenon occurred as had transpired in the previous workshop in which two opposing forces co-existed side-by-side outside by the pool. The students in my current workshop hadn't complained and, in fact, seemed totally unaware of any distractions. So, I let the conflicting juxtaposition go on the whole afternoon.

That evening when we came together in a sharing circle to end the day, I decided to take the defense of a good offense.

Before someone had a chance to yell at me for not keeping their space quiet and safe, I asked the group to forgive me for the disruptions. I apologized, saying, "I could have taken care of the noise this afternoon. I could have told the intoxicated young men they couldn't use our refrigerator. I didn't do that. I'm sorry if it interfered with your meditation today."

Mouths gaping in puzzled bewilderment, my students stared at me. Almost in unison, they told me they had no idea what I was talking about. "What disturbance? What men?"

I then explained to them what I'd witnessed in the clubhouse during the day. As with the earlier poolside incident, I watched the expressions on my students' faces transform as they "remembered" the sports fans coming and going during their quiet meditations. And, as in the poolside instance, the students and I anchored the newfound phenomenon in our collective reality by openly acknowledging that conflicting universes did co-exist peacefully that afternoon.

The first two encounters with co-existing, parallel realities—in "Cops and Robbers of Time" and the just discussed poolside harmony—were flukes, accidents, in terms of me having any prior conscious intention in creating them. This last beer incident, however, was a deliberate creation on my part. The group's shared experience was directly related to my conscious, focused intention to have harmony between the two conflicting parties. At the time that it occurred, no one except me saw or heard the intoxicated men stagger in and out of the room. No one except me was aware of the two incongruent worlds existing in the same place at the same time.

Attention flows to the focus of strongest intention to become a reality. In order to create the outcomes you desire in life, you can deliberately use this knowledge and strategy to harmonize situations with "apparent" built-in conflicts.

How the Hopi Create Their World

God gives food to every bird, but does not throw it into the nest.

MONTENEGRIN PROVERB

"Do you hear that?" I whispered to my friend Tobias.
"No, what?" he answered under his breath.
"Drumming. The sound of soft, distant drumming."
"No, but I see a faint glow over there by the cliff. Like a small fire. A vague, flickering light cast against the rock face."

My friend Tobias and I love to explore old Indian ruins in Arizona's desert canyons and mesas. Our favorite ones are the secluded, out-of-the-way remains not normally visited by other people. These remnants of a bygone civilization are quiet, dreamy and somewhat desolate. Many of the aged, abandoned fortresses and homes are over a thousand years old. These timeworn vestiges of ancestral life are extremely serene—and mystical. When Tobias and I sit and meditate within their eroded walls, we often see a dim, blurry campfire, or hear subtle, muffled, elusive drumming, chanting or the sound of children playing. Experiencing visual and auditory glimpses of the distant past is enthralling to us and serves to heighten our interest in learning more about the ancient ones who lived in the American Southwest so long ago.

One day, while exploring a windy, arid, remote mesa in the high northern desert of Arizona, Tobias and I happened upon an Anazazi Indian ruin with several partial dwellings still standing. The crumbling abodes were awash in relics of antiquity. Delighted to find a site that obviously hadn't received many visitors over the years, we dropped to our hands and knees, and sifted through the dirt for artifacts to help us understand the long-departed residents. Our efforts were rewarded with arrowheads, pottery shards and corncobs preserved by the extreme dryness.

In the center of this native village is a large oval pit about sixty feet wide. Surrounded by a wall of very carefully fitted slate stones, the pit sinks approximately five feet into the ground. This submerged ring of stones is called a kiva by Native Americans. The structure served as a ceremonial circle for Indian rituals. Spellbound by the aura and electricity we sensed within the ceremonial pit, Tobias and I speculated about its history. As we sat on the sun-warmed stones in the kiva, we longed to know the specific nature and focus of the ancient rituals conducted by the Anazazi Indians so long ago.

The absolute quiet and serenity of the kiva reminded me of a psychology experiment I read about in college. The research project revealed a fascinating quality inherent in a vacuum. Relaxing in the ominous silence of the kiva, I related the experiment to my fellow explorer.

Scientists set up a near vacuum in a completely empty room. Installed in this vacuum-sealed room were a speaker and a listening device. From outside the room, one of the researchers spoke distinctly one secret word, known only to him, through the speaker into the room. The chamber was then locked and sealed for five years. At the end of the five years, the scientists returned. From outside the room, they turned on the highly sophisticated sound sensing equipment to listen to whatever they could hear from inside the room. The device picked up the secret word spoken into the vacuum five years earlier! The sound vibration of the word was still alive and detectable within that environment after five years.

The kiva was almost as still and empty as I imagined a vacuum to be. It was the kind of quiet that absorbs every sound. Even the intermittent whistling of the wind was consumed by the all-prevailing silence.

Sitting in this timeless place, we allowed the tranquility to envelop us. I sensed the space around us had been this serene for the last thousand years. That's when the notion came to me. *Was it possible that whatever happened in the kiva a millennium ago still exists on some subtle, vibrational level, just like the sound of the spoken word in the scientists' vacuum? And, like the word, is that vibration accessible and perceivable now?*

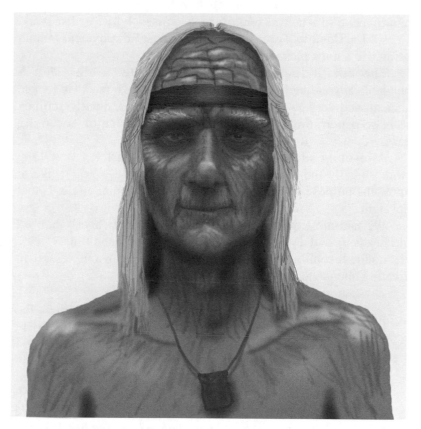

What an exciting concept! I turned to Tobias to share my proposal, "Maybe we could contact whatever occurred in this kiva long ago. Perhaps even hear part of a ceremony."

Tobias caught my enthusiasm. Blond, blue-eyed and innocent, Tobias had the adventurous curiosity of his Norse forebears. He was as anxious as I to see if such a feat was possible. We were flush with excitement. We were on a mission to connect with the kindred souls who had preceded us on the planet!

We decided to sit quietly inside the circle and open ourselves to sensing any vibrations remaining from previous activities in the kiva. The most we expected was something along the lines of what we'd experienced before—a faint vision, a vague mumbling, or, if extremely fortunate, a hazy, dreamlike apparition.

After about half an hour, neither of us had picked up any sound or sighting. Then suddenly, to our right sat a Native American Indian—in the flesh! I tentatively reached over lightly touching him to make sure he was real. I was taken aback by my discovery. "Yes," I nodded to Tobias, "the man is a solid, physical human being. He's not a phantom!"

The stoic Indian sat cross-legged on the bare ground. A hundred canyon-like lines etched his noble, bronze face. He looked ancient, and very sweet and gentle. His soft eyes, quietly smiling, were so penetrating I kept losing myself in his calm, accepting gaze.

A reverent silence engulfed the three of us for a very long while. Finally the Indian elder smiled and stated, "You'd like to know the purpose for which we used this ceremonial circle. Is that not right?"

We had not expected a living tour guide and eagerly bobbed our heads up and down to indicate "yes"—a thousand times "yes!" He nodded, took a long, quiet breath and began our lesson in creating abundance:

"Many, many moons ago, when the antelope ran free, the buffalo grazed across all the land, and my brothers and sisters lived in harmony with each other and Mother Earth, we would meet in this circle every fall for the most important ceremony of the whole year. This most sacred, vital ritual was attended by the chief of the tribe, the medicine man, the tribe elders and all of those who had achieved the status of a brave—the hunters of the tribe. After many days of purification through chanting, drumming and praying in our sweat lodges, we sat around this circle in silence and waited until the Great Spirit honored us with a vision.

"Then, one by one, each brave would see and feel the specific animals they would kill and bring to the village as food for the tribe in the coming year. Each animal's spirit made an agreement with the warrior who would be killing the animal. For a period of time, their spirits would commune in the beauty and harmony of their shared intention. In this time-honored way, the warrior would connect with each bison, antelope and deer that he would be providing for the tribe. When his vision was complete, the brave announced to the rest of the group what he had seen and experienced."

At this point, the Indian took a full breath and said in a very deliberate manner:

"And on this day, the entire year's food supply for the tribe was created."

He stared at us closely to see if we heard his last statement. Satisfied, he continued:

"Each warrior waited until he saw, greeted and came to a mutual understanding with the spirit of each buffalo, antelope and deer before announcing to the circle, 'I will bring so many buffalo, antelope and deer to the tribe in the coming year.' And so it went until, one by one, each brave met the spirit of each animal that would come to him to be killed in the next year. One by one, each warrior announced the food they would provide to the tribe in the coming year."

Again, the venerable, timeworn storyteller paused. With great passion, he looked directly into our eyes—first mine, then Tobias'. I have never felt such a piercing gaze. His look penetrated the depths of my soul. Dramatically, he drew air into his lungs. Repeating his message, he declared:

"And on this day, the entire year's food supply for the tribe was created."

Once again, he waited until he sensed that the import of his words was fully absorbed before resuming:

"After all the braves had proclaimed the food they would bring for the coming year, the chief, medicine man and elders would bless the ceremony. All would leave the kiva knowing that on this day, the entire year's food supply for the tribe was created."

Again, he waited, watching to see if we were fully digesting his last sentence before speaking again. He continued in a very emphatic tone:

"In the winter when the warriors could not go out hunting because there was a blizzard with snow drifts twenty feet high, the chief, medicine man, elders and braves would meet again in the kiva and wait in silent, expectant meditation. Soon, from the wind-swept prairie and the snow-covered plateaus would come a bison, a deer or an antelope. On its own, the animal would find its way into the tribal encampment and then into the kiva circle. The creature would stand in the center of the circle until it recognized the brave with whom it had made a spirit agreement. Then the animal would walk over to the warrior, stand right in front of him, and calmly allow itself to be killed in a very quick and painless way. The creature gave itself up to the brave, as previously agreed in the kiva, so that the people would have food during the harsh, winter months. For, on that special day the previous fall, the entire year's food supply for the tribe had been created."

It wasn't until the Indian told us about the animals coming into the circle in the winter and recognizing the warriors with whom they had an agreement that Tobias and I finally realized what the Indian was telling us. And at the exact moment we got the point of the story, the old man disappeared in front of our eyes. Not believing our vision, we scanned the kiva quickly, thinking he must have been a very fast escape artist. It was thirty feet to the edge of the circle and neither of us saw him leave. He vanished the second we understood his message!

Driving back to Phoenix later that day, Tobias and I discussed our shared encounter at great length. We agreed the Indian was telling us something far more important than how the Hopi used to create food for a year. He was opening a gateway for us to understand how creation itself works.

The message Tobias and I received in the kiva was simple, yet profound; the power to create lies in the Present, not in the future. Creation happens *now* when declared with power, heart and strong intention. Then, that which is created in the Present unfolds in future time and space according to our mutual agreements with the rest of the living beings of Mother Earth.

Conjuring Up Sid Caesar

If one advances confidently in the direction of his dreams,
and endeavors to live the life which he has imagined,
he will meet with a success unexpected in common hours.

HENRY DAVID THOREAU

Love focuses attention. When you really love something, you are naturally pouring your interest and appreciation toward the object of your love. The driving core of this concern and care, on an electro-magnetic level, is creative life force. As our love flows toward the object of our love, the object is filled with our vital energy, enthusiasm and joy. This energetic connection to the object magnetically pulls the object into our sphere of experience. We attract that which we love. It becomes created within our world.

I love the humor of Sid Caesar, one of our culture's most talented and observant comedians. I especially enjoyed the wild and batty characters he presented on his television show in the 1950s. One of my favorite caricatures was called "The Professor." An exuberant, pompous man, The Professor pontificated in an exaggerated, self-absorbed way about scholarly subjects, using long words, complex phrases and complicated logic. In taking these qualities to the extreme and the absurd, Sid Caesar helped me to release the frustration and impatience of a lifetime of having to listen to people just like The Professor: my father, athletic coaches, countless school teachers, and many other authorities and experts.

It was almost time to break for lunch at a workshop I was conducting in New York City. To illustrate a certain point, I was describing to the group a particular bit of schtick Sid Caesar had done in the early days of television. Playing The Professor, he lectured verbosely about his subject, as usual, using convoluted sentences and ridiculous reasoning. As he built up to a dramatic climax and was just about to make his main point, his tie—rigid and stiff—would flip up into his face. Each and every time the tie unceremoniously interrupted his presentation, the studio audience broke into gales of laugher. Knowing his tie was going to snap up in his face every time The Professor built to a crescendo, I laughed in anticipation along with the audience. We couldn't wait for that tie to flip up into his face again. The more arrogant and pompous The Professor became, the more we anticipated his forthcoming humiliation. There was also a mild sexual undertone to the skit which, while never discussed, was always present in regards to the rigid, erect tie. With unbounded respect and admiration for the humor of Sid Caesar, I acted out the skit for the group. To our shared delight, I was able to demonstrate the hilarity of The Professor, as well as convey the keen insight into human nature Sid Caesar possessed.

My good buddy and co-presenter Tobias was in the class. He grew up in Sweden and had never heard of Sid Caesar. My loving re-enactment stirred an acute curiosity in Tobias to know more about this icon of American comedy. The rest of the participants in the gathering had been raised on American television. Lunch forgotten for the moment, members of the group began to share their own fond memories of the beloved comedian with Tobias. Like me, several people even acted out their favorite routines. It ended up being a Sid Caesar "Love-In" as people remembered how much they looked forward to his performances on The Ed Sullivan Show and how much they treasured his talent and comedy.

We finally broke for lunch. Tobias and I decided to eat our meal in Central Park. As the elevator made its way to the main floor, Tobias mused aloud, "You know, I'd really like to meet this guy, Sid Caesar."

I replied nonchalantly, "He probably lives in Hollywood, and I'm not even sure if he's still alive."

With an air of uncommon determination, Tobias countered, "No, I really must meet him. He sounds like a unique and wonderful man."

Then, as we crossed the street bordering Central Park, I saw a stately gentleman coming toward us who looked exactly like Sid Caesar! I couldn't believe my eyes. He appeared older than I remembered Mr. Caesar, but he bore an uncanny resemblance to the comedian. I whispered to Tobias, "You know, that man looks just like Sid Caesar."

Peering closely at the man approaching us, my friend—who had never seen Mr. Caesar in person or on television—pronounced in no uncertain terms, "He is Sid Caesar. I can tell."

"No, it couldn't be," I responded incredulously.

Tobias' solution was to find out for sure. We walked over to the stranger. Tobias introduced himself as being from Sweden. He asked the gentleman if he was Sid Caesar. Sure enough, he was! Not only did he not mind identifying himself, but Mr. Caesar was very willing to spend some time chatting animatedly with us. What a treat!

For ten minutes, we listened to jokes and stories, enjoying the man who was the same funny, friendly being we'd all talked about before lunch. Tobias' wish was granted. He met Sid Caesar and experienced firsthand the joy, warmth, openness and humor of this extraordinarily gifted man.

Like vibration creates like vibration by attracting that which exists on the same wavelength or frequency. The vibration of our love pulled to it the object of our love. The affection and admiration we had poured into the personage of Sid Caesar vibrationally attracted his very real spirit to meet us in Central Park. What a magical and wondrous universe we live in!

The Fickle Finger of Fate

Be realistic: Plan for a miracle!

BHAGWAN SHREE RAJNEESH

A very brief, but potent incident early in my workshop career showed me that the human ability to heal has no limits—not even in regard to the past.

We're told there's nothing we can do about an incident that has already occurred. From birth, we're bombarded with the collective tribal agreement: "That's water over the dam" and "Don't cry over spilled milk." The mainstream cultural belief is that once an event occurs a certain way, that's it. It's done. It's fact. Nothing and no one can change the past.

I also was at the mercy of this limited way of thinking until I accumulated several healing experiences that were an exception to this paradigm, like Kriya's burn disappearing in "E.T. to the Rescue" and Joe's broken wrist reconstituting in "The Seven Sacred Pools." I began to strongly suspect that human beings have more power than we give ourselves credit for. I saw the past can be changed. I learned it's very effective to "cry over spilled milk."

A challenging, new workshop in New York loomed ominously on my horizon. I wasn't looking forward to conducting the event. In fact, I was dreading the trip. During my previous stay in New York, the person who had so supportively facilitated seminars with me for years decided to quit his career as a workshop leader because of personal issues. He hit a wall of fear about being so visible and vulnerable to the public. I felt alone and shaky going back to the Big Apple to teach a brand new program without a trusted and able comrade by my side. He was also my best personal friend, so I felt a strong sense of sadness and loss as well.

To add to the discomfort level, it was a very hot, humid summer on the East Coast. The apartment where I was staying had no air-conditioning.

So, I was experiencing a lot of resistance to going through with the whole affair. Nevertheless, canceling was not an option. Many people already had enrolled in the class. Some were traveling long distances to attend. I was committed to going.

I rushed to make breakfast before the taxi arrived to take me to the Phoenix airport. In my haste, I was careless and cut myself slicing homemade bread for my toast. The knife slashed deeply into my left index finger. Blood spurted like a geyser all over the cutting board and kitchen counter. I grabbed my finger, squeezing it tightly to try to stop the bleeding.

My heart sank. I cried out loud, "Oh, God, this is too much!" Immediately, my mind and emotions focused on and exaggerated a worst-case scenario: *With the throbbing pain of a severely cut finger, I won't be able to relax on the five-hour flight to New York. I'll never get a restful night's sleep in a sweltering hot, humid apartment. Nor will I be able to deliver a seven-day seminar in a composed, professional way. And my finger will probably become infected.* The projected nightmare of having to pretend to be happy, healthy and together with this injury while leading a workshop for seven days quickly became a totally overwhelming and unbearable prospect.

Suddenly, from the depths of my being, welling up from a place I didn't know existed, came a thunderous wail, "NOOOO!" For what seemed an eternity, I screamed out loud at the height of my voice from the depths of my soul, "NOOOOOOOO, I WILL NOT DO THIS! IT CANNOT BE!" It was an absolute refusal from the core of my being. I cried "NO" to the cut and to the nightmarish problems I imagined it would create.

Finally, I ran out of breath and the "NO" started to trail off. Shaking uncontrollably, I concentrated on catching my breath after the exertion of my despairing wail. Then I heard a sound unlike any other I've ever heard. It came from inside me and resembled the whir of a tape recorder when it rewinds. I instinctively shook my head trying to dispel the strange noise, but the sound continued for several minutes, finally winding down to silence.

With the quiet came a sense of calm. Peacefulness replaced my apprehension. I noticed I no longer had any pain in my finger,

still wrapped in the vise of my right fist. Slowly, I relaxed my grip
on the injured finger and, very cautiously, withdrew my hand. The
cut was gone! It no longer existed. There wasn't even a scratch to
indicate where the knife had sliced my flesh. The blood was gone.
I looked at my right hand, which had squeezed the cut finger. No
blood. My eyes went to the cutting board and countertop. I saw the
partially sliced bread and the knife. But no blood!

I stumbled to a nearby chair and sat down, totally confounded.
What happened? Did I imagine the whole thing? I examined my
finger again. Nothing unusual.

Disoriented and discombobulated, I must have sat there for
twenty minutes contemplating the details of the event I was sure I
just experienced in my kitchen. Over and over, I replayed the
incident in my mind's eye. I pictured myself holding the bread and
picking up the knife. I felt the knife slice through my flesh. I heard
myself scream as I had never cried out before. Then the injury and
the blood disappeared. My ordered, rational world turned upside-
down. How could I make any sense of this? My mind whirled in
circles, trying to comprehend the unexplainable phenomenon.

Shocked out of my bewildered state by the sharp intrusion of a
taxi horn outside my door, I was spurred into action. I grabbed my
suitcase with my now whole and healthy left hand and lumbered
down the hallway to the waiting cab.

As the taxi whisked me away from my old world to begin a
new adventure in the Big Apple, I realized I had just traveled on
an inner journey of transformation to a new, bigger reality. Born
of necessity, I'd learned how to tap into the place within my being
of profound will, decision and intention. Owning this natural
power has changed my conception—and enjoyment—of reality
forever.

Saved by the Kosmic Lady

God is a comic playing to an audience that's afraid to laugh.

VOLTAIRE

Staying focused on your intention despite *apparent* setbacks is one of the keys to creating what you want in life. Trust isn't always easy in the face of the unconscious human habit of trying to control how the universe operates. We often have an urge to micro-manage the way the universe delivers our intentions. However, what may *seem* to be a drawback or delay is often only the unique and inventive way Spirit has chosen to fulfill our dreams.

My new career as a national workshop facilitator was just beginning. I scheduled a one-evening affair in San Francisco sandwiched between a two-weekend workshop in Milwaukee, Wisconsin. During the midweek break of my workshop, I planned to fly all the way to San Francisco for just one evening to give a free introductory seminar, spend the night, and then fly back to Milwaukee to continue my workshop.

This was my first professional visit to San Francisco. For the past six months, I spent several thousand dollars advertising in and around the city to attract people in a geographical area known to contain a sizeable population interested in spiritual and human growth. I rented a large meeting room for the affair at a major downtown hotel. My intention was to draw so many people to the free introductory evening that enough of them would sign up for my main workshop, which carried a substantial price tag.

The affair was scheduled to take place at seven-thirty in the evening at the Jack Tarr Hotel.

On the afternoon of the big day, I settled into my seat on the plane in Milwaukee. Tingling with anticipation, I waited impatiently for the flight crew to announce our takeoff. Finally, after numerous delays, we were instructed to fasten our seatbelts. The plane taxied down the runway. But instead of gaining momentum and leaving the ground, the plane returned to the gate. The captain announced an engine malfunction had been detected. In his opinion, the aircraft was not safe to fly. Disgruntled, all the passengers shuffled off the plane.

I was crestfallen. My itinerary was extremely tight. This flight would have gotten me into San Francisco with just enough time to secure a cab to the hotel by seven-thirty. Even if I were able to find another flight right away, I'd be hard pressed to get to the hotel on time.

My mind had a field day of doom and gloom concerning the repercussions of missing the meeting. My emotions ran wild. *I'm a one-man operation. I don't know anyone in San Francisco who can give the talk for me. There's no way to reach the people who've seen the promotional ads to inform them of the delay. If I don't show, my investment will be down the drain. My reputation will be ruined in the San Francisco area before I have a chance to build it. My cherished intention to serve the awakening planetary consciousness through seminars will be lost.* Just a little excess of self-importance!

Shuffling off the plane with the other disgruntled passengers, I re-entered the terminal and checked all the airlines for a scheduled flight that would get me to San Francisco on time. There were none. Discouraged beyond words, I stood in the middle of the busy terminal and began calculating my losses. The total ran into thousands of dollars. I sat down on my luggage and basically gave up. I surrendered, thinking, *Well, this fiasco is a very expensive lesson. I won't plan my schedule so tight next time. If there is a next time! Maybe I'm not even supposed to facilitate workshops.*

Abruptly, I realized what I was saying to myself and the message of failure I was sending out into the universe. In an attempt to reverse the tide of my conjectures and the direction of my energy, I willed myself to become very quiet and check in with my inner guidance. I felt and released my feelings as fully as I could and rededicated myself to divine purpose. Suddenly, I saw a vision of me standing in front of a large audience in San Francisco sharing the words of wisdom and the tools of empowerment taught to me by so many shamans and spiritual teachers throughout my life. Apparently, I was destined to deliver this talk!

A tap on my shoulder snapped my awareness back to the airport lobby. Standing before me was an impeccably dressed young woman approximately twenty years of age. In a soft but firm voice, she stated, "You wanted to get to San Francisco this evening, too."

I nodded. I didn't have a clue how she knew. *Maybe she saw me on the earlier flight.*

"I must get there by seven-thirty this evening," she stated emphatically.

"That's when I need to arrive," I replied.

With a quick "Follow me," she turned in the direction of the gates for departing flights.

I started to question her, but she was already walking away. What did I have to lose? I didn't have any viable alternative plan. I couldn't find a flight that would get me to San Francisco on time. Having nothing else productive to do with myself, I ran to catch up with her.

"What about my baggage?" I asked breathlessly.

"Never mind," she answered. "It will be taken care of."

I followed her to the gate of another airline that was just about to close its boarding process. The agent took my ticket from the original airline without comment. Once on the plane, I lost track of the helpful young lady and took the last empty seat on the aircraft.

I buckled myself into the seat and deliberately avoided looking at my watch or listening to any discussions about the time. I've learned not to watch the clock when focusing on the intention of altering time. I kept my attention riveted on the vision I had at the terminal of me speaking to a full house of attentive, curious people.

Several times during the flight I walked the aisle searching for my "guardian angel" without success.

Just as the confident stranger had predicted, my luggage was waiting for me in San Francisco. I jumped into a cab. Walking through the lobby of the Jack Tar Hotel, I pulled my watch out of my pants pocket where I had hidden it so I wouldn't peek at the time during the flight. Impossibly, I had arrived five full minutes before my seminar was advertised to start!

Astonished, I pondered to myself, *How could this be? . . . a time warp? I'll figure it out later . . . or not!* Quickly I set out to find my reserved lecture hall. The space was set up perfectly with row after row of neatly aligned chairs. There was only one problem. I was the only person in the auditorium! I rushed out of the room hoping to find people milling around. No one. I searched the hotel foyer. Not one person was lingering about as if waiting for something to begin. I checked the events marquee in the hotel lobby. It clearly announced the correct name, location and time of my seminar. But, obviously, no one cared!

I was crushed. I might as well have stayed back in the Milwaukee air terminal. Magically, I'd been given my wish to arrive on time for my seminar only to find one important element missing. People!

My emotions plummeted into an abyss of despair. I knew I had to pull my focus back from drawing disastrous conclusions. Finding a quiet place to sit in a corner of the hotel vestibule, I once again willed myself to become very quiet and check in with my inner coach. To divert my attention from the feelings of failure, I focused on examining other vocations. A career as a car mechanic popped into my head. *Yes,* I theorized, *that's a simple job. You know what you're dealing with. A car needs work—you fix it!* But I quickly realized this train of thought was a dead end. It would solve nothing in my present predicament. It was only distracting my creative energies from the goal at hand.

I reminded myself of the clearing and centering that had been so successful at the Milwaukee airport. I needed to unblock my creative life force. I redirected my focus toward fully experiencing my emotions. When I dug myself out of the despondency and dire predictions, I recommitted myself to my core intention of expressing my soul's purpose, doing what I came here to Earth to do this lifetime. The lobby became brighter. I lightened up, too. I felt an intuitive pull to go back to the meeting hall. Returning to the room, I discovered . . . Hey! One person had shown up!

And what a person! A shade over five feet tall, she was a somewhat elderly lady with long, gray hair radiating out in all directions from under a feathered, wide-brimmed hat. She was decked out in what one might call a dress for lack of another term. Her frock-like attire was composed of hundreds of bright, exotic shreds of different fabrics unceremoniously sewn together by hand

254 Inner Coach: Outer Power

in a random, helter-skelter manner. Her whimsical gown was decorated with little pieces of glass diamonds, mirrors, glitter and other shiny objects obviously gathered from the streets and back alleys of San Francisco. Adorned with a hippie shoulder bag with beaded dangles, she was altogether a colorful and eye-catching sight!

The garish garment caught and reflected the dazzling lights of the room's chandelier at her slightest movement as she stood on a chair in the middle of the vacant meeting room. Ignoring my presence, this crackpot crone in her resplendent recycled robe was pontificating to the sea of lonely chairs. To my extreme consternation, the zealot railed to the deserted room in a shrill, loud voice about the imminent coming of the Great White Brotherhood/Sisterhood. These heavenly saviors would arrive in spaceships to carry humans safely away when the drastic Earth changes begin. The catastrophic upheavals were to begin very soon. Her hands waving frantically, she clutched homemade flyers covered with detailed maps showing the Bay Area parks in which our extraterrestrial brothers and sisters would land to carry the "chosen ones" away. Basically, she was being a very responsible and informative civil defense worker, except she wasn't working for the U.S. government—and she had no audience!

Suddenly, she stopped her tirade and turned her gaze on me. In a sweet, quiet voice, she said, "Oh, hello, Keith. Would you mind if I handed out my flyers to the people who are coming to your seminar? I'm sure the same people who come to your gathering will want to know where to be picked up by the spaceships when the Earth changes come."

It was easy for me to be magnanimous since she could hardly distract an absent audience from the focus of my talk. So I replied, "Oh, sure, it's no problem. Do whatever you want . . . uh, what did you say your name was again?"

"Everyone knows me, Keith. I'm the Kosmic Lady."

I nodded and smiled. I'm sure it was a condescending smile. My calm, friendly response was a façade. I was angry. *What's going on? Have I invested over five thousand dollars in publicity, room rental and travel costs to attract one person? Am I supposed to give a seminar to one crazy old lady who isn't even interested in what I have to say? She's obviously an unbalanced person who only came to use my meeting room to present her own agenda!*

Humph! Well, she's wasted her time, too. There isn't a single
person to take her stupid flyers! Serves her right!

Vexed beyond words, I stalked out of the room. Sitting in a
corner of the lobby, I gazed out at the city lights and allowed my
disappointment, anger and frustration with the whole affair—and
particularly with this Kosmic Lady character—to consume me. I
was distraught at the image of her grandstanding from a chair in
the middle of an unoccupied meeting room, preaching and waving
her hands full of flyers as if she were addressing a huge crowd.

As I succumbed to my feelings, my mood began to shift.
Then, to my surprise, I found myself appreciating the woman's
spunk and passion. The Kosmic Lady really did care about people.
She sincerely wanted folks to be picked up and taken to safety
during the coming crisis in *her* universe. She had nerve and heart.
Why, I liked her! Furthermore, I was no longer angry or frustrated.
In appreciating this unusual, yet obviously compassionate woman,
I began to feel less alone and abandoned by God. At least *she*
showed up! I chuckled to myself. I'd become so serious about the
whole financial fiasco, I'd actually resented the woman for
wanting to hand out flyers to *my* nonexistent people! Go figure!

It appeared I was meant to spend five thousand dollars and fly
all the way to San Francisco just to meet the Kosmic Lady. What a
cosmic comedy!

I began to feel so accepting of the Kosmic Lady and the
apparent failure of the event, I decided to go back to the seminar
room to enjoy her. It was almost okay with me to have come this
far and spend this much money just to meet this lively character.

By now, it was around eight o'clock. To my shock, when I
walked into the meeting hall, I discovered six new people sitting
there. In chatting with them, I discovered each had come to my
talk *because of* the Kosmic Lady! Each had either been handed
one of my flyers by her personally, or picked up a flyer at a public
location where the Kosmic Lady placed them. This wild and
wacky dame had taken stacks of my flyers from a metaphysical
bookstore and distributed them to other stores and cafés throughout
the city. She even handed out my notices individually to people on
the streets.

What an angel! How could I possibly be angry with her!
I mused.

Then I wondered, *what made me change my mind about her even before I was given the miracle of six people showing up because of her?*

I replayed what I'd done while sitting in the hotel lobby. I'd focused on what I liked about the Kosmic Lady, rather than what I disliked about her. I'd found something about her I could agree with, even enjoy. I had shifted my attention from judging her to respecting her. Driven by a strong, intuitive urge, I excused myself from the small group and returned to my seat in the lobby. My goal was to find and release all my remaining negative feelings and judgments about this divine messenger in disguise. As I embraced and transmuted each emotion and evaluation, my perception of her shifted from derision to total appreciation. As my criticisms of her dissolved, I discovered many qualities I could wholeheartedly admire about her Celestial Ladyship: her contagious enthusiasm and joy, her willingness to help, and her boundless concern for the well-being of all people on the planet.

I realized the Kosmic Lady's presence forced me out of the dire somberness and self-absorption of my important workshop and my oh-so-significant, new career. Her spirit of spontaneous, unreserved sharing with people was catching. Her delight in the play and mystery of life was freeing me from the psychological prison of trying to control the unfolding of the universe.

I returned to the seminar room to discover my current, open, flowing state was continuing to produce miracles. There were over thirty more people in the hall, many of whom had come through the efforts of my cosmic friend.

The presentation was loads of fun. Filled and emboldened with the supportive magic of the entire day, I was very relaxed and natural. I loosened up, let my hair down and became more like the Kosmic Lady.

Then, near the end of my talk, right when everyone was very quiet and peaceful in a meditative state, the Kosmic Lady stood up on her chair. In her grating voice, she waved her flyers and exhorted *my* audience to watch for the coming of the spaceships of the Great White Brotherhood/Sisterhood. She was the cosmic civil defense worker again, declaring to *my* people where to go to be picked up by our extraterrestrial friends when the drastic Earth changes begin. I started shouting at her. Then I quickly halted my words and chastised myself, *My audience? My people? She was*

responsible for attracting more than half of them! I realized
what an arrogant, inaccurate idiot I was being. And I was still
judging her. So, right on the stage, I closed my eyes to find what
evaluation was still lingering in my consciousness. *Yes, I was still
critical about the way she dressed and the crazy way she acted.*
I acknowledged and released all remaining negative feelings about
the Kosmic Lady. This purging process moved me into a state of
total love and appreciation for her just as she was.

As soon as I released my last judgment, my personal celestial
messenger stopped shouting about the end of the world and the
space people coming. She shifted tone and tact one hundred and
eighty degrees. Calmly, with great dignity, the Kosmic Lady
declared to the group, "The Brotherhood and Sisterhood of the
Ascended Masters are very grateful to Keith for coming to San
Francisco to bring this empowering program to us." She looked
directly at me. "All the angelic and devic realms in all dimensions
fully support everything you're doing. They're going to make sure
you have plenty of people for your workshops. Thank you, Keith."
Then she daintily sat down.

After the seminar, twelve people signed up for my complete
weeklong workshop. The trip ended up being a very successful
excursion to San Francisco, professionally and personally.

Perhaps you think, as I did, that the Kosmic Lady was a flash-
in-the-pan occurrence. Not so! Let me share "The Rest of the Story."

A year later, I discovered the metaphysical mystery of the
Kosmic Lady was even grander than her physical appearance.
During another free talk in New York City, I related my mystical
encounter with this cosmic jester to my audience. I shared the
delightful story of the Kosmic Lady because I knew New Yorkers
would enjoy the tale. They encounter a lot of their own Kosmic
Lady types on the streets of Manhattan. The anecdote is also an
excellent example of the creative power of freeing oneself of rigid
judging and labeling of people and situations. After I finished the
story, a very well-dressed man stood up in the back of the room
and introduced himself as a doctor of psychiatry and a member of
the board of New York City's public television station.

"I know the Kosmic Lady," he said. "And she's not a loony
street person. She's on four prominent community boards in
San Francisco. She's on the governing board of the city's public

housing authority, an organization for the homeless, and two special committees set up by the mayor of San Francisco. She has two master's degrees and four published books. She's a respected professional consultant in New York, as well as in San Francisco. The Kosmic Lady is a frequent television and radio panelist because of her down-to-earth wisdom and compassion for all life."

This woman, whom I initially labeled a maniac and nuisance, was not at all as she appeared on the surface. I have grown to understand that the universe's messengers come in many forms to assist us to fulfill our spiritual goals and heartfelt dreams. Now, whenever I stay focused on my intent and on my trust in the universe, cosmic angels appear to help and guide me—as they will for whomever leaves open the door of innocence and acceptance for them to enter.

The Message of the Wild Stallion

People say that what we're all seeking is a meaning for life.
I say that what we're really seeking is
an experience of being alive,
so that our life experiences on the purely physical plane
will have resonance within our innermost being and reality,
so that we can actually feel the rapture of being alive!

JOSEPH CAMPBELL

Hiking in the Arizona canyonlands one winter, I had a chance encounter with a timeless creature—a wild stallion. The bronco's raw, vibrant spirit opened a doorway for me to my own true nature.

Rounding a bend in the dry riverbed, I abruptly came face-to-face with this enchanted, primal creature as he froze in his tracks just across the creek. This lead mustang then broke from the herd and walked toward me. He stopped a few feet from where I stood. Holding my breath in awe, I stayed very still as he inspected me, and I him. He was curious and innocent in a very childlike way, yet majestic, strong and totally sovereign.

Eyes locked, we felt, enjoyed and marveled in each other's being for an eternal moment. The mighty steed and his pack run free on Federal land and have never been ridden or domesticated. I pulsated with the raw and explosive, yet soft energy that emanated from his core. Then he tossed his head, snorted and turned to rejoin his herd. I glowed and quivered in his vibration for the rest of the day.

That night, the spirit of the stallion came to me in an awake vision. He spoke to me gently, as a brother—not in words, but in a direct transmission, in a capsule of complete communication, heart to heart.

"For a long time you humans have been using techniques and processes in an effort to free yourselves from limiting artificial structures and constraints. Your goal is to return to a more relaxed, happy, natural state. Your various approaches have been only partially successful. This is because the very way you have been going about freeing yourself—studied, linear, and logical—has inhibited and, in the end, prevented the very goal you seek: to experience a free-flowing, natural aliveness.

"The only way to recapture the fire you have lost is to reconnect with it directly. Technical and methodical approaches can't sever the ancient layers of deadness and fear surrounding your every breath and movement. Only by touching your original essence—your core life force, infinite spirit, alchemical cauldron of life—will you have enough power to burn your way to freedom and restored vitality.

"Rediscover the fire in your belly, the primal exhilaration that is life itself. Nurture it as you would a pilot light, as if it is the very survival of your soul—which, in fact, it is. Put your attention there and only there. For that passion will not only heal, it will transform. Because that is the prime directive. Because that is what your heart longs to do. Because that is where life itself resides. In this way, you will begin to live again. You will become what you actually are—an energy, a vibration, a star!"

The next day I happened upon one of Carlos Castaneda's accounts of don Juan, a Native American shaman. In this particular story, don Juan spoke about a man whose "spirit is broken," just as a horse is domesticated by "breaking its spirit." As I read the passage, I recalled the power of my meeting with the wild stallion. Realization, like the sun piercing through an early morning fog, dawned on me, "That's it! My spirit was broken. That's what happened!"

I was emotionally shaken by the words I spontaneously spoke aloud. I decided to follow the trail of my strong feelings and find the source of my dramatic reaction. With focused determination, I closely examined my life in an intuitive meditative journey until I returned to the very incident in which my spirit had been broken. I discovered one exact moment when I gave up completely on myself. That was the day I buried deep within me the excitement that life is really about. That was the day I gave up on life itself.

The shutdown occurred when I was a vulnerable teenager in my hometown in western Pennsylvania. I was just beginning my sophomore year in high school. Even though I played first string in my freshman year, I was considering not going out for the school football team this next year. On my Steeltown USA, local football squad, we were trained not only to tackle hard and win, but to hit hard enough to deliberately maim the opposing team players for the length of their high school playing career! This extremely barbaric approach to winning ran so against the grain of my natural human connection with other players that I was willing to buck the system by dropping out of the "program" and everyone's expectations of me.

Several of my teachers took me aside on the first day of classes. I was informed in a very explicit, unsubtle way that I wouldn't pass my courses if I didn't play football for the sake of the school and the town. I felt I needed the cooperation of the system to be accepted at a college and escape the narrow, limited world of my provincial hometown. With the intense pressure and persuasion, I buckled under and went out for the team.

In order to play football, I had to shut down my connection to my true self. I resigned myself to "getting with the program." I decided to follow outside authority, accept the town's values and "adapt to the real world." My spirit died that autumn. In fact, I entombed my enthusiasm for life so well that I hadn't remembered until I did this meditation that natural exuberance and joy ever existed within me!

The act of consciously returning to the exact moment I shut the door to my aliveness had the effect of reconnecting me to the energy of my own eternal spirit. Relinking to the power of my real self immediately shattered the chains of oppression from that fateful decision to close down. Resuscitating my natural vitality had the effect of reopening all the other doors I'd shut in my life to my original, spontaneous, primal passion.

As the stallion promised, the fire of feeling alive returned to me—this time forever!

The Magic of the Present Moment

To see the World in a grain of sand,
And a Heaven in a wild flower,
Hold infinity in the palm of your hand,
And eternity in an hour.

WILLIAM BLAKE

While walking through my home in the Southwest one balmy afternoon in March, a breath of fresh truth blew through an open window. It rode in on a wisp of memory brought forth by a quote I'd just heard from Carolyn Myss, a medical intuit:

"If you could stay fully present for forty-eight hours straight, all the connections and synchronicity would take place that are necessary for your entire life purpose to unfold from that moment on."

I knew instantly those words held very timely and compelling wisdom for me. I felt a forgotten understanding trying to surface into my consciousness. A knowing was attempting to claw its way up to the light of day through eons of dark, entangling vines of illusion, fear and distraction. I tried to reach down past my personality to this intuitive truth, but couldn't quite connect with this dearly missed, orphaned awareness struggling to find its way home.

As I usually do in such situations, I asked for clarity and guidance from Spirit. I requested my inner coach to send me a direct experience so compelling it would lance the veil obscuring my recognition of this truth. Having turned the matter over to divine direction, I continued with my day's activities, confident the answer would come at the right time and in a form I would readily identify.

The next afternoon my buddy Tobias and I were sitting in the backyard welcoming spring back to the desert. Tobias remarked about all the bees hovering around a bottlebrush bush just a few feet from where we were lounging. Spontaneously, I launched into an unexpected, effusive tribute to the plant. I explained to Tobias how the fiery bush was almost always in bloom with brilliant red blossoms radiating in every direction; and how excited bees, hummingbirds and dragonflies constantly converged upon it. I talked about how vital and giving the bush was, and how willing it was to share its life with me and any other creatures who wanted to partake of its energy.

As I was extolling the plant's virtues, I suddenly realized how unabashedly I loved and appreciated this bush!

At that precise instant, a seedpod on the bush burst open and one of its seeds shot toward me, landing gently on my cheek. Startled and delighted, Tobias and I watched in awe at the simple, yet profound return of affection by the bush. I'd never been kissed by a plant before! I felt intimately honored and loved.

For a timeless hour, Tobias and I sat in silence, aware of every sound and sensation, yet noticing nothing in particular. I vibrated with the wind. I pulsated with the peaceful primal rhythm of the Earth. Once we were able to talk, Tobias recounted experiencing the same eternity of connection with all life surrounding him.

Over the next four days, I encountered uncanny movement and change in my life. Long-stuck problems were suddenly resolved. Dead situations found new life and transformed. My health improved markedly. Money showed up at my door out of the blue. It was quite puzzling, for all of this happened with no effort or action on my part. Then it hit me. This renewal and transmutation was a result of the hour I spent *being fully present* in the backyard with the bottlebrush plant.

I remembered Carolyn Myss' prophetic words and asking my inner coach for guidance on the subject. My soul had used the bottlebrush bush to help me slip into being totally present in the moment, so that I'd experience the extraordinary effect being fully present can have on one's life.

Sometimes the truth is so obvious, it's illusive. Conceptually, I'd always understood the importance of living in the present moment—the value of "being here now." My encounter with the bush took me to a realm beyond the concept. The benefit of being in the present moment was dramatically demonstrated to me in a way that was undeniable and life-changing. Suddenly, a spiritual *philosophy* became *reality*. I *experienced* that the blueprint for our lives exists only in the Eternal Present—not in the past or the future.

I absorbed the fact that our true purpose—design, script, dream—only abides in the present. Each person's specific, detailed life plan lies woven within his or her eternally present vibration. The plan and the vibration are one in the same. When our attention, our creative life force, is fully absorbed in the moment, it is also automatically focused on our unique life plan. Thus, all the necessary connections in consciousness are made for the individual blueprint to unfold. During the times we are fully in the present, our precise dreams are fully energized into existence.

To have everything in life work perfectly—to have life manifest just as the heart desires—all we need to do is consciously stay as fully present as possible. Each moment that we are in the Eternal Now, our dreams are being energized into existence. Our soul (sole) task is to stay present being simply who we truly are—spontaneously, purely. In the present is the seed of destiny. Whenever we show up for our dream, our dream will show up in our world.

These insights have brought me to a new understanding of the awesome power of arriving and remaining in the vibration of the Eternal Present Now Moment. The Present is the matrix for our personal dream, as well as for the collective divine dream. The Now is the seat of magic, alchemy and grace. The Moment is the home of the heart and all its accumulated wisdom. The Eternal Present Now Moment is the gateway to all that is, was and ever will be. It is the portal to freedom and union.

The Plant Fairy Speaks

Every blade of grass has its angel
who bends over it and whispers,
"Grow, grow!"

THE TALMUD

"How can I cultivate communication with the nature spirits of trees, animals, wind, birds, rocks and plants?"

"What approach or attitude opens the door to seeing and talking with elves, fairies, gnomes, angels and Ascended Masters?"

People often question me about how they can deliberately develop a personal connection with nonphysical beings in other dimensions of reality. Since this form of communication unfolded naturally for me, I've never had a good answer. My process was invisible to me. Finally, so many people came to me expressing a sincere longing to see and talk with angels, nature devas and spirit guides, I felt compelled to find a way to help them. So I asked my inner coach the same question my many friends asked me:

"Why is direct connection to beings in other dimensions a natural ability for a few people and yet seemingly impossible for so many others?"

A piece of the puzzle revealed itself to me during a casual early morning conversation in San Francisco. The previous day, I'd asked for intuitive guidance on how people could foster multisensory perception in order for them to have direct personal communication with diverse nonphysical realms. The following morning, I was eating breakfast with a dear friend. Lois is a delightful, adventurous, spunky woman well into her eighties. At one point in the conversation, she shared how she'd been opening up spiritually for sixty years, but was still unable to see or talk with her spirit guides—St. Germain, Jesus and Sai Baba—or with angels and nature spirits.

"So many times I'll feel a warmth akin to a presence in the room with me. The connection gives me a vivid sense of serenity and comfort. But that's as far as it goes. I'm still not able to make further conscious contact with the energy or entity."

Questioning her further, I learned that she enjoys a distinct resonance with plants. She can sometimes feel an energy emanating from her plants, but is never able to see the plant's aura or subtle body, or to have a dialogue with the spirit of the plant.

"Keith," she implored, "How do I do it? How can I connect with my guides and my plants in a more conscious and meaningful way?"

Her expression and words were so poignant. I could feel how significant this issue was for her. Then, at that very moment, a faint glow began to radiate from the little houseplant she had on the breakfast table. As Lois continued to express her desire and longing to interact more directly with nonphysical friends, the light at the center of the plant shown brighter and brighter.

I knew the light was the deva, the nature spirit, of this plant. Upon my recognition of its presence, the fairy deva shone so brilliantly it almost hurt my eyes. I breathed a sigh of relief. Obviously, this dramatic light demonstration was a direct response to Lois' prayers and desires. I speculated to myself, *This is great. Here's her answer. Thank you, Spirit!*

Pointing to the brilliant glow radiating from the heart of the plant, I exclaimed, "Well, there you go! There's your answer."

Lois said nothing. She simply sat there with a puzzled look on her face, staring in the direction of my outstretched finger. "What answer? I don't see anything unusual. I don't understand what you're pointing at!"

She didn't see the light. She saw nothing! "What about that light there, Lois," I coached. "That deva, that fairy, that glow?"

She strained and squinted. She still didn't see anything unusual.

I urged, "Do you sense anything? Do you feel a presence, a warmth, any unusual sensation at all?"

Discouraged, she sighed and responded, "No, nothing."

By now I was perplexed and becoming extremely frustrated. I asked my inner knowing, "How can I help her?"

The plant spirit spoke right up:

"Ask her: 'If you saw me, would you tell anyone?'"

I took the deva's cue. I softly inquired, "Lois, if you saw the glow of this deva right now . . . if you communicated with it in some way . . . if you had any definite interaction with it at all . . . would you tell anyone?"

"No, absolutely not!" she replied immediately, abruptly sitting up straight in her chair. "I've gotten in such trouble talking about things like that. You can lose friends that way."

Lois' reply was so terse and fearful, I realized instantly why she never experienced spiritual visions, multisensory awareness or communications with other dimensions. The barrier was *her own* unconsciously held, internal, emotional belief system. She believed if she communicated with the nonphysical world and people found out, they would think she was a foolish old woman. Lois was afraid people would say she was crazy. This, in turn, would cause her an enormous degree of shame. Lois was in denial. Unconsciously, of course, as with all denial. She was actually refusing contact, *blocking herself* from opening to the connection she so desperately longed for in her life.

Now I understood. I thought to myself, *Each of us is in charge of what kind of spiritual experiences we can and do have. By the receptivity level of our own unconscious, emotional beliefs, we determine how much we can open to the full array of all the possible dimensions and aspects of life. We are the keepers and creators of our own magic and miracles.*

I shared my insight with Lois. She definitely saw how she psychologically hindered her own ability to have the spiritual experiences for which she so longed. I assisted Lois to feel, release and integrate her strong emotions about publicly expressing her natural spiritual abilities.

Lois was a trooper! She went deep inside and experienced her emotions as "sensations," instead of calling them "fear," "shame" and "loneliness." Holding her emotions within a neutral, generic framework such as "sensations," "energy" or "vibration," she was willing to open to and fully feel these energies she normally identifies as specific emotions. When she didn't define or name the sensations she was feeling with a "negative" label, she didn't resist feeling the emotion. When she approached the feelings in an emotionally uncharged way—as "vibration"—she was willing and able to fully experience and embrace the energy of each feeling.

Fully feeling the energy of an emotion allows the energy of the emotion to fully express itself. When the energy of a feeling is given the space—the acceptance—to fully express itself, it is complete, done, fulfilled. The energy of the emotion dissipates by the act of being integrated—embraced—back into our neutral field of energy, our creative life force. The feeling is no longer a block or hindrance to our intentions and actions.

After a short while, Lois was much lighter and a lot freer of the vibration generally called "fear." In fact, she remarked that the sensation she used to label "fear," now felt like excitement! She felt very open to the possibility of developing her innate spiritual skills no matter who found out about them!

The last time I connected with Lois, she reported she's seeing a distinct glow around certain flowers in her garden. She's also feeling a definite, strong presence and a long-desired tranquility when speaking to her roses. Last week, a daffodil actually talked back!

And, she no longer keeps her magic to herself. She's told two friends so far. And they don't think she's a crackpot. In fact, they'd like to learn themselves how to converse with plant spirits.

Enjoying a Near-Death Experience

Nothing real can be threatened.
Nothing unreal exists.
Herein lies the peace of God.

THE COURSE IN MIRACLES

Out of the blue, I felt dizzy. I grabbed for the nearest chair to stable myself. It was early afternoon. I was walking around my house contemplating an upcoming seminar when, without warning, I became faint and very nauseous. Sitting down quietly for a while, the symptoms passed. But the minute I went back to planning, the strange sensations started all over again. The room started to spin, the nausea returned, and I became extremely lightheaded. At one point, I tried walking across the room, but couldn't. I sat down in the middle of the floor, incapable of making it back to my chair until the room quit orbiting around me.

Finally, I made it back to my desk, and the phone rang. My friend Jill asked about the workshop I was scheduled to deliver that evening.

"Yes, I have a class tonight, but I don't see how I can possibly do it." I explained the symptoms I experienced all afternoon. "I certainly can't drive a vehicle in this condition," I concluded.

"Oh, Keith, so many people will be disappointed if the evening is cancelled. If I drove you there, do you think you would be able to conduct the seminar?" she asked.

"I think so. I seem to be fine as long as I'm sitting down. I could refrain from walking about or becoming too physical during the presentation."

Jill immediately volunteered to chauffeur me to the event, and we agreed upon a time.

Nestling the telephone back in its cradle, I checked my watch. I had four hours to relax. I distinctly remember thinking, *Perhaps I should simply lie down and take a nap*, when all of a sudden my body was lifted as if some outside force was carrying me! The next thing I knew, I was driving my truck to the post office about a mile down the hill to mail a letter—a letter that could have easily gone out the next day. As if in a trance, I walked from the vehicle to the post office, mailed the letter and started back home.

I remember driving up the hill. Then total blackness. I couldn't feel anything, see anything or hear anything. Gradually, I began to experience a very familiar sensation. It was the feeling I have when I meet with my guides, whom I call the Council of Elders.

My Council of Elders is comprised of nonphysical friends who make themselves available to me when I need spiritual advice, emotional help or simply friendly support.

We meet in consciousness in our subtle bodies. Being Spirit, they are always around me, always available to call upon for guidance or encouragement. I call the psychic space we meet in the "Great Hall."

My subtle body was in the Great Hall. My physical body was upside down in my overturned truck in a ditch.

When my spirit guides appeared, the first words they spoke to me were:

"We've been trying to reach you all day. We tried to contact you in the usual ways. We sent messages through your intuition. We flashed the usual, external, visual signs. We let ourselves be known. You ignored us. You kept slamming the door on our efforts to connect with you. It's very important we speak with you now. Because it is a matter that cannot wait, we had to force a meeting."

As soon as they spoke, I deduced, *Of course, that's what the dizziness was all about! A message was trying to come through and I was blocking it. I tried to knock myself out of commission by getting dizzy, becoming nauseous and fluctuating between consciousness and unconsciousness. A communication portal was opening in my living room, and I was ignoring it. It's so obvious now. I was in resistance to connecting with my inner coach and Spirit through my guides.*

Then it dawned on me, *I was in denial. I was suppressing fear. I didn't want to connect with my inner coach and guides because I'm afraid to find out the next step in my soul's expression in the world. I can see why my spirit friends had to force me out of my unconscious resistance with a car crash!*

The meeting was about me, and my mentors were very blunt. They implored:

"You have been spending your time, energy and attention relating with people in ways which are not nurturing to you. Nor are these ways nurturing to the people who you are supposedly assisting. You are spending your time, energy and attention involved in overly dramatic, obsolete patterns of dependency with other people. Even though both parties in each situation *think* the relationship is supportive, it is not. These patterns of interacting with people no longer serve you. Nor do they serve the other people involved. We realize you *believe* what you are doing is beneficial and loving. It is not. The manner in which you connect is not helping you; it is not helping them. It is not loving to you; it is not loving to them."

Next, the Elders visually showed me all the relationships in which I was perpetuating outmoded, unnurturing patterns. I saw where I was going along with arrangements that were no longer right for me. I reviewed situations in which I was engaged in activities I really didn't want to do any more. I felt how I was continuing to interact with people in ways that had lost their meaning and integrity for me—and for the other folks involved. In many various roles—as therapist, healer, business partner, friend or lover—I was on automatic, running old tapes, trying to connect in ways that had long since lost their original realness, aliveness and value. I was no longer on my heart path, neither personally nor professionally.

Fully awake and conscious, I observed these scenes from my life as if watching a movie. After viewing many examples, it finally registered with me what my guides were attempting to convey. I was operating out of habitual patterns. And these ways of being helpful and being loving weren't reflecting the real me anymore. And because this behavior was no longer authentic for me, it was no longer my truth. And, therefore, I wasn't being of real assistance to these people. I was actually keeping them—and myself—stuck in old places!

I took a quick breath and said, "Okay, I see it. I see what you're saying."

Expressing the will and wisdom of my inner coach, my dear friends, the Council of Elders, continued:

"You have to stop these ways of relating now. It is time for you to move to a higher level of energy and vibration in your life expression on Earth. In order to evolve to your next stage of soul unfoldment, you must let go of these outdated interpersonal routines, dependencies and addictions.

"There is a second reason why you must retire your long-existing habits, open yourself to your next level of spiritual evolution, and act more from fresh intuition. The consciousness of Planet Earth is unfolding at an accelerated pace. The number of people awakening spiritually is increasing. Events are happening faster now. Actions trigger quicker reactions. Karma is more instantaneous. Human behavior results in almost immediate consequences. Your inner consciousness reflects more rapidly in your outer world.

"In the past, you could plateau at one spiritual level for a while. You could coast on the same level of awareness for a long time. It worked out all right to be a little sloppy—not fully present, not totally in your integrity and not completely honest. You could get away with it, Keith, because there was a lot of leeway then. Human affairs were evolving more slowly.

"However, with the current quickening, every thought and every emotion not dealt with consciously is going to have instant repercussions in your personal universe. For your own safety, happiness and health, you must be more aware and impeccable in thought and action. You need to be unequivocally honest about what is intuitively right—and not right—for you to do, for the sake of yourself and for the people you love. There simply is not as much room for sloppiness, fudging and hedging as there was in the past."

One of the most enriching aspects of conversing with these celestial entities is the total absence of judgment or evaluation on their part. When I'm with them, I bask in the feeling of being fully supported and loved just as I am. In their presence, the aura of total acceptance is palpable. Within this space of tangible grace, they assist me to move toward my highest good and my best interest.

Therefore, even though the Elders were using harsher words than ever before, I didn't feel reprimanded. I simply felt, *Oh. Yes. Right. This meeting is about my spiritual evolution. If I make these changes, I'll be happier. The people I love will be happier. We'll all be more in tune with who we really are and with the accelerating spiritual awakening of Earth.*

I was very aware I received a great gift from my mentors that day. I understood I needed to shift my whole being and lifestyle. I needed to "up" my level of alertness, integrity and accuracy big time.

My guides and I were so intimately connected in the space of Oneness, there was no need for me to speak my feelings. They knew how I felt *as I felt it*. My advisors concluded:

"Good! However, this meeting has taken longer than we anticipated. Your body in the physical realm has died. Now you must make a choice. You can go back to the life where you left off on Earth, or you can continue with your soul's evolution in another Earth lifetime or in another dimension."

I took a quick inventory of where I had left off on Earth: my close friends, *The Dream Workshops* I was facilitating, and my connections to other people on our shared spiritual path. In my heart, I knew at once I couldn't ask for a better set-up for my soul to learn and grow. I didn't have to think about my answer. I resolved within myself, *I'll go back and pick up where I left off.*

No sooner had I reached my conclusion than POP! I was upside-down, back in my physical body, inside my overturned vehicle, blood flooding over my face. With ambulance emergency workers pulling me out of my nearly totaled truck, I was back in my present lifetime. They quickly hoisted me onto a gurney, strapping down my head, arms and legs to stop any movement on my part until my neck and spine were X-rayed.

The ride to the hospital was short and quick. On a Friday night with a full moon rising, the scene was very hectic and busy.

The emergency room was packed with too many patients and not enough doctors, nurses or examination booths.

Rushed first to X-ray for pictures of my neck and spine, I was returned to the emergency room, still strapped tightly against the gurney. The attendant deposited me in a crowded, narrow hallway, reassuring me, "Someone will be back to get you once your X-rays are read." I asked him to call my friend Jill and gave him the number.

People in pain were everywhere, moaning, crying and begging for assistance. The place was in absolute chaos! Two policemen propped a profusely bleeding man against the wall by my head. Each of the officers held a gun pointed directly at the detainee whom they obviously considered a dangerous person. They wanted the offender sewn up so they could take him to jail. A harried nurse told them abruptly that they would have to wait their turn along with everyone else.

Blood from the captive's wounds spurted onto my face. Passing people bumped into me. Since I was securely tied down, I couldn't position either my arms or head to shield myself from the mania. I reflected, *I can't move. I can't protect myself. I should be freaked out. I should be terrified.* As a child, I didn't like cramped spaces and I never let myself be tied up playing cowboy and Indians. As an adult, I still panic when enclosed in tight places or unable to flex my arms or legs. Yet I felt no anxiety. An ecstasy of being totally cared for and loved enveloped me.

Jill showed up. Taking one look at me, she began to cry. I had to persuade her that I was fine—better than fine. She reported later to me that I repeated the same phrase over and over—"Oh, there is so much love, just so much love!"—for the entire time I was immobilized in the hallway waiting for my turn to see a doctor.

The X-rays came back negative. There were no broken bones or internal injuries. My restraints were removed. I was wheeled into a private booth. A plastic surgeon was called in to attend to a couple of severe cuts. A serious gash disfigured my face from the top of my forehead to my chin. The wound missed my left eye by a whisker. Also, my right arm was severely slashed at the elbow.

The surgeon examined my face. "I don't know if I'll be able to close this lesion or not. You're going to need a lot of plastic surgery when this heals, my friend." Sixteen stitches later, he grunted satisfaction with his work and turned his attention to my left elbow. That took another twenty-four stitches. "This laceration will be quite a bit more painful due to the location," he remarked. "Hard to keep together. The arm will probably remain swollen for a while. I'll see you in my office in three weeks, and we'll discuss plastic surgery for your face. The discharge nurse will set the appointment for you and give you instructions about how to care for the wounds until I see you. I'll write out a prescription for some pain medication."

Patting my shoulder, the surgeon motioned for an attendant to wheel me back to the hallway. While I awaited discharge, several strangers wished me well. One of the policemen took the time to say a few encouraging words to me. I continued feeling intense love wash over me from everyone with whom I came in contact. Finally, a nurse handed me release papers to sign, an appointment card for the plastic surgeon, several prescriptions, the usual instruction sheet on what to do if this or that happened, and orders to see my personal physician within the next couple of days. After driving me home, Jill helped me get settled in, and then dashed to the druggist for medication to ease the pain in my arm and face.

Every time I moved my left arm, the stitches on my elbow were stretched. The wound wept a lot and continued to bleed. My entire limb was still swollen almost three times its size and caked with blood. I cleaned it as much as possible, but the slightest touch caused excruciating pain. Yes, I was healing, but it was a slow process. Sore and stiff, I found it difficult to walk and move around. My thinking was still somewhat cloudy.

One of my *Dream Workshops* was scheduled in Boston just four days after the crash. I should have rescheduled the seminar immediately after the accident, but *something* kept me from taking action. It was as if my inner self *wanted* me to go to Boston. And, after the meeting with my guides during the car incident, I was definitely into paying attention to my inner coach!

It was painfully evident that four days were not enough time to heal sufficiently, physically or mentally, to travel and then facilitate a seminar consisting of thirty people. But it was too late to back out. The workshop was sold out. A friend packed my bags. I hoped for the best—and prayed!

The flight from Phoenix to Boston is a long one. I tried to secure a window seat on the left side of the airplane to keep my bloody, swollen arm out of the sight of a seat mate, and out of harm's way from flight attendants and passers-by. I ended up on the left side, but on the aisle. Some poor passenger in a middle seat would have a bloody limb in their face unless the swelling went down enough for me to put on a long-sleeved shirt or jacket.

The day arrived. Still swollen and sensitive, my arm would not tolerate the pain of any covering. Even though it was going to be extremely cold in Boston, I boarded the plane wearing a short-sleeved shirt.

The ride to the airport took its toll on me. I was asleep before the airplane left the ground without even noticing that someone had sat in the seat next to me. Every so often throughout the trip, I remember stirring from my slumber and finding myself touching my sore limb. Each time, my arm hurt less. Dully registering the improvement, I would quickly doze off again. Astoundingly, by the time the plane descended into Boston, the swelling had disappeared and all the pain was gone!

Fully awake now, I turned to the woman sitting next to me, apologized for my bloody arm, and briefly explained about my truck accident. "And now, it seems to be mended," I exclaimed wondrously.

"Oh, yes. I know. I've been doing Reiki energy healing on your arm since we left Phoenix."

"Did you notice that I woke up every hour or so and touched my arm?" I asked.

"Yes," she smiled. "It was very gratifying. I could tell you noticed some improvement."

I thanked her profusely for her generous and effective healing. The plane landed. I found I could move my arm easily and painlessly. I could touch it. I could put a jacket on. In fact, the functioning of my limb was totally recovered from that time on, and I was able to maneuver very well wearing a jacket during my entire stay in Boston.

At the workshop, another miracle occurred. Even though my arm was totally restored, my body was extremely sore. Walking and moving about was still difficult, and my mind continued to move in slow motion. The seminar was going well when one of the female participants named Sherry became very emotionally reactive and started screaming at me. She was intensely angry about a personal issue not connected with me or the group. However, the facilitator is usually the first target for anyone who is upset in a workshop. After all, the seminar leader is trained and paid to deal with people's emotional expressions in a compassionate and professional manner.

In the past, I handled this type of situation with tricks of the trade learned over the years. I'd deal with someone's anger with diplomatic, neutralizing words, tone of voice, gestures and actions. Still handicapped with my recovering condition, my usual quick wit, articulation and creativity failed to surface. I was unable to muster any strategy, defense or even reaction to Sherry's attack. Without any apparent alternatives, I surrendered to the predicament, whispering to myself, *God help me!*

To my surprise and delight, my confrontation with the woman's anger transformed into an experience radically different from anything I've ever encountered before. I "saw" the anger coming at me as a kind of frenetic, frazzled, jagged wave of energy. Yet I *knew* I was protected from the force of the anger!

Encircling me, I perceived a translucent bubble of energy, or aura, through which no harmful emotions or vibrations could pass. I watched the oncoming wave of anger—that irritating, destructive, harsh, sharp energy we call anger—split apart as it reached the protective vibrational shield surrounding me. The anger couldn't reach me! The threatening energy of the wave never got within three feet of me. However, what did reach me through my protective bubble was a flow of pure love. That's how I experienced the emotional energy coming from the attacking woman. The very person who was screaming at me was feeding me love. What a blessing!

Sharing, later, from her perspective, Sherry reported that she became increasingly angry as I stared back blankly at her verbal attacks without responding in any expected way. She said that her frustration with my lack of reaction combined with her rage to form a powerful wave of cresting energy, which she directed toward me. Astonishingly, this overwhelming emotion went out from her and then inexplicably returned, washing over her in a blissful shower of total acceptance. She said she tried to resist the flow of euphoria, but finally realized her folly, surrendering to the love. The energy she had been labeling "anger" then dissipated into a sea of calm and self-compassion. After I survived this emotional eruption, the rest of the workshop was a breeze and a resounding success.

Returning to Phoenix, I picked up the task of dealing with the consequences of the auto accident: the doctors, lawyers, hospital staff, insurance agents, car rental personnel and the body shop workers. You know, "regular" people in the "regular" world. To my knowledge, there wasn't a metaphysically minded person in the group. During my interaction with these ordinary folks, whom I presumed to be very disinterested in spiritual affairs, another life-changing gift from the accident surfaced.

For some mysterious reason, every person I dealt with was enormously curious about the intimate details of my *personal* experience of the accident.

"Why did you go off the road?" they each asked.

"I blacked out," I replied, not wanting to go into any specifics.

"Why did you black out?"

"I don't know," I answered, trying desperately to end the questioning.

They persisted. "What happened when you blacked out?"

With each person, I tried to change the subject or ignore the queries. My meeting with the Elders was not something I felt I could possibly tell total strangers, especially people I prejudged as not being able to hear or handle the spiritual truth of my revelation during the accident. But people refused to be swayed from being told the complete story. They pressed me to tell them more. Everyone wanted to know what happened when I blacked out.

So, eventually, I threw in the towel. Over the next two or three months, I recounted in depth my near-death experience to the personnel I interacted with at the doctor's office, law firm, hospital, insurance company, car rental and body shop.

I told them I met with Jesus, St. Germain, Sai Baba, Mother Mary and my other spiritual guides. I explained those mentors are beings who comfort, console and give me advice when I need it. Because these folks insisted on hearing it, I related the whole story.

And the more I shared the "Rest of the Story," the easier it became. You see, before my accident, I believed I couldn't tell my whole truth publicly. I felt I couldn't discuss the spiritual aspect of my life with so-called "regular" people because I had the preconception they didn't want to hear it, wouldn't understand it, or would be scared by it. Over the years, I'd developed a defensive barrier between me and others based on beliefs about people's limited interest in—and capacity to hear—my truth. Fortunately, with the openness and receptivity I found following the accident, those beliefs bit the dust—along with the wall of separation between me and "regular" people. Thank God!

The doctors, nurses and staff I saw for my post-operative follow-up kept me in their offices several times to discuss my inner experience in great detail. One doctor held my hand and asked if we could just sit in silence for twenty minutes in his office. I've never before encountered a doctor who wanted to simply be with me in silence in the middle of a busy day to contemplate the wonder of my spiritual unfoldment!

When I went to see the plastic surgeon to have him remove my stitches, he didn't believe I was the person he'd treated in the hospital emergency room. In fact, the good doctor asked to see my driver's license to confirm I was Keith Varnum. He said the person he sewed up couldn't possibly be the same person standing before him. The wound on my face was too well healed for the short amount of time involved. Also, the manner in which the injury had mended astounded him. There was no scarring at all and no need for "a lot of plastic surgery." The gash had sealed so well the stitches were barely visible. Their removal was difficult because they'd become imbedded in healed flesh.

In the weeks after my accident, my old beliefs, judgments and prejudices against hospitals, doctors, insurance companies, judges, lawyers and policemen began fading away in a very gentle and graceful manner.

My altered experience of life after my accident reminded me of a movie called *Blown Away* with Jeff Bridges. The film is about a few individuals who miraculously survive a plane crash in which the crew and all the other passengers perish in the extreme devastation. The gripping movie dramatizes how the people's unlikely survival changes their lives in a very profound way. The survivors discover they've entered a strange, new world in which old relationships and connections feel awkwardly unfamiliar, uncomfortable and in need of change. My world also was radically shifted after my return from the brink of death. I found I was having fresh, new feelings and reactions to old, familiar situations and relationships.

I remember the way I was before my accident. I recall my old ways of doing things. I used to have to control everything and everybody. Those old controlling ways are no longer necessary, for now I move within a bubble of protection and knowing. As I turn more and more of my personality—identity, ego, mind—over to the guidance of my inner coach, my sense of well-being increases and my need to micro-manage every detail of my life decreases.

The truck crash was the breakthrough to this new me. In talking to my asute mentors, the Council of Elders, about the extraordinary outcomes of the accident, I gained more insight into the ways and means of self-transformation. My guides shared that the extreme measures of the car crash and the injuries were necessary in my case because my inner coach was in immediate need of more freedom within which to influence my spiritual development. My personality was holding on tightly to a bygone reality and outmoded ways of trying to feel in control and safe— so tightly my soul plan couldn't unfold to my next stage. My guides explained that my fierce grip on those obsolete patterns and beliefs had to be shaken loose. "Strong medicine" was needed, as my Native American friend Medicine Cloud would say. It took a car crash to shake me free of my death grip on an outdated image of myself and old, unnurturing ways of living.

The crash was the day the personality of Keith Varnum died and the spirit of Keith Varnum took charge. It was the day Keith Varnum began to truly live from his heart and soul.

Indiana Jones and the Volcano

There are three kinds of people:
those who are immovable, those who are movable, and
those who move!

ARAB PROVERB

Experiencing a live volcano was on top of our agenda when my friend Rob and I visited the exotic land of Costa Rica. The plane touched down in the capital city of San Jose, and, after clearing customs, we headed for the car rental to pick up a 4x4 and a map to Mt. Arenal, the nearest active volcano.

After an arduous drive through torrential rain, we finally arrived in a quiet village supposedly at the foot of a fire-belching monster. I say *supposedly* because it was so foggy, we weren't even sure a volcano existed. We couldn't see a tree a block away, let alone a volcanic mountain looming 5,000 feet above us.

Locals claim if you really listen closely, you can hear the beast rumble. We never heard a whimper. By the second misty day and night of no sighting, I suspected the local population had fabricated the story of an erupting volcano in order to attract tourist dollars. A volcano of convenience. No muss, no fuss. Just some imaginary rumbling every so often that only the locals hear from a volcano no one ever sees because of the rain and fog!

Near the end of our second day of waiting out the rain, we were eating a tasty native dinner of red beans and rice at a colorful local dive when the owner of the café strolled over to our table. Without hesitation or invitation, he plopped himself down. Miguel appeared to me exactly as I've always imagined don Juan of Carlos Castaneda fame to look. His face was dark and swarthy with a kind but inscrutable expression. Staring straight into our eyes, he declared in halting English, "You want to *know* volcano, not just *look* at it."

Being a veteran traveler, I have learned to be agreeable in a foreign country and, in general, say "yes" to practically everything spoken to me by the locals. Not realizing the full import of the distinction between the words Miguel had used, I responded amicably, "Yeah, yeah, of course, we'd like to *know* the volcano."

Without another word, Miguel turned over one of our paper place mats and, pulling a broken stub of a pencil from his shirt pocket, began to draw a crooked line. We watched in silence for the next twenty minutes as he guided the pencil over the grease-stained paper in absorbed concentration. What emerged was a detailed map of twists and turns with landmarks indicated by little, kid-like pictures of trees, stone walls and tiny shacks to represent a village.

Finished, Miguel put the pencil back in his pocket, sighed and spoke directly into our souls with piercing, green eyes. "This," he said, tapping the crude map with its meandering trail, "take you to volcano. To be *with* volcano." With his finger, Miguel softly tapped his chest over his heart, "to *feel* and *know* spirit of volcano." Then he laughed softly and cautioned us we would be scared because the volcano would *definitely* erupt when we were there. "But volcano not harm you," he added hastily. With a wistful look in his face, Miguel shared how he and his friends have picnicked at the edge of the volcano his whole life and the towering inferno had never harmed him. His words only mildly consoled me.

The sound of the cold, drenching rain woke us at dawn. We still couldn't see or hear the volcano. Since the downpour discouraged us from any other tourist activity, we decided we may as well get soaking wet following Miguel's map to wherever it led. Maybe the rain would stop once we were out of the village. Fat chance!

We drove up the steep mountainside of what the villagers below insisted was the volcano until the rugged jeep road ended abruptly at a craggy cliff. I was very surprised Miguel's rough, hand-drawn map actually corresponded to what we found on our journey. His drawing indicated the sheer cliff and the small, hidden opening we found nestled between the rock wall and a weather-beaten wooden fence. We followed our friend's makeshift chart through the hole, up a circuitous rocky path, over many collapsed lava rock walls and past long-deserted fruit orchards.

The trail ended abruptly at an imposing 300-foot wall of solid volcanic lava flow so jagged and sharp we couldn't climb it.

Fortunately for us, Miguel had anticipated this challenge. At the left edge of the lava flow, his map showed a naturally camouflaged trail through the dense rainforest. Our confidence in both our friend and his diagram strengthened over the past several hours, we plunged into the dark primeval forest. The jungle growth was so thick with vines and roots, the path so muddy and slippery, I felt we'd dropped into a comic scene right out of the Harrison Ford movie "Indiana Jones and the Raiders of the Lost Ark." During one hilarious moment, Rob and I both lost our footing and, clutching each other, slid back down fifty feet of the mudslide trail. Grabbing overhanging vines, Tarzan-style, saved the day— and our necks! Our guardian angels must get a lot of overtime pay!

Undaunted and filled with the rush of adventure, Rob and I helped each other stand up, pull ourselves together and restart the climb. Clawing and scratching our way through the rainforest, we finally reached the top of the lava flow. My first impression was how very windy and cold it was up there for a tropical climate. The pouring rain and dense fog had persisted, obliterating the view of anything more than a foot in front of us. As we inched our way along the top of the volcanic rock, I remembered how Miguel had told us of his many idyllic picnics here with his friends. Not very conducive weather for a picnic on this morning!

Suddenly, a booming roar filled the air, followed by a very powerful rumble that reverberated throughout our bodies. We felt the Earth roll in one undulating wave after another! Even though Rob and I had never experienced an eruption before, we instinctively knew this was the volcano showing its might. The ground continued to heave in unnerving spasms. People-size boulders sped past us down the slope. Flying rocks were propelled into nearby trees, the sheer force imbedding the projectiles cleanly into their trunks. We heard and felt nearby avalanches crashing their way down the mountain. We could only see a fraction of the devastation because of the blinding downpour, but our bodies definitely registered the massive rearrangement all around us.

A sharp electric terror shot through every cell of my body. Its message was explicit and commanding, *"Leave! Now! You must go now to save your life."*

I shouted to Rob, "We're out of here! It's not safe!" To my astonishment, he shook his head from side to side indicating he didn't want to go.

"I'm staying. This is too cool!" he yelled over the roar of the wind and falling rock. He was nineteen years old. His sense of novelty and exploration was still stronger than his sense of danger and good judgment. I started to argue. I made zero impression on the brash, young daredevil.

Then another explosion rocked our world. I watched in horror as the heat, ash and force of the blast denuded a huge 200-foot tree in one second, stripping off all its leaves and limbs. If this volcano could do that to a tree, it could do the same to us! I knew with certainty I was supposed to leave posthaste.

Jumping off the top of the lava mound right into the rainforest, I bolted without another thought. I threw myself into the "Raiders of the Lost Ark" express mudslide, riding the flowing water and sludge through the dense jungle growth down the side of the still-quaking mountainside. In what seemed like only a few seconds, I arrived at the bottom of the lava flow. The path was certainly faster and easier going down than climbing up! For a brief moment, I lay soaked to the bone, resting in a mud puddle, my ripped clothes covered with brown muck.

Recovering some of my composure, I became aware for the first time of heat radiating from the lava flow smoldering several feet to my left. I crawled in the direction of the flow until I was within a few inches of the mass. To my surprise, the air felt like I had just opened a 400-degree oven. The surface was so hot, I instinctively jumped back a few feet. When we first arrived earlier in the morning, the extremely cold wind and pelting rain had so neutralized the radiant heat from the lava, we didn't even notice the temperature.

But the heat was not the only aspect of the lava that the elements had concealed from us. I picked up a small twig and approached the foot of the black mound that had gushed from the top of the mountain. Getting as close as I could to the sulphurous heat, I stuck the branch into the rain-drenched ground about two inches in front of the lava. Within a minute, the lava hill reached the stick and buried it!

Suddenly my whole body reeled with the involuntary shudder of recognition. For the last hour Rob and I had been walking on a

live, moving lava flow! And Rob was still up there running around on the molten granite.

Another eruption, three times louder than the first one, filled the air. My ears throbbed from the deafening boom. My feet and body registered avalanche after avalanche of crashing rock careening down the side of the volcano. Descending the rough trail, I ran head over heels in a panic, determined to outrun any rockslides coming my way. After a half-hour of the fastest, long distance race I've ever run, I arrived at our jeep safely sheltered under a broad-armed tree. Collapsing into the front seat, I fought to catch my breath.

As my pulse and mind quieted, I was overcome with fear for the safety of my friend still walking around on the moving bed of liquid rock in the midst of periodic violent explosions. I began feeling intensely responsible. I'd left a young kid in my charge on top of an erupting volcano! A nightmarish vision bombarded me. I saw his parents, who had entrusted their son with me, watching local authorities dig through the rubble of the volcano searching for the body of the lost American youth. Feeling so guilty and worried I could neither relax nor rest, I decided I must leave the jeep and hike back up the volcano. I had to find Rob.

No sooner had I opened the door of the jeep than an insistent inner impulse told me to stay put and listen inside for further instructions. When I receive such forceful commands from my inner coach, I usually obey. Quieting myself as much as possible under the circumstances, I endeavored to get in touch with my next best intuitive move. I challenged myself, *Was it wrong what I did? Was it selfish and self-absorbed to look after my own safety and leave a young kid behind?*

After I felt all the intense emotions stirred up from asking these soul-searching questions, I received a very strong message directly from Spirit. My inner knowing spoke to me emphatically, saying:

"You did the right thing. You followed *your* intuition. If you recall specifically, your inner coach told you that it was dangerous for *you* to stay, and that *you* needed to leave immediately. It said nothing about your friend Rob. Nothing at all. You were right to follow your guidance and leave. In fact, had you stayed, you may very well have endangered your friend's safety! Had you stayed, you would have been out of alignment with your intuition and, therefore, out of harmony and integrity with yourself. This discordant state has a strong tendency to interfere with another person's ability to tap into and follow his or her own knowing. Had you stayed, you may have hindered Rob's ability to hear and heed *his* inner direction. You took the most helpful, loving and appropriate action by following the letter and spirit of your intuition. You following you own internal urging allowed your friend the space to realize he must rely on his own internal wisdom."

Spirit's message was a fascinating new lesson in intuitive guidance for me. In general, and for its reassurance in my present predicament, I was grateful for this fresh perspective. I never before realized the precision of intuition. I never before understood the independence of one person's guidance from the inner counsel of another person in a shared situation.

At the exact moment I realized the import of what I was being told by my inner coach, Rob came streaking down the trail toward the jeep. In the fury of the last violent eruption, Rob received his own internal signal to vamoose. Guided by his own inner compass, he immediately took the Mudslide Express through the jungle to safety. I was extremely relieved—and appreciative to Spirit—that my nightmare vision of Rob's demise was averted. I gave silent thanks for the eternal lessons I learned from our escapade.

Back on solid ground, Rob and I were anxious to leave the mountain rains and clouds. We hopped into the jeep and sped toward the sunny western coast of Costa Rica. Driving down the mountainside, we both lapsed in and out of thankful silence for being alive. Perhaps the next day, the morning's events would seem a great adventure, but, right then, the very real danger we'd just survived remained very palpable and raw. Our minds, emotions and physical bodies were still remembering and replaying our narrow escape.

Suddenly, Rob and I experienced simultaneous intuitive hits to pull over and get out of the jeep. Leaning against the vehicle, we turned as one toward the top of the mountain we'd just descended. As if waiting for us to stop our downward trek away from the mountain and turn our gaze upward, the clouds parted to reveal the awesome Mt. Arenal volcano for the very first time since our arrival in Costa Rica so many days earlier. The dense mist lifted. We saw exactly where we had been hiking on the lava flow. We pinpointed where the tree line ended and the lava flow began. We'd been standing only a hundred yards from the open mouth of the volcano when it erupted!

The restaurant owner Miguel had promised we would be with, we would feel and we would *know* the spirit of the volcano. He said the mountain would definitely erupt when we were there. And he'd promised the volcano would not harm us. The rain and his crude map tricked us into going so close to the volcano that we did, indeed, get to *know* the volcano, not just view it.

Was it the spirit of the volcano that sent Miguel to us? . . . and turned the skies into a torrential downpour in order to obscure the treacherous nature of our journey so we wouldn't be scared off? Rob and I agreed, stranger things have happened. One thing was certain. If we'd been able to see where we were going, we would never have walked as close as we did to the mouth of the cauldron.

Now, viewing the majesty of Mt. Arenal, we were humbled and ever so grateful for the experience of having been able to safely feel the mountain's power and personality. As we were sending out our thankfulness to and admiration of the volcano, the mountain erupted again with an explosion twice as high as the volcano itself. Two miles of elegant ash plume shot up into the dark blue sky. The event was quite dramatic and very humbling.

We knew the volcano was responding to our love and appreciation for its gift to us that day. Then the clouds closed back in and our mighty friend said good-bye, leaving us forever changed and enriched by its friendship.

Tapping Primal Life Force

*When the residents of the Scottish spiritual community of
Findhorn first encountered Pan in the forest,
Pan asked them to convey a message from
the Beings of Nature to the rest of humanity. Pan said:*

"Tell them, 'We never left—you did.'"

The colorful toucans squawked from within their tiny cage:

"Why would any free spirit ever confine another free being?"

The incarceration had rendered the once vibrant birds withdrawn
and lifeless captives. Their eyes cried this piercing question just as
the same bewilderment echoes from the dull gaze of every animal
in every zoo:

"Why would any being with heart ever drive the dagger of
imprisonment into the heart of another being?"

The answer is obvious. No being *with heart* would shackle another
free being. No being *whose spirit still lives* would ever kill the
spirit of another being—by any means.

The beseeching toucans were on exhibit at the country inn
where I stayed in Costa Rica. The innkeeper explained he was building
a huge cage around a tree so the birds would have a whole tree
around which to fly and live. But the confined birds told me
they didn't want a larger enclosure. No cage would ever be big
enough. Their spirits needed to be free. After a few days, I could
no longer look into the toucans' eyes. Before long, I avoided going
near their cage altogether.

Instead of focusing on the plight of the caged toucans, I was guided by my inner coach to explore the free and untamed treasures of the stunningly vibrant and beautiful country of Costa Rica. During my travels, I was blessed by direct encounters with wild animals, virgin forests, raging rivers and an erupting volcano. In their natural state, these diverse elements of life were undomesticated, unbridled, unfettered and unspoiled. Every cell of my body *felt* the raw, free essence of each basic kingdom of nature: mammal, reptile, bird, plant, water and mineral.

I connected with a sloth hanging out in its jungle haunt, a tabor scouring the forest carpet for grubs, a crocodile sunning in a sultry swamp and a very curious iguana checking me out through the mist of a waterfall. I shuddered at the primitive roar of jaguars too close for comfort. I witnessed reptiles called "Jesus lizards" with so much aliveness they literally walk on water, skimming across the surface on webbed feet.

I reveled in the unrestrained, exuberant expression of brilliant orchids, enticing mushrooms and outlandish fungi. The beauty and grace of exotic parrots, wild toucans and resplendent quetzal birds awed me. I was gratefully battered by the uncontrollable strength of ocean surf. Standing at the edge of an exploding volcanic cauldron, I exalted in the undiluted rapture of the fiery, flowing lava.

Soon I began to appreciate my soul's purpose in sending me to this lush, virgin land. My spirit's strategy was for me to encounter so many dynamic examples of the exhilaration of raw nature that I would break through to the other side of my rigid, conditioned, overly civilized state of being. And I did!

Through diverse *outer appearances* of vitality, I connected with the *inner source* that animates all forms of life. I danced with deer riding waves of natural electricity over grassy hills. I soared with caracara hawks spiraling with wind currents above luxuriant valleys. I clamored with howler monkeys playing in the rain forest canopy. I surrendered with meandering sea turtles to rhythmic tidal currents.

On the surface, animals, plants, rocks and volcanoes appear to be solid forms. Through intimate contact, I discovered firsthand that what creates these seemingly immutable shapes is primal life force, the basic *essence* generating and driving all *forms* of life.

A volcano in Costa Rica was the natural element that shared this secret with me in the most dramatic, effective and revealing way. When the molecules of mountain granite are sped up by intense heat, the true nature of this *solid* form is disclosed as being *fluid, moving, alive* energy. Universal life force is so fundamental and powerful, it melts granite. It transforms the most condensed form of matter into molten lava, liquid rock. Primordial life force is so alive, pure, wild and basic that it's potent enough to liberate the most rigid crystallized matter into free-flowing life expression.

My soul arranged for me to "accidentally" stumble through the dense fog onto an active lava flow for the purpose of exposing me in a very palpable, tangible way to the true nature of all reality. Walking on this semi-solid river of fire, I absorbed the raw, innocent, spontaneous vital energy lying at the core of all physical manifestations of life. I merged with the alchemical power of basic life force—uncontrollable, undiluted and pristine.

The direct transmission I received from the volcano and all the other wild creatures of Costa Rica is that this fundamental life force energy is as available to us humans as it is to them! If we choose to unite with this energy and allow divine alchemy, we also can become one with the pure, primal, passionate, undivided, unqualified, unlimited expression of life. This underlying flow is referred to by the Chinese as the *Tao*—the river of knowing, the central stream of consciousness, the God current that is our true nature and essence.

The harsh contrast between the toucans in captivity and the toucans in the wild awakened me to the magnitude of the aliveness and connection we humans lost somewhere along the way in our collective life journey. The fact that we cage toucans and other animals in zoos and homes around the world is a clear indication of how far we have removed ourselves from the natural vitality and joy of freedom—both our own and that of other inhabitants of Earth.

Our human quest for love, security and energy cannot be achieved as long as we remain in a state of consciousness in which we systematically seek to control the freedom of our fellow beings—human and otherwise. In the process of "civilizing" our species, we humans have become conditioned to not feel deep, dynamic passion and love for life. Our collective heart, the world's heart, has become so crystallized and armored that it is now as hard and cold as the granite of a mountain. Our collective heart has turned to stone. Only a granite heart could do what we are doing to the natural expression of life—within ourselves and on the planet.

The original Old English meaning of the word *panic* was "of the nature of Pan: wild and free-flowing." But now we humans are so shut down, controlling and cut off from nature—and from our own vital electric nature—that we experience "wild and free-flowing" energy as scary and threatening. Life's creative enthusiasm sends us into a *panic* in the modern sense. Most of us are terrified of living fully alive and free.

How can we humans reverse this process? How can we melt the granite façades of our public institutions—and our own faces—that so starkly reflect the state of our hardened soul? How can we re-light the pilot light and stoke the cosmic fire within us?

As I melded with the effusive wildness of Costa Rica, I unearthed an answer. We humans can re-connect to our natural aliveness by opening to a force that is more powerful than our programming, more compelling than our collective conditioning. The force that can liberate us is universal life energy, primal life force. This unbridled exuberance abounds everywhere around us—and within us. Fortunately, cultural conditioning cannot control primal life force. This raw creative energy is free and innocent of all human concepts and beliefs. Primal life force doesn't *follow* its own drumbeat; it *is* the drumbeat.

Primal life force is more fundamental, more basic, than our human psychological and cultural creations. In reality, this power provides the lifeblood, essence and juice that sustains and supports the entire human culture currently existing on the planet. Primal life flow is the natural energy source that literally runs our human creations.

Several years ago, a wall of red-hot lava streamed down the side of a volcano on the Big Island of Hawaii cutting right through a village located between the volcano and the ocean. So intense was the temperature of the boiling lava, its radiant energy vaporized the wood and cement foundations of the human structures *before the lava physically touched the foundations.* All traces of the village and human habitation were annihilated in the wake of the lava inferno as it made its way to the sea.

Modern science doesn't know a way to stop the power of the Goddess Pele, the impassioned expression of the spirit of the volcano. The human structures were not as real, fundamental or substantial as the energy of the volcano. Human concepts, beliefs and paradigms trying to overlay and dominate nature are no match for the raw, creative primal power of natural vigor.

The vibration of original vitality, passion and excitement is strong enough to melt our *collective granite heart.* Just as primal life force vaporized the not-so-solid foundations of the Hawaiian physical structures, primal life force can dissolve the foundations of the psychological structure that makes us *think* we need to control and feel separate from other life in order to get enough energy to survive.

One key to becoming fully revitalized is to reconnect with universal life force in such a way that we are not only *fed* by it, but also *transformed* by it. If we resonate with the abundant aliveness all around us, divine alchemy will transmute us into the experience of *being* that eternal essence of life energy. When we *become one* with universal life force, we are able to draw our very sustenance, supply and security from our own source within. We are sovereign, self-generating, in terms of where we get our energy. Sourcing our own energy, we then have enough personal power to melt the crystallized granite heart within ourselves and our culture. And until we walk with the authentic sovereignty of natural vitality, we won't have the courage and strength to go out and love with true spirit and fulfill our core purposes on Earth.

Another crucial aspect of the message I received from the wildness of Costa Rica is that to be successful on our quest, we humans need to open to this primordial energy *through direct, pure, spontaneous, innocent and fresh means.* We cannot approach this enterprise from an old paradigm or model. For, if we seek natural, organic vitality in an unnatural, nonorganic way, we won't uncover the pure source we seek. To approach aliveness in a sequential, methodical, linear manner prevents us from contacting its basic nature. This natural aliveness does not exist within the framework or box in which we currently exist as a society. Pure, free life expression lives outside of our cultural conditioning, underneath it, behind it—*beyond* it.

We can reclaim our natural power only if we approach the challenge in a manner that is new, wild, free, unexpectant and in-the-moment. If this alive space is sought in any way that is familiar or known, it won't be found. Where we're going and what we're looking for isn't located on any existing cultural map.

The way to natural vitality is uncharted because the very finding of this energy transforms us and our universe to such an extent that no previous map, blueprint or paradigm is relevant. By the very nature of the goal—aliveness—the path to the goal remains fresh and spontaneous, impossible to document or plan.

No methodology, technique or structured approach can ever remain valid for any period of time—or even a second time—to assist us in reaching this vibrant state. This space, once achieved, once embodied, once lived, is so free, transforming, creative and constantly changing that any *existing* map, chart or way won't take us there a second time. *Strategies previous to this moment* take us to old places and old experiences. Really cool, but not current. Pleasant, but not present. Potent, but not profound.

To undertake this odyssey in the most advantageous way, my inner coach suggests a simple, direct, personal approach. To rekindle our fire of aliveness, we can open to peak moments in our life when we experienced a strong connection to the vibration of raw, creative primal life flow. Many of us can't *think* of—or *remember*—a time when we did merge with this basic life force. Fortunately, it doesn't matter that our memory of our true nature is blocked by our mind. We can employ our intuition as a guide, instead of the *mind*. Our intuition knows where and how to access this vibration of vitality. Our intuition knows how to remove or go around any barriers or denial. Behind our veils of fear, dismissal, distraction, invalidation and misinterpretation are hundreds of firsthand encounters with this universal fire. Within each of us lies a treasure house of direct personal experiences readily available for the enhancement and transformation of our everyday life.

The heart of Costa Rica radiated one primal message:

"Go for the juice, the electricity. Forget the form."

If whatever is happening in the moment looks and sounds right, but doesn't *feel intuitively right* to *you*, then it's not right. It isn't what you're meant to be doing at that moment—it isn't what is spiritually appropriate or indicated for you to be doing at that precise time.

In regard to any situation, the key question to ask yourself is:

"For me, in the moment, is there passion, aliveness, heart?"

If there is not, then you are not in the right place, no matter how convincing the outer appearance might be. Let it go.

The spirit of the Earth urges:

"Move on. Stay open. Keep flowing."

In an Arizona canyon twenty years ago, a venerable Hopi medicine man named Medicine Cloud shared a keen observation with me:

"Everything you need to know about life you can learn from streams and clouds."

I now know what he meant.

Getting Our Power Back

You are in grave danger!
At any moment—you may be loving, laughing, alive—
you may accidentally find God!

RABINDRANTH TAGORE

During many years of observing others and myself searching for fulfillment, I've noticed an essential ingredient is often missing. I call this ingredient *sovereignty*—self-sufficiency, self-generation or total independence from outside sources. Without this quality in its authentic form, no one I know has been able to achieve the happiness, health and peace they are seeking.

Throughout the years of assisting others and myself to feel truly joyous and free, I've watched people try to ignore, deny, invalidate or rationalize away the importance of sovereignty. I've witnessed friends and other people attempt to fake it, substitute for it, and try to steal and borrow it from others. All these efforts have been in vain. Their time, energy and intention would have been put to better use by focusing on allowing this quality to become a solid personal reality.

In my experience, a true, conscious state of sovereignty is absolutely critical for genuine, lasting satisfaction during the Earth experience. If you're not entirely clear as to the nature of this state, it's not surprising. In deliberate accordance with our personal and collective design, there is a subtle, pervasive individual and cultural prohibition against tasting too deeply the nectar of sovereignty.

Throughout history, this cover-up has been very successful and almost completely impenetrable. There is a good reason for this. When you authentically recognize the fundamental truth of your own sovereignty, the gig is up! The ego's charade of imminent destruction is exposed as a lie and, in fact, as an *impossibility*. This revelation is a death knoll for the aspect of you that tries to destroy your joy by threatening you with disapproval, disagreement, disease and destruction. This part of you that doesn't want to "give up the ghost" (illusion) is variously referred to as the ego, mind, intellect, conditioning, programming, personality, identity or persona. This aspect of yourself bought into the tribal collective agreement, mainstream mass consciousness, that you are ultimately vulnerable to body and soul annihilation if you don't tow the party line, as dictated by . . . who else? . . . the ego.

In reality, nothing could be further from the truth. One of my spiritual mentors, Lester, was fond of musing:

> "The thing people fear the most is non-survival. And non-survival is the only thing that can't ever happen to us."

You are an eternal being, whether you like it or not—whether you are aware of it or not! Sovereignty is the personal recognition of your everlasting, eternal permanency!

Sovereignty isn't a concept, idea, principle, possibility, option or creation. It doesn't need to be affirmed, declared, visualized, asserted, defended or manifested. The immutability of your sovereignty doesn't depend on whether you believe in it or not. It is a fact of your existence, an inescapable, immutable reality. Your awareness, appreciation and enjoyment of sovereignty may come and go to one degree or another, but eternalness never waivers as your fundamental, inalienable true nature.

Sovereignty is knowing you are the ultimate source of every experience you have in your life. You know for certain you are a sovereign being when you generate your own energy, love, power, health, wisdom, clarity, security, peace and fulfillment on a daily basis.

Lester often reminded me, "You only know that which you can do!" In order to operate on a practical basis as the creator you are, it's crucial to tap directly into the universal life force in a real, tangible, lasting way. You need to connect fully with the fire within, with the essence that nurtures the fullness of your being.

One very effective and immediate way to access your true nature and power is to shift your identification away from thinking (believing) that you are *only* your human personality, that you are *only* a body, and that you are *separate* from other people and other forms of life. As your creative attention shifts from who you *think* you are to who you *truly* are, you experience the total security and certainty of your basic essence. Our true essence is an eternal energy field of consciousness. This energy field of consciousness is connected with all life and gives us the freedom to create whatever we choose.

It's helpful to be aware that this shift of attention cannot be just a mental exercise. A wholesale re-identification of *your entire being* with the everyday reality of self-generation is required. This re-identification has to be fully integrated on the emotional, spiritual, biological and molecular levels. And it's crucial for you to create direct, firsthand, tangible, demonstrable and repeatable evidence that you *can*, in fact, manifest and attract all the love, safety, energy, well-being, joy, peace and abundance you desire in your life.

The benefit of giving yourself this factual personal validation is that this firsthand evidence takes sovereignty from the realm of the *conceptual* to the reality of the *practical*. When you can *prove* your sovereignty to yourself repeatedly, at will, on your own terms, in your own way and in your world, then self-generation becomes real for you.

One very useful resource you can use to validate sovereignty for yourself is tapping into the accurate, comprehensive recall of your inner coach—intuition. Your intuition is the aspect of your consciousness that can remind you accurately, without ego filters and bias, of everything that has ever happened to you in your lifetime. Using intuitive, meditative, shamanic soul journeying you can guide yourself to reconnect with peak moments in your life when you personally experienced the vibration, energy and reality of sovereignty. These are moments when you knew with certainty your true nature of power, passion and creativity.

In this way you can re-light your pilot light and stoke your inner fire to burn more brightly. As you come alive again within, you naturally remember how to continuously fuel your own courage, safety, power, prosperity, compassion and happiness. As you begin to vibrate at the frequency of sovereignty in your everyday life, you attract and experience more of the direct personal evidence that makes the state of sovereignty even more authentic and lasting for you. Like vibration attracts—and creates—like vibration.

The more *experientially* convincing it becomes to you that you are in charge of your own energy and survival, the more you will keep your creative attention focused on the realness of your own sovereignty. As more attention is focused on your true personal power, less attention is available to slip back into energizing old patterns of dependence and helplessness. Old fears of victimhood, insecurity and abandonment diminish and eventually dissolve from lack of sustaining attention. Threats of your personality's limited perspective become less and less convincing. It becomes less crucial to control other people or the environment to make sure you get enough love, energy or safety. It becomes less necessary to resist or defend against others trying to control you or steal your energy. It becomes less imperative for you to withhold, hide, alter or disguise your true feelings, desires and excitement for fear of upsetting or threatening somebody else's world.

As you reclaim your natural power, you become self-sustaining. The whole process of truly owning your sovereignty snowballs in the direction of freedom and abundance. The more time you spend in the vibration of sovereignty, the easier it becomes to keep all your attention there. Soon, you find yourself living every day in an ocean of infinite supply. You possess all the clarity, wisdom, power and joy you previously searched for and found so fleeting. All your awareness is nurtured daily by this direct experience of being completely connected, loved, energized and supported *on the Earth in a very practical way.*

From this authentic inner security emanates the courage and strength to be who you really are. This honest expression keeps your creative attention flowing to what is naturally right for you and truly gives you happiness. You have all your personal power available to fully energize your soul's innermost impulse to express and create. Your attention flows unhindered—without distraction, detour or derailment—into funding your heart's deepest desires and fulfilling your fondest dreams. You have returned to your natural state of sovereignty.

Sharing who you really are—and all your natural spiritual abilities—with the world is the ultimate act of love. Being self-generating, you are able to allow all other inhabitants of Earth to do whatever they choose. You can offer others the space to be just as they are. You become capable of giving the greatest gift we can bestow on another being: unconditional love, total acceptance.

About the Author

For 30 years, Keith Varnum has focused his unique spirit on helping people explore, enjoy and embrace the adventure of life. From the wisdom of native, tribal cultures and ancient spiritual traditions, Keith shares his distillation of the underlying principles of all healing and transformation. He has applied his approach to human dynamics in a practical way as a life strategy coach, international seminar leader, therapist, acupuncturist, gardener, author, filmmaker, radio talk show host, owner-chef of two gourmet restaurants and vice president of the country's largest natural food company. When not exploring consciousness in the canyons of Arizona, he travels around the world assisting people to open to life's wonders and surprises in his *Dream Workshops*.

Keith Varnum
Life Strategy Coach

As a Life Strategy Coach, Keith assists people to enjoy life by opening to support from the universe through fully expressing their unique gifts and personal passion. "I help people close the gap between where they are and where they want to be," Keith relates. "Together we develop the plans, strategies and approaches to increase a person's personal power and joy in everyday life. As a personal coach, I am a powerful ally in the person's life journey. Your life can be as big, bold and brilliant as you wish it to be!"

Keith helps his clients define their goals and intentions in life and supports people in applying their action plans. With time-tested techniques, Keith facilitates the discovery of hidden potentials, strengthens confidence and resolve, and helps anchor and celebrate successes.

"As a soul consultant," Keith shares, "I hold a vision of who people can be—and align with their hearts' fondest dreams. Intuitively, I recognize clients' true destinies, encourage natural creativity and tailor my style to their needs to champion their soul blueprint. I help people discover their worth, disarm fears, master money, deepen intimacy and refresh their spirit. I assist people to hear and follow their own intuition, and to express their special calling by clarifying personal vision, focusing power, unleashing courage and developing hidden talents."

In his many-faceted approach, Keith employs intuitive journeying, Reiki energy balancing, shamanic healing, soul retrieval, past life regression and acupuncture.

Keith consults in person in Arizona and by phone nationwide. You can contact Keith for a free consultation at 800.736.7367 or keith@thedream.com.

The Dream Workshops

In *The Dream Workshops* we have assembled some of the most powerful transformational tools available currently on the planet. Using shamanic intuitive journeys, movement, music, painting, laughter and fun, you learn to access the wisdom of your intuition and free yourself from limiting patterns. The workshops provide easy, efficient processes to discover your life purpose and ignite the passion to create that purpose as a personal reality.

On our workshops, we come together as *Gatherings of Equals*. You play together with the other participants and the facilitator Keith Varnum as peers, conscious equals—equal in wisdom, power and compassion. The space encourages you to show up as the creative, knowing being you truly are—naturally clear, inventive and free.

Then, by keeping attention focused solely on your desires—not on the distractions of life—your soul's intentions manifest with no effort or doingness. You create by achieving vibrational harmony with the object of your desire. Drawing from your own peak life experiences, you go directly to the quality you want and allow that core energy to manifest itself in the perfect form in your life. You reclaim your innate wisdom, inner strength and natural aliveness and make lasting life changes. These proven techniques bring the mind, body and spirit together to manifest what truly makes you healthy and fulfilled.

The purpose of life is to share love. *The Dream Workshops* help you to recover your ability to embrace and express love in your own individual way.

We invite you to join us for a profound adventure of opening to the real you—the you that knows how to fly—the you that is Spirit. You are *one of a kind*, with unique talents and expressions to offer the world.

There is nothing more attractive and powerful than an authentic person living the life he or she truly desires.

The Dream Workshops offer easy, effective tools to:

- Develop a clear, lasting connection to your inner coach
- Attract a livelihood with heart and meaning that supports you financially and spiritually
- Transform personal and professional relationships into mutually satisfying soul partnerships
- Liberate you from patterns that block happiness, love, money and health
- Create your life as a fun, joyous adventure

Contact us for a:

Free Empowerment Tape and

Free Subscription to spiritual quarterly, *The Dream Daily Sun*

The Dream Workshops, 11248 N. 11th St., Phoenix, AZ 85020

800.736.7367 or keith@thedream

Visit us online at

www.thedream.com

Nature Speaks
Sedona and Hawaii Vision Quests

Double your chances of getting the message from Spirit
by reading the outer signs from your inner guidance

Keith Varnum shares easy and effective ways to apply Earth's wisdom to bring more prosperity, meaning, aliveness and balance to your life. This dynamic outdoors adventure is a joyous journey of self-discovery employing the physical universe as an accurate, liberating reflection of your own consciousness.

Often we are able get clearer answers from the external physical signs Spirit gives us than from meditative contemplation. In the quiet, empty, ageless spaces of Sedona and Hawaii, you're able to read the helpful outer signals from your soul more easily than in the busyness of everyday life.

You experience everything in nature supporting and guiding you, giving you messages and direction to bring you back into balance with your soul and with the wholeness of life. You learn to transform the lessons absorbed in wild spaces into concrete results in the urban canyons of life back home.

- Clouds show you how to shift positions to greater advantage
- Water demonstrates how to get into the flow of abundance
- Spiders teach how to weave new patterns to catch new dreams
- Eagles reveal how to lift yourself to higher realms of vision
- Hummingbirds help you increase your vibration, ease and fun
- Rocks share how to build a solid foundation for your dreams
- Flies show you what's really bugging you in your life
- Ancient oaks whisper the wisdom of flexible, bending strength

In the *Quest*, you learn to use Nature to create:

The love your heart longs for
A job with soul and passion
The courage to find life purpose
The clarity to make wise choices

Discover from the Earth how to:

Finance and support your dreams
Heal and re-vitalize your body
Stay centered in your power
Renew personal creativity

Questing is for everyone:

Gentle, non-rigorous approach for all backgrounds
Easy hiking by cool streams along tree-shaded trails
Refreshing, rejuvenating waterfalls and swimming holes
No previous outdoor experience necessary
Not a physically strenuous adventure
Nature is safer than the average urban environment

Sedona and Hawaii have for centuries expressed an irresistible spiritual magnetism on the hearts and minds of people desiring to increase creativity, develop spiritual powers and awaken the soul to a knowing of its true purpose in life. There is low cost lodging and free camping in Sedona and Hawaii. Free rides are available to and from Phoenix and Sedona—and around the islands in Hawaii. It's usually not necessary to rent a car.

Enjoy stunning pictures of Red Rock Sedona on our web site:

sedonavisionquest.com

Living the Dream—It's Time

A Chronicle of the Gathering of Equals, 250 page book

By Keith Varnum and Mark Conrad

Living the Dream is a chronicle of one year of *The Dream Workshops*—human spirits who have come together to learn from others while they rediscover the deep knowing within themselves. Share the experience of the participants as they individually express their hearts while exploring their original vibrations, essences and gifts.

This is a journey to the innermost level of knowing, an adventure into a world that shakes the paradigms of mainstream thought. This is where magic happens and you can be part of it.

Align with your true purpose and unique destiny here on Earth. Rediscover who you are and play in the realm of pure vibration, energy and essence. Rekindle the fire in your belly, the primal excitement that is life itself. Nurture your passion as you would a pilot light, as if it meant the very survival of your soul—which it does.

The sleeping spirit within each of us is waking up. It is now time to know our magnificence and openly share what we know with others. It's time to awaken and live the Dream.

Explore the spirit, power and process of *The Dream Workshops* in a dynamic, play-by-play presentation of this dynamic approach to transformation. Filled with practical, experiential exercises you can do at home to embrace and master Alchemy, Sovereignty, Universal Supply, Synchronicity, Unconditional Love, Grace, Equality and many other natural, miracle-producing states of being.

QUICK ORDER FORM

Phone order: 800.736.7367 toll free
Email order: keith@thedream.com
Mail order: The Dream, 11248 N. 11th St., Phoenix AZ 85020

Name_____

Address_____

City_____ State_____ Zip_____

FREE *Empowerment Tape*   ☐
  with guided processes to unfold your dream

FREE Subscription to *The Dream Daily Sun*   ☐
  quarterly journal of metaphysical articles

FREE Information on:

  Life Strategy Coaching   ☐   The Dream Workshops ☐
  Vision Quest   ☐   The *Yes!* Center   ☐

Inner Coach: Outer Power Book   ___ copies @ $16.95 ____

Living the Dream Book   ___ copies @ $12.95 ____

Adventures of the Heart
  Six 60-min. Tape Set   ___ copies @ $29.95 ____

Dream Tools 60-min. Audiotape   ___ copies @ $ 7.95 ____

Shipping: $2 first item and $1 for each additional item   ____

Total $____

MC/VISA BILLING
Cardholder Name_____
Card No._____ Exp. Date_____

SHIPPING ADDRESS IF DIFFERENT:
Name_____
Address_____
City_____ State_____ Zip_____

Dream Tools

Tools to Build Your Dream

60-minute audiotape

Keith Varnum, founder and facilitator of *The Dream Workshops* leads you through five extremely effective, experiential guided meditative processes from *The Dream Workshops* that empower you to connect with your intuitive core self, remove limiting blocks and create your heart's desires.

You can also use these processes to open to your soul purpose, own your sovereignty and develop your special spiritual gifts and talents.

The tape assists you to:

- Connect with your soul
- Reclaim your worth
- Energize your body
- Maximize your money
- Master your mind
- Dissolve your fears
- Free your shadow
- Awaken your heart
- Embrace your emotions
- Celebrate your sexuality
- Make lasting changes

QUICK ORDER FORM

Phone order: 800.736.7367 toll free

Email order: keith@thedream.com

Mail order: The Dream, 11248 N. 11th St., Phoenix, AZ 85020

Name_____

Address_____

City_____ State_____ Zip_____

FREE *Empowerment Tape*   ☐
  with guided processes to unfold your dream

FREE Subscription to *The Dream Daily Sun*   ☐
  quarterly journal of metaphysical articles

FREE Information on:

  Life Strategy Coaching   ☐   The Dream Workshops   ☐
  Vision Quest   ☐   The *Yes!* Center   ☐

Inner Coach: Outer Power Book   ___ copies @ $16.95 ____

Living the Dream Book   ___ copies @ $12.95 ____

Adventures of the Heart
  Six 60-min. Tape Set   ___ copies @ $29.95 ____

Dream Tools 60-min. Audio Tape   ___ copies @ $ 7.95 ____

Shipping: $2 first item and $1 for each additional item   ____

Total $____

MC/VISA BILLING

Cardholder Name_____

Card No._____ Exp. Date_____

SHIPPING ADDRESS IF DIFFERENT:

Name_____

Address_____

City_____ State_____ Zip_____

Adventures of the Heart:
Breaking Your Belief Barrier

Set of 6 audiotapes in handsome album

Jump start your life with these riveting, real-life exploits of Keith Varnum designed to pierce your veil of forgetfulness, uncover the treasures of your own buried past and reveal to you the exciting lost adventures of your soul! Fascinating, liberating true tales of levitation, soul travel, time tripping, parallel realities, deva communication, radical healing, out-of-body experiences, miracles and magic. An intimate, informal rendering of many of the stories in *Inner Coach: Outer Power,* told through the voice and spirit of a master storyteller to a small group of close friends sitting in a cozy room warmed by a soothing fire.

As you listen . . . Keith's dynamic, revealing stories inspire you to tap into the power of your own peak life experiences in which you.

- Healed spontaneously
- Broke "out of the box"
- Glimpsed other dimensions
- Met your nonphysical guides
- Were touched by real-life magic
- "Knew" your true spiritual nature
- Opened to multisensory awareness
- Expressed the potential of your unique gifts

QUICK ORDER FORM

Phone order: 800.736.7367 toll free

Email order: keith@thedream.com

Mail order: The Dream, 11248 N. 11th St., Phoenix, AZ 85020

Name_____

Address_____

City_____ State_____ Zip_____

FREE *Empowerment Tape*   ☐
  with guided processes to unfold your dream

FREE Subscription to *The Dream Daily Sun*   ☐
  quarterly journal of metaphysical articles

FREE Information on:

  Life Strategy Coaching   ☐   The Dream Workshops   ☐
  Vision Quest   ☐   The *Yes!* Center   ☐

Inner Coach: Outer Power Book   ___ copies @ $16.95 ___

Living the Dream Book   ___ copies @ $12.95 ___

Adventures of the Heart
  Six 60-min. Tape Set   ___ copies @ $29.95 ___

Dream Tools 60-min. Audio Tape   ___ copies @ $ 7.95 ___

Shipping: $2 first item and $1 for each additional item   ___

Total $___

MC/VISA BILLING

Cardholder Name_____

Card No._____ Exp. Date_____

SHIPPING ADDRESS IF DIFFERENT:

Name_____

Address_____

City_____ State_____ Zip_____

The *Yes!* Center

An Invitation to Play

We at *The Dream Workshops* invite you to play in a new, exhilarating adventure. We are founding a Center for Aliveness to be built in pristine countryside somewhere in the United States. The focus of The *Yes!* Center is to empower people to not only discover their Life Purpose and Passion, but to share that purpose full-time—creating a sustaining income and making a good living doing what they love.

We'd enjoy co-creating this dream with you! The *Yes!* Center will be for everyone to use as practical, logistical support to further their journey toward fully expressing their unique abilities and gifts with the world. A vital, integral aspect of The *Yes!* Center will be venues, resources and opportunities on-site for you to express and demonstrate your special talents and distinct contribution to the public.

We welcome your participation in the realization of this shared dream in whatever way your inner coach directs you:

- Contribute land, equipment or resources
- Invest money, time, expertise or energy
- Share ideas, suggestions and feedback
- Send us your love and spiritual encouragement
- Be inventive in discovering other supportive actions

Feel free to contact us to share your response to our invitation.

We'd love to hear from you,

Keith

800.736.7367
keith@thedream.com

QUICK ORDER FORM

Phone order: 800.736.7367 toll free

Email order: keith@thedream.com

Mail order: The Dream, 11248 N. 11th St., Phoenix, AZ 85020

Name_____

Address_____

City_____ State_____ Zip_____

FREE *Empowerment Tape*   ☐
   with guided processes to unfold your dream

FREE Subscription to *The Dream Daily Sun*   ☐
   quarterly journal of metaphysical articles

FREE Information on:

   Life Strategy Coaching   ☐   The Dream Workshops   ☐
   Vision Quest   ☐   The *Yes!* Center   ☐

Inner Coach: Outer Power Book   ___ copies @ $16.95 ____

Living the Dream Book   ___ copies @ $12.95 ____

Adventures of the Heart
   Six 60-min. Tape Set   ___ copies @ $29.95 ____

Dream Tools 60-min. Audio Tape   ___ copies @ $ 7.95 ____

Shipping: $2 first item and $1 for each additional item   ____

Total $____

MC/VISA BILLING

Cardholder Name_____

Card No._____ Exp. Date_____

SHIPPING ADDRESS IF DIFFERENT:

Name_____

Address_____

City_____ State_____ Zip_____